'Decker is a rare scholar, combining the empirical fastidiousness of a business historian with the conceptual and theoretical skills of an organization theorist, producing a book that should contribute to a more global and historical appreciation of the role of multinationals.'
– **Stewart Clegg**, *Distinguished Professor, University of Technology Sydney Business School*

Postcolonial Transition and Global Business History

British multinationals faced unprecedented challenges to their organizational legitimacy in the middle of the twentieth century as the European colonial empires were dismantled and institutional transformations changed colonial relationships in Africa and other parts of the world. This book investigates the political networking and internal organizational changes in five British multinationals (United Africa Company, John Holt & Co., Ashanti Goldfields Corporation, Bank of West Africa and Barclays Bank DCO). These firms were forced to adapt their strategies and operations to changing institutional environments in two English-speaking West African countries, Ghana (formerly the Gold Coast) and Nigeria, from the late 1940s to the late 1970s. Decolonization meant that formerly imperial businesses needed to develop new political networks and change their internal organization and staffing to promote more Africans to managerial roles. This postcolonial transition culminated in indigenization programmes (and targeted nationalizations) which forced foreign companies to sell equity and assets to domestic investors in the 1970s. *Postcolonial Transition and Global Business History* is the first in-depth historical study on how British firms sought to adapt over several decades to rapid political and economic transformation in West Africa.

Exploring both postcolonial transitions and development discourse, this book addresses the topics with regard to business and economic history and will be of interest to researchers, academics and students in the fields of organizational change, political economy, African studies and globalization.

Stephanie Decker is Professor of Strategy at the University of Birmingham Business School, UK, and visiting professor in African Business History at the University of Gothenburg, Sweden. She is co-editor-in-chief of Business History, on the editorial board of Organization Studies and Accounting History, and Co-Vice Chair for Research and Publications at the British Academy of Management.

Routledge International Studies in Business History

Series editors: Heidi Tworek and Ai Hisano

Leading the Economic Risorgimento
Lombardy in the 19th Century
Edited by Silvia A. Conca Messina

Pervasive Powers
The Politics of Corporate Authority
Edited by Sara A. Aguiton, Marc-Olivier Déplaude, Nathalie Jas, Emmanuel Henry, and Valentin Thomas

Internationalisation and Strategic Control
An Industrial History
Morten Pedersen

Politics and Rhetoric of Italian State Steel Privatizations
A Gramscian Analysis
Edoardo Mollona and Luca Pareschi

A History of Business Cartels
International Politics, National Policies and Anti-Competitive Behaviour
Edited by Martin Shanahan and Susanna Fellman

Industrial Clusters
Knowledge, Innovation Systems and Sustainability in the UK
Edited by John F. Wilson, Chris Corker and Joe Lane

Postcolonial Transition and Global Business History
British Multinational Companies in Ghana and Nigeria
Stephanie Decker

For more information about this series, please visit: www.routledge.com/Routledge-International-Studies-in-Business-History/book-series/SE0471

Postcolonial Transition and Global Business History

British Multinational Companies in Ghana and Nigeria

Stephanie Decker

Routledge
Taylor & Francis Group
NEW YORK AND LONDON

First published 2023
by Routledge
605 Third Avenue, New York, NY 10158

and by Routledge
4 Park Square, Milton Park, Abingdon, Oxon, OX14 4RN

Routledge is an imprint of the Taylor & Francis Group, an informa business

Library of Congress Cataloguing-in-Publication Data
Names: Decker, Stephanie, 1977-author.
Title: Postcolonial transition and global business history : British multinational companies in Ghana and Nigeria / Stephanie Decker.
Description: New York City : Routledge, 2022. | Includes bibliographical references and index.
Identifiers: LCCN 2022026184 | ISBN 9780367428105 (hardback) | ISBN 9781032386829 (paperback) | ISBN 9781003001058 (ebook)
Subjects: LCSH: International business enterprises--Ghana--History--Case studies. | International business enterprises--Nigeria--History--Case studies. | Postcolonialism--Economic aspects--Ghana. | Postcolonialism--Economic aspects--Nigeria. | Africanization--Ghana. | Africanization--Nigeria. | Great Britain--Foreign economic relations--Ghana. | Great Britain--Foreign economic relations--Nigeria. | Ghana--Foreign economic relations--Great Britain. | Nigeria--Foreign economic relations--Great Britain.
Classification: LCC HD2928.3 .D43 2022 | DDC 338.88866709046--dc23/eng/20220602
LC record available at https://lccn.loc.gov/2022026184

ISBN: 978-0-367-42810-5 (hbk)
ISBN: 978-1-032-38682-9 (pbk)
ISBN: 978-1-003-00105-8 (ebk)

DOI: 10.4324/9781003001058

Typeset in Bembo
by MPS Limited, Dehradun

Contents

Data statement

The data that support the findings in this book are available from public and private archives, and not digitally available. Restrictions apply to the use of this data, which were used with the kind permission of the data owners. A list of archives, and sources consulted in those archives, can be found at the end of the book.

Acknowledgements

This book started off as my doctoral thesis and has been a long time in the making. Returning to the thesis manuscript to turn it into a book after so many years was initially daunting, but I am glad I have done it. Debates have moved on, but the subject remains relevant and important. I would like to thank the editorial staff of Routledge for their patience, and the past and present series editors for their continued interest in the project, as I struggled to pull this book manuscript together amid too many other commitments.

This book would not have been possible without the many excellent archives in the United Kingdom and Ghana, both private and public, and the work of the archivists who keep the past accessible to researchers. I would like to thank the staff of The National Archives, UK, and the Public Records Administration and Archives Department, Ghana, for their help in identifying records relating to the operation of British businesses in West Africa. Some of the most fascinating historical files can be found in company archives, and in the United Kingdom, we are fortunate that many large companies maintain their own historical archives, and that their archivist work hard to ensure these remain open to external researchers. I am grateful for the continuing support for researchers by the Barclays Group Archives (Manchester) and the Unilever Historical Archives (Liverpool) and their excellent archival staff. Corporate records can also be found in public and university archives, and I am indebted to the staff of University of Oxford Rhodes House, University of Cambridge Churchill College, Liverpool Records Office, and the Manuscripts Section of the Guildhall Library in London, where I originally consulted the archival records that are now housed in the London Metropolitan Archives. A detailed list of archival records consulted, and the archives they are in, can be found at the end of the book.

1 Introduction

British business decided at an early stage to stay in West Africa after independence. Indeed, that they would outlast the empire was not a matter that anyone doubted, according to John Holt & Co's (Holt) chairman:

> Merchant houses in West Africa by years of good service and honest dealing have built up a fund of goodwill. Our company has been trading in West Africa for 90 years and I am confident that we shall still be there 90 years hence.[1]

Such firms and their managers 'have long managed not just variation and shifts in technology, but also shifts in the political and social environment'.[2] While contemporary management studies are interested in corporate political activities, business diplomacy and legitimization strategies, only rarely do they acknowledge the long history of firms developing such capabilities to 'harness the trajectory of political and social change'.[3]

1.1 Periodization

The 1950s and 1960s marked a critical time period for global business, as formerly imperial companies were faced with the emergence of many newly independent states. Mistrust of firms as agents of a neo-colonial presence, nationalism and simmering internal tensions about ethnicity, social division and redistribution in new states presented a diverse yet increasingly familiar and repeating mix of challenges for multinational companies (MNCs). They constituted a postcolonial transition for international business (IB), and across the developing world, MNCs began to explore how to respond to these challenges strategically.[4]

This coincided with the creation of IB as an academic field of study. Early IB scholars were concerned with the 'liability of foreignness', economic nationalism and later expropriation.[5] Yet, many changes that stemmed from MNC responses to postcolonial transitions were often normalized as a sign of the times and forgotten after the resurgence of neoliberal orthodoxy in the 1980s.[6] However, economic and political nationalism and the enduring

DOI: 10.4324/9781003001058-1

legacy of global empires have gained increased relevance in recent years, thus highlighting the importance of understanding the legitimization strategies of MNCs faced with postcolonial transitions.[7]

Such legitimization strategies were often based on MNCs' role in promoting economic development. The 1950s and 1960s were characterized by a post-war consensus on orthodox development theory. Ghana (formerly the Gold Coast) and Nigeria were good examples of these dynamics. Most West African nationalist politicians accepted the tenets of development theory, as did the Colonial Office and practically all British firms in Ghana and Nigeria.[8] While the state was envisaged as taking a leading role in this process; foreign investment was seen as beneficial because it was a source of capital, for example, for industrialization, or aided the transfer of skills to Africans. This study focuses on formerly imperial British firms that sought to fit in with this new approach to the economy and adapted their strategies to gain the goodwill of colonial officials and nationalist politicians.[9]

Development policies in West Africa came into their own only at the end of World War II, and the late 1940s and early 1950s saw a surge of economic nationalism and criticism of foreign merchant companies. This became less common through the rest of the 1950s and early 1960s when attention focused on decolonization. By the late 1960s and 1970s, however, economic nationalism returned in the form of promoting indigenous business, expropriations, the expulsion of foreigners and stricter immigration controls. Frederick Cooper, for example, has argued that 'the shifting tendencies of the world economy [...] do not fit a breaking point coinciding with political independence. Rather, they suggest a break a decade later, in the mid-1970s, when modest progress turned into a prolonged crisis. The period 1940–1973 can be dubbed the development era'.[10] This account finishes in the late 1970s, coinciding with the second indigenization programme in Nigeria, which marked the breakdown of the development framework that was so formative for Africa's independence. In the late 1970s, the wave of expropriations worldwide also slowed down noticeably after reaching its peak in 1975, and by 1981 global incidences became increasingly rare.

1.2 Terminology, company selection and country context

The terminology of economic nationalism in West Africa was complex. Localization, Indigenization and Africanization were frequently used interchangeably. Here, I use the term Africanization to denote the replacement of expatriate staff with Africans. This can also be referred to in terms of nationality, for example, Ghanaianization or Nigerianization. For Nigeria, regional rivalries also found an expression in terms such as Northernization. The UAC and Unilever coined their own parlance on the issue, referring to Africanization as Ization more generally (and hence encompassing their global operations).

In contrast to this, I use indigenization to refer to changes in ownership or shareholding that led to part or total ownership of an enterprise by local interests, whether private, public or corporate. Local incorporation refers to the local registration of a formerly extraterritorial firm, whereas localization is used as a general umbrella term for all these processes. There is also a terminological issue regarding Ghana, whose colonial name was the Gold Coast. Throughout this study, the last name is used exclusively for the colonial period; otherwise, the name Ghana is used if a reference is made to the country during the colonial and postcolonial periods.

The selection of companies was driven by the question of how existing businesses coped with the postcolonial transition from a colonial presence to operating in a newly independent country. Hence the oil industry is not included because these companies entered Nigeria towards the end of the colonial period. Moreover, due to their economic importance, they were not subject to the general indigenization legislation, as negotiations with oil and petroleum firms were dealt with separately.[11] The firms featured in this book dominated the West African colonies in the post-war years and continued to be significant at least until the 1970s. In Nigeria, for example, eight business representatives, among them four of the five companies chosen for this study – Bank of British West Africa (BBWA) (later Standard Bank of West Africa), Barclays Bank DCO (later Barclays Bank International), the Unilever subsidiary United Africa Company (UAC) and John Holt & Co. (Holt) (Liverpool) – were consulted by the governor on business representation in parliament, an indication of who the key economic players were at the beginning of the period.[12]

Barclays and BBWA remained predominantly branch bankers, but they increased their local business substantially. They also began to compete – often unsuccessfully – with African banks for government accounts, and advertised themselves to African customers instead of serving almost exclusively expatriates. UAC and Holt changed their primary fields of operation in these years. At the end of the war, they were still mainly produce and general merchants, but commercial and official pressure led to their withdrawal from many small retail activities and to some extent from produce buying as well. They went increasingly into wholesale and distribution, and the UAC opened a chain of department stores (Kingsways). Holt invested in construction and building supplies, often with technical partners, as did UAC. The Unilever subsidiary expanded significantly into textile printing, packaging and highly profitable beer brewing. The fifth firm in the sample is Ashanti Goldfields Corporation (AGC), which operated a major gold mine in Ghana in one location (Obuasi).

Nigeria and Ghana are, despite some similarities, two very different countries, especially in terms of their economic and political development. But they also differ in their geographical and human endowments regarding size, natural resources, ethnic diversity, levels of wealth and education. During decolonization, however, political events in the Gold Coast affected

Nigeria and vice versa, for example, the speed of constitutional devolution or the introduction of a central bank. The Gold Coast was considered the better-developed country, capable of quicker advances. Nigerian politics became dominated by regionalism and ethnic rivalries to a greater extent than Ghana. In the 1960s, their economic fortunes diverged as Nigeria began to exploit the oil resources in the East, while prices for Ghana's main export and the source of its wealth, cocoa, declined. But there were also political differences. While Nigeria was a federation with a fragile alliance at its centre, which pursued essentially liberal economic policies, Ghana's more centralized political system was initially dominated by its first independent head of state, Kwame Nkrumah, who experimented with African socialism, 'big push' industrialization schemes and protectionist policies. This difference remained significant until the 1970s when military dictatorships controlled both countries. Ghana blocked remittances from foreign investors during this time period and went into a prolonged economic crisis, whereas Nigeria remained open to foreign investment and experienced an economic boom because of its oil revenues.

British business reflected on these differences, and most companies shifted their attention in the late 1960s towards the more profitable Nigeria. Previously, decision-making on dealing with African economic nationalism after the war was more determined by experiences in Ghana, especially to consumer protests and political campaigns by new nationalist parties. But they were also aware that they were faced with similar policies of local participation in foreign investment across Africa, and they interpreted events in Ghana and Nigeria in this light.[13] The indigenization programmes that occurred in both countries were also remarkably similar, more so than the nationalizations in Tanzania or Uganda.[14]

1.3 Decolonization and development

MNC strategies for dealing with postcolonial transitions reflected their potential role in the process of economic and social development. Frederick Cooper and Randall Packard discussed the importance of the idea of development for the social sciences.[15] They emphasized how the notion of development reverberated in local contexts, giving peripheral groups a sense of entitlement and a place in the global economy from which they could make demands based on the moral and political right of development: 'Development in the 1940s was a framing device through which colonial regimes tried to respond to challenges and reassert control and legitimacy, but it was a device that could itself be challenged and seized, used for different ends'.[16]

Their conception of development as an ideological framework that frames redistributional struggles, political alliances of different groupings and the participation of several conflicting interests in the same discourse, none of whom were entirely in control of the contents and the boundaries of the debate. Corporate responses reflected this concern with 'development', especially in their corporate political activities and commercial decisions. For British companies in West Africa, the nationalist mobilization after the war created the prospect that firms would not be allowed to continue unless they adapted to the demands of future independent nations. The nature of this development discourse, and its interpretation by companies, is the subject of chapter 2.

However, did decolonization truly end the imperial presence of more powerful countries in the newly independent states? Gallagher and Robinson argued that the nature of British imperial expansion shifted between formal and informal control.[17] Whereas on the African continent, the lack of effective large-scale states and imperial rivalries led to the imposition of formal rule. The notion of local collaborators and informal modes of control returned in the form of neo-colonialism, which cast British companies in the role of new imperial agents.[18]

1.4 MNCs and the postcolonial transition during decolonization

Research focusing on MNCs in developing countries tended to consider the activities of firms separately during decolonization, and the political risk they faced from expropriations in formerly colonial countries. This book views both as connected – decolonization marked a transition from a colonial institutional framework to an independent one. Still, colonial legacies meant that the new institutional arrangements were not stable. Postcolonial transition refers to this process of change that was not complete with independence and that culminated in a period of economic nationalism and expropriation of foreign property.[19] The experience of MNCs in Ghana and Nigeria was repeated, with variations, in other formerly colonial states. The legitimization strategies firms employed were deployed in different regions at different times.[20] These continuities become visible when considering how consistent corporate strategies remained before and after independence.

Nevertheless, several historiographical debates have focused only on business-government relations during decolonization. Here the focus has been on whether colonial governments collaborated with companies during decolonization. Imperial historians such as Sarah Stockwell, Roger Tignor, Larry Butler and Nicholas White have addressed whether colonial governments continued to support the interest of imperial firms during decolonization. Stockwell, for example, seeks to counter an earlier study by Milburn, in which the author maintains that British businesses had not prepared for independence.[21] Nwankwo, in his history of British banks in Nigeria, came to a similar conclusion to Milburn.[22] Stockwell demonstrated that companies did indeed prepare, but that their attempts to influence official policies were not universally successful. She concluded that distance bordering on mistrust developed between the colonial government and imperial business during decolonization. As British companies became increasingly sidelined in the process of decolonization, they began to develop new corporate strategies that maintained some influence and failing that, at least some sympathy in official circles. The merit of Stockwell's study is that she demonstrates that businesses aimed to be involved in wider political, social and economic concerns and projects. To be accepted as partners meant that they were potentially able to influence the course of political decision-making. Butler similarly researched the political activities of mining companies in Northern Rhodesia/Zambia.[23]

They document a change from the rather closer relationship between imperial business and colonial governments before and during World War II. Deutsch argued that the collaboration between business and the Nigerian government peaked in 1940 and subsequently declined; the same year that Cooper and Randall suggest for the adoption of 'development' as the new colonial rationale by Britain.[24] Tignor's comparative study of British companies during decolonization in Egypt, Nigeria and Kenya comes to a similar conclusion. He offers a sustained comparison between the official economic policies of three former colonies that developed very differently after decolonization. He deplores that nationalism and politics take over economic questions during decolonization in all three countries and argues that nationalism remained a powerful force throughout this period.[25] One of his central arguments, that Nigeria became a mixed economy, mainly through the introduction of marketing boards, which were crucial instruments of state control of the economy in the name of development. Deutsch analyzes the rationale and interests behind their inception in *Educating the Middlemen*, which makes it clear that the experience of World War II was central in creating a more active role for the colonial state in the economy.[26] The key insights were summarized by White, who drew on his research on colonial Malaya and a range of international studies.[27]

These conclusions have been challenged by Uche, who has highlighted the close relationship between British business and the British government.[28] However, his evidence reflects the post-independence period, specifically the late 1960s and 1970s, in which the position of the British government vis-à-vis its companies operating abroad changed back to a more supportive position due to the international competition between investors.[29] This study is more concerned with the strategies employed by MNCs to manage both the challenges and opportunities that emerge from the actions of host and home governments. At all times, MNCs sought out political contacts and aimed to gain the acceptance and goodwill of politicians. In Ghana and Nigeria, their attention shifted from colonial governments towards the emerging African elites in politics and business (see chapter 3).

1.5 Economic nationalism and expropriations

Economic nationalism became an issue of greater relevance in the 1970s, as a wave of expropriations unsettled the post-war development discourse.

This coincided with critical scholarship at the time such as the rise of Latin American dependency theory. These ideas reached Africa via Walter Rodney's *How Europe Underdeveloped Africa*. He argued that the political and economic inequality in the world was due to imperial exploitation and, more recently, MNCs.[30] Other authors defended the role of MNCs in the world economy.[31] UNCTAD took a keen interest in these issues and began to publish research and overviews of its own, supporting demands for a New International Economic Order and generally favouring a moderate internationalist view, which nevertheless favoured closer host economy control of foreign investment, and applauded the indigenization programmes.[32]

Indigenization programmes were, however, controversial, and viewed as mistakes by defenders of MNCs, or failures by their critics. UNCTAD criticized many programmes for their focus on ownership, which undermined attempts to extend host country control over foreign investors.[33] Some, however, took a more differentiated position towards economic nationalism: Collins pointed out that Nigerian indigenization often masked internal redistributional struggles over definitions of citizenship.[34] In the most extensive and detailed study of the Nigerian Enterprise Promotion Decrees, Biersteker emphasized the role Nigerian businessmen played in the formulation of the first NEPD and in the subversion of the second. Despite being cautiously positive about the impact of indigenization on local manufacturing, he concurs that real control over investment only rarely changed hands (he cites banking and insurance as exceptions).[35] Chapter 4 specifically addresses the indigenization programmes in Ghana and Nigeria from the perspective of the MNCs.

IB history often covers time periods of economic nationalism in long-run corporate histories, for example, the extensive work of Geoffrey Jones.[36] The history of British imperial business has benefited especially from Mira Wilkins' concept of the free-standing company (FSC).[37] This type of business was normally conducted from a metropolitan head office, often in the City, which specialized in one country or one region of the world. By the 1960s and 1970s, this organizational form became less common due to a wave of mergers. Most of the companies in this sample followed this pattern at least at one stage of their development: UAC and John Holt were predominantly active in West Africa and Africa (and the UAC was managed at arm's length, operating very independently within the Unilever group), Ashanti Goldfields (only Ghana) and the BBWA (only West Africa), were FSCs.[38] Barclays Bank DCO's three predecessors had been focused on specific areas: Egypt, South Africa and, in the case of the Colonial Bank, West Africa and the Caribbean. The UAC acquired interests in the Congo and Eastern Africa and was not an FSC, because it was a wholly-owned subsidiary of Unilever, which operated worldwide. Holt (which opened French and US American subsidiaries in the 1930s) and AGC were bought during the 1960s and 1970s by Lonrho and BBWA by Standard Bank.

Unilever and the UAC have seen the greatest scholarly interest of all the companies in this study. Jones published a commissioned corporate history of Unilever, which assesses the importance for Unilever of UAC and the African business, particularly in Ghana and Nigeria.[39] Previously, Fieldhouse's corporate history of the UAC attributed the decline of the company to the increased politicization of the economy.[40] Economic nationalism and poor financial performance led to greater protectionism, something Fieldhouse refers to as a 'shadow'. He defines economic decolonization in an earlier book as something that was happening almost simultaneously with political decolonization.[41] However, in his history of the UAC, he extends this to a much wider and less clearly defined timeframe: 'the economic evolution of many of the African countries from the mid-century threatened UAC's life-blood. I have loosely described this process as "economic decolonization", by which I mean the process by which the African countries, once politically independent, used their sovereignty to cast off, or at least limit, the power of foreign merchant capital'.[42]

While not a well-defined concept, economic decolonization is significant because it connects decolonization and economic nationalism. This fusion of anti-colonial and nationalist sentiment with demands for economic asset redistribution defines the postcolonial transition. Hodgkin described African nationalism in 1956 partly as a 'revolt against an inferior economic status'. Still, such economic nationalism became submerged in the transfer of power, only to emerge in the early 1960s and more forcibly in the late 1960s and 1970s, when the development agenda had failed to deliver economic prosperity.[43]

The economic nationalism of the postcolonial transition shared many similarities with other countries such as Canada. Breton describes economic nationalism as focused on the redistribution of wealth, not on economic growth, by shifting sources of income away from the lower-income groups and agricultural producers towards the (educated) middle classes.[44] This aspiring new middle class, which often suffered from a lack of career opportunities, benefited from nationalist policies that increased the state's control of employment in key sectors such as administration and manufacturing. Bates described similar dynamics in African countries as development coalitions, which were made up of producers and commercial interests that benefited from political patronage.[45] Johnson defined economic nationalism as a community deciding to exchange actual private consumption for the collective consumption of a 'public good', i.e., the national ownership and control of the economic system. This involved actors not taking decisions on purely economic grounds, but also considering factors such as social prestige and national pride in their 'imagined community'.[46]

Economic nationalism and firms' responses to local content requirements and expropriations are often considered in isolation from MNCs' staffing decisions. However, the workforce of MNCs became more diverse during this period, a process described by Perlmutter at the time in almost natural terms.[47] Yet historical research into corporate files shows that political considerations influenced human resource policies. The second part of the book connects the internal changes within the firms to the corporate responses to the broader institutional changes.

1.6 The postcolonial transition and Africanization

Curiously, the subject of Africanization has not attracted a great deal of historical attention. The Africanization of the civil service was a hotly debated topic during decolonization in West Africa, but few works devote more than a couple of pages to the subject.[48] It was more explicitly the focus of Nicolson's work on *The Administration of Nigeria* that offered the perspective of a former expatriate civil servant and Olusanya, a Nigerian historian, who addressed the racism within the service.[49] Even less attention was paid to corporate Africanization, with Milburn the first to analyze the Ghanaian case.[50] Stockwell only briefly mentions the advance of African managers in her study and mostly refers to their role in corporate representation.[51] A more in-depth, sociological analysis of relevance is Burawoy's enquiry into the Zambian copper mining industry.[52] His research is unique as he worked for one of the mining companies and conducted interviews during and after his formal employment contract when Africanization was still ongoing. The importance of Africanization as a legitimization strategy has not been fully recognized in business historical research.[53]

Research into Africans as workers and employees of foreign firms rather than managers saw greater interest, especially in the 1970s and 1980s. The political aspects of Africa's labour movements, or the lack thereof, remained a particularly controversial area. Initially, interest in the history of organized workers in Africa began with Hodgkin's book *Nationalism in Africa*, whose central premise, that all protest movements in colonial countries were essentially national or proto-national, was disputed in an influential work by Coleman.[54] Coleman's critique changed the interpretation of nationalist politics in Africa, emphasizing that they were not as all-encompassing as they were portrayed in the early years. The importance of the global discourse on economic development in the 1940s and 1950s was also evident in the decolonization of the French and British Empires in Africa. Cooper's *Decolonization and African Society* argues that governments wanted to create a bounded working class with whom they could negotiate through an essentially metropolitan system of industrial relations.[55]

This was essential, especially after World War II, to ensure the steady output of tropical commodities and rising productivity needed for Britain's post-war reconstruction. Labour, however, turned these development theories into a basis for entitlements, and the increase in strikes, consumer protests, riots and nationalist agitation gave rise to fears of losing control. Subsequently, social issues were subsumed by the 'nationalist struggle', as colonial governments could now conveniently deflect demands for universal entitlements. In contrast, the nationalist politicians, who took over government step by step, showed more remarkable ability to contain conflict, at least until independence.[56]

This debate ignored the corporate context, in which increasing numbers of Ghanaians, Nigerians and other Africans worked. Chapter 5 compares the speed of Africanization between the public and private sectors and between the companies and industries selected for this study. Corporate Africanization lagged that of the public sector and only showed signs of significant progress several years after independence. Chapter 6 considers the experience of African staff in MNCs, including the tensions and challenges that accompanied the change from a majority expatriate workforce to a majority domestic African one.

1.7 Legitimization strategies and the postcolonial transition

This book takes an organizational focus and seeks to understand the significant changes in Ghana and Nigeria in this time period through the lens of corporate archives. While this requires an appreciation of the political and social transformations that occurred at the time, MNCs interpreted these in sometimes idiosyncratic ways. Even though specific strategies could differ between firms and change over time, the overarching goal was to ensure the legitimacy of MNCs in newly emerging states. Legitimacy here refers to organizations' actual and metaphorical social license to operate. It is defined as the 'generalized perception or assumption that organizational activities are desirable, proper, or appropriate within some socially constructed system of norms, values, beliefs, and definitions'.[57] The relevance of legitimacy theory for business historical research is demonstrated by a growing body of theory-informed studies, which encompass MNCs operating in Africa, Latin America and Asia.

On the African continent, business historical research often investigates the social expectations of MNCs without explicitly referencing the concept or theory of legitimacy.[58] Yet legitimization strategies are evident across a range of corporate activities.[59] Indeed, legitimization attempts were not only limited to host countries, but MNCs were also under pressure to justify their actions in their home countries due to expanding international media coverage.[60] In Latin America, MNCs in the oil industry, in particular, have been the focus of research on responses to economic nationalism.[61] Yet, companies in other sectors also faced the threat of obsolescing legitimacy.[62] The drivers of expropriations and economic nationalism can be found in political alliances, as highlighted by a comparative study of Latin American and African states.[63]

On the Asian continent, Malaysia and India have been the focus of business historical research. Both colonial Malaya and the actions of the independent state of Malaysia have seen substantial research on issues related to legitimacy, if not overtly labelled as such.[64] Research on India, in particular, has highlighted the often counter-intuitive and original strategies employed by foreign investors keen to disassociate themselves from colonial identities.[65] While not all of these contributions explicitly conceptualize their research as dealing with legitimization strategies of MNCs; they do engage with very similar concerns about how MNCs engage with host and home countries and the societal expectations they face. In all these cases, such expectations fluctuate and rapidly change as countries find themselves in a postcolonial transition. The companies in this study began to reflect on the similarities of these processes that their subsidiaries encountered across Latin American, African and Asian host countries and often deployed strategies based on the experience they had accumulated in more than one location. Hence, corporate legitimization strategies emerge as a significant conceptual framework that allows us to compare the experience of IB in the middle of the twentieth century across the developing world.

Notes

1 Chairman's statement at the annual general meeting, 8 March 1957, Liverpool Records Office (hereafter LRO) 380 HOL II (formerly Acc 4888).
2 Witold J. Henisz, "The Dynamic Capability of Corporate Diplomacy," *Global Strategy Journal* 6, no. 3 (2016): 184, https://doi.org/10.1002/gsj.1121.
3 Henisz, "The Dynamic Capability of Corporate Diplomacy," 195.
4 Stephanie Decker, "Postcolonial Transitions in Africa: Decolonization in West Africa and Present Day South Africa," *Journal of Management Studies* 47, no. 5 (2010): 791–813, https://doi.org/10.1111/j.1467-6486.2010.00924.x.
5 R Vernon, *Sovereignty at Bay: The Multinational Spread of US Enterprises* (New York: Basic Books, 1971); S Hymer, *On Multinational Corporations and Foreign Direct Investment: The Theory of Transnational Corporations* (London: Routledge for the United Nations, 1960); SJ Kobrin, "Expropriation as an Attempt to Control Foreign Firms in LDCs: Trends from 1960 to 1979," *International Studies Quarterly* 28.3 (1984), 329–48.
6 HV Perlmutter, "The Tortuous Evolution of the Multinational Corporation," *Columbia Journal of World Business* 4.1 (1969), 9–18; S Decker, "Africanization in British Multinationals in Ghana and Nigeria, 1945–1970," *Business History Review* 92.4 (2018), 691–718.
7 C Lubinski and RD Wadhwani, "Geopolitical Jockeying: Economic Nationalism and Multinational Strategy in Historical Perspective," *Strategic Management Journal* 41.3 (2020), 400–21; I Minefee and M Bucheli, "MNC Responses to International NGO Activist Campaigns: Evidence from Royal Dutch/Shell in Apartheid South Africa," *Journal of International Business Studies* 52.5 (2021), 971–98.
8 Tony Killick, *Development Economics in Action: A Study of Economic Policies in Ghana, Studies in the Economics of Africa* (London i.a.: Heinemann Educational, 1978), 17–24.
9 David Kenneth Fieldhouse, *Merchant Capital and Economic Decolonisation: The United Africa Company 1929–1987* (Oxford: Clarendon, 1994), 413.

10 Frederick Cooper, *Africa since 1940: The Past of the Present* (Cambridge, UK, and New York, NY: Cambridge University Press, 2002), 85.
11 Thomas J Biersteker, *Multinationals, the State, and the Control of the Nigerian Economy* (Princeton, NJ: Princeton University Press, 1987).
12 The fifth company, Ashanti Goldfields Corporation, was only active in Ghana. RWT Bateson (General Manager Holt, Lagos area) to AC Walker (Administrative Department Liverpool), 26 August 1951, Rhodes House Oxford (RHO) Mss Afr. s 825 421 (v).
13 At Barclays the board members concluded: '[...] you can see the political/economic changes in Swaziland following the normal pattern we've so often seen elsewhere and it is not a question of "if" we have to go local but "when".' See "Swaziland – Note of discussion with Mr. R. Stephens, Minister of Finance, Johannesburg," 8 November 1972, p. 4, Barclays Group Archive (hereafter BGA) 80/5666.
14 M Bucheli and S Decker, "Expropriations of Foreign Property and Political Alliances: A Business Historical Approach," *Enterprise & Society* 22, no. 1 (2021), 247–84.
15 Frederick Cooper and Randall M Packard, *International Development and the Social Sciences: Essays on the History and Politics of Knowledge* (Berkeley, CA, London: University of California Press, 1997).
16 Cooper and Packard, *International Development and the Social Sciences,* 12, 18.
17 John Gallagher and Ronald Robinson, "The Imperialism of Free Trade," *Economic History Review* 6, no. 1 (1953): 1–15.
18 Kwame Nkrumah, *Neo-Colonialism: The Last Stage of Imperialism* (New York: International Publishers, 1965); David Kenneth Fieldhouse, "'A New Imperial System?' The Role of the Multinational Reconsidered," in *Imperialism and After,* ed. Wolfgang J Mommsen and J Osterhammel (London: Allen & Unwin for the German Historical Institute, 1986), 225–40.
19 Decker, "Postcolonial Transitions in Africa: Decolonization."
20 Stephanie Decker, "Corporate Legitimacy and Advertising: British Companies and the Rhetoric of Development in West Africa, 1950–1970," *Business History Review* 81, no. 1 (2007): 59–86, https://doi.org/10.2307/25097298; Marcelo Bucheli and E Salvaj, "Multinational Corporations' Obsolescing Political Legitimacy: ITT in Chile, 1920–1972," *Business History Review* 87, no. 3 (2013): 729–55, https://doi.org/10.1017/S0007680513001116.
21 Sarah E Stockwell, *The Business of Decolonization: British Business Strategies in the Gold Coast* (Oxford: Clarendon Press, 2000); Sarah E Stockwell, "Political Strategies of British Business during Decolonization – the Case of the Gold-Coast Ghana, 1945–57," *Journal of Imperial and Commonwealth History* 23, no. 2 (1995): 277–300.
22 GO Nwankwo, "British Overseas Banks in the Developing Countries," *Journal of the Institute of Bankers*, no. June–October (1972): 148–58, 253–61, 329–39.
23 Larry J Butler, *Copper Empire: Mining and the Colonial State in Northern Rhodesia, c. 1930–64, Cambridge Imperial and Post-Colonial Studies* (Houndmill: Palgrave Macmillan, 2007); Larry J Butler, "Business and British Decolonisation: Sir Ronald Prain, the Mining Industry and the Central African Federation," *Journal of Imperial and Commonwealth History* 35, no. 3 (2007): 459–84, https://doi.org/10.1080/03086530701523455.
24 Cooper and Packard, "International Development," 7; Jan-Georg Deutsch, *Educating the Middlemen: Political and Economic History of Statutory Cocoa Marketing in Nigeria, 1936–1947* (Berlin: Das Arabische Buch, 1995), 234.
25 Robert L Tignor, *Capitalism and Nationalism at the End of Empire: State and Business in Decolonizing Egypt, Nigeria, and Kenya, 1945–1963* (Princeton, N.J.: Princeton University Press, 1998), 287–88.
26 Deutsch, *Educating the Middlemen.*

27 Nicholas J White, "The Survival, Revival and Decline of British Economic Influence in Malaysia, 1957–70," *Twentieth Century British History* 14, no. 3 (2003): 222–42; Nicholas J White, "The Business and the Politics of Decolonization: The British Experience in the Twentieth Century," *Economic History Review* 53, no. 3 (2000): 544–64; Nicholas J White, *British Business in Post-Colonial Malaysia, 1957–70: Neo-Colonialism or Disengagement?, RoutledgeCurzon Studies in the Modern History of Asia 21* (London: RoutledgeCurzon, 2004); Nicholas John White, "Imperial Business Interests, Decolonization and Post-Colonial Diversification," in *The Oxford Handbook of the Ends of Empire*, ed. Martin Thomas and Andrew Thompson (Oxford and New York: Oxford University Press, 2017), 1–27, https://doi.org/10.1093/oxfordhb/9780198713197.013.35.

28 Chibuike Uche, "Oil, British Interests and the Nigerian Civil War," *Journal of African History* 49, no. 1 (2008): 111–35, https://doi.org/10.1017/S0021853708003393; Chibuike Ugochukwu Uche, "British Government, British Businesses, and the Indigenization Exercise in Post-Independence Nigeria," *Business History Review* 86, no. 4 (2013): 745–71, https://doi.org/10.1017/S000768051200181X.

29 Stephanie Decker, "Less than an Empire and More than British: Foreign Investor Competition in Ghana and Nigeria in the 1960s," in *Imagining Britain's Economic Future, c.1800–1975: Trade, Consumerism and Global Markets*, ed. David Thackeray, Andrew Thompson, and Richard Toye (London: Palgrave, 2018), 183–203, https://www.palgrave.com/gb/book/9783319712963.

30 WL Bernecker and T Fischer, "Rise and Decline of Latin American Dependency Theories," *Itinerario* 22, no. 4 (1998): 25–45; Colin Leys, *The Rise and Fall of Development Theory* (London UK: James Currey, 1996); C Kay, *Latin American Theories of Development and Underdevelopment* (London: Routlede, 1989); Cooper and Packard, 'International Development.'

31 Vernon, *Sovereignty at Bay: The Multinational Spread of US*; Charles Lipson, *Standing Guard: Protecting Foreign Capitalism in the Nineteenth and Twentieth Century* (Berkeley and London: University of California Press, 1985); Paul E Sigmund, *Multinationals in Latin America: The Politics of Nationalization, a Twentieth Century Fund Study* (Madison, WI, and London: University of Wisconsin Press, 1980).

32 United Nations Report by a Group of Eminent Persons, *The Impact of Multinational Corporations on Development and in International Relations* (New York NY: UN Department of Economic and Social Affairs, 1974); RL Rothstein, *Global Bargaining: Unctad and the Quest for a New International Economic Order* (Princeton, NJ: Princeton University Press, 1979).

33 UN Commission on Transnational Corporations, "Transnational Corporations in World Development – Third Survey," 1983; Ankie Hoogvelt, "Indigenization and Technological Dependency," *Development and Change* 11, no. 2 (1980): 257–72.

34 Paul Collins, "The Political Economy of Indigenization: The Case of the Nigerian Enterprises Promotion Decree," *African Review* 4, no. 4 (1974): 491–508.

35 Biersteker, *Multinationals*; see also Ankie Hoogvelt, "Indigenisation and Foreign Capital: Industrialisation in Nigeria," *Review of African Political Economy* 14 (1979): 56–68; M Adejugbe, "The Myths and Realities of Nigeria Business Indigenization," *Development and Change* 15, no. 4 (1984): 577–92.

36 Geoffrey Jones, *Merchants to Multinationals: British Trading Companies in the Nineteenth and Twentieth Centuries* (Oxford University Press: Oxford, 2000); Geoffrey Jones, *British Multinational Banking, 1830–1990* (New York: OUP, 1993).

37 Mira Wilkins, "The Free-Standing Company, 1870–1914: An Important Type of British Foreign Direct Investment," *The Economic History Review* 41, no. 2 (1988): 259–82, http://onlinelibrary.wiley.com/doi/10.1111/j.1468-0289.1988.tb00465.x/full.

38 Stephanie Decker, "Return to Imperial Trade? John Holt & Co (Liverpool) Ltd. as a Contemporary Free-Standing Company, 1945–2006," in *The Empire in One City?*

Liverpool's Inconvenient Imperial Past, Studies in Imperialism (Liverpool: Liverpool University Press, 2008), 300–335.

39 Geoffrey Jones, *Renewing Unilever. Transformation and Tradition* (Oxford: Oxford University Press, 2005).

40 Fieldhouse, *Merchant Capital and Economic Decolonisation*, 674, 758–62.

41 David Kenneth Fieldhouse, *Black Africa 1945–1980: Economic Decolonisation and Arrested Development* (London: Allen & Unwin, 1986), https://doi.org/10.4324/9780203838525.

42 Fieldhouse, *Merchant Capital and Economic Decolonisation*, vii.

43 Thomas L. Hodgkin, *Nationalism in Colonial Africa.* (London: Frederick Mueller, 1956); Axel Harneit-Sievers, "African Business, 'Economic Nationalism', and British Colonial Policy: Southern Nigeria, 1935–1954," *African Economic History* 24 (1996): 25–68.

44 Albert Breton, "The Economics of Nationalism," *The Journal of Political Economy* 72, no. 4 (1964): 376–86.

45 Robert H Bates, *Markets and States in Tropical Africa: The Political Basis of Agricultural Policies* (Berkeley, Los Angeles, CA, and London: University of California Press, 1981), 6–7, 62–77, 121.

46 Harry Gordon Johnson, *Economic Nationalism in Old and New States, a Publication of the Committee for the Comparative Study of New Nations, University of Chicago* (London: Allen & Unwin, 1968); Benedict Anderson, *Imagined Communities: Reflections on the Origin and Spread of Nationalism* (London and New York: Verso, 1993), https://doi.org/10.2307/2056089.

47 Perlmutter, "The Tortuous Evolution."

48 FM Bourret, *Ghana: The Road to Independence 1919–1957* (Stanford CA: Stanford University Press, 1969), 40–3, 66–8, 145, 155, 160–2, 171, 178–9, 184, 215; JS Coleman, *Nigeria: Background to Nationalism* (Berkeley, CA: University of California Press, 1971), 90, 154–9, 312–14, 427, 448 fn36; Dennis Austin, *Politics in Ghana* (Oxford: Oxford University Press, 1964), 8, 158, 166.

49 IF Nicolson, *The Administration of Nigeria 1900–60: Men, Methods, and Myths* (Oxford: Clarendon, 1969); GO Olusanya, *The Evolution of the Nigerian Civil Service, 1861–1960: The Problem of Nigerianization* (Yaba and Lagos, Nigeria: University of Lagos, 1975); see also FG Burke and PL French, "Bureaucracy and Africanization," in *Frontiers of Development Administration*, ed. Fred W Riggs (Durham, NC: Duke University Press, 1970), 538–55.

50 Josephine F. Milburn, *British Business and Ghanaian Independence* (London: C. Hurst, 1977).

51 SE Stockwell, *The Business of Decolonization: British Business Strategies in the Gold Coast* (Oxford: Clarendon, 2000), 140–5, 171–5.

52 Michael Burawoy, *The Colour of Class on the Copper Mines: From African Advancement to Zambianization* (Manchester: Manchester University Press, 1972).

53 Decker, "Africanization."

54 Hodgkin, *Nationalism in Colonial Africa.*; Coleman, *Nigeria: Background to Nationalism.*

55 Frederick Cooper, *Decolonization and African Society: The Labour Question in French and British Africa, Africa: Journal of the International African Institute* (Cambridge, UK: Cambridge University Press, 1996), https://doi.org/10.2307/1161082.

56 Cooper, *Decolonization and African Society*, 468–70.

57 Mark C Suchman, "Managing Legitimacy: Strategic and Institutional Approaches," *Academy of Management Review* 20, no. 3 (1995): 574.

58 Marie Claire Loison, Celine Berrier-Lucas, and Anne Pezet, "Corporate Social Responsibility before CSR: Practices at Aluminium Du Cameroun (Alucam) from the 1950s to the 1980s," *Business History* 62, no. 2 (2020): 292–342, https://doi.org/10.1080/00076791.2018.1427070; Ian Phimister, "Corporate Profit and Race in

Central African Copper Mining, 1946–1958," *Business History Review* 85, no. 4 (2011): 749–74, https://doi.org/10.1017/S0007680511001188.

59 Decker, "Africanization"; Decker, "Corporate Legitimacy and Advertising."

60 Nikolas Glover, "Between Order and Justice: Investments in Africa and Corporate International Responsibility in Swedish Media in the 1960s," *Enterprise and Society* 20, no. 2 (2019): 401–44, https://doi.org/10.1017/eso.2018.87.

61 Marcelo Bucheli and Ruth V. Aguilera, "Political Survival, Energy Policies, and Multinational Corporations: A Historical Study for Standard Oil of New Jersey in Colombia, Mexico, and Venezuela in the Twentieth Century," *Management International Review* 50, no. 3 (2010): 347–78, https://doi.org/10.1007/s11575-010-0036-1; Marcelo Bucheli, "Canadian Multinational Corporations and Economic Nationalism: The Case of Imperial Oil Limited in Alberta (Canada) and Colombia, 1899–1938," *Entreprises et Histoire* 54, no. April (2010): 67–85; Marcelo Bucheli and Gonzalo Romero Sommer, "Multinational Corporations, Property Rights, and Legitimization Strategies: US Investors in the Argentine and Peruvian Oil Industries in the Twentieth Century," *Australian Economic History Review* 54, no. 2 (2014): 145–63, https://doi.org/10.1111/aehr.12042; Stephen Haber, Noel Maurer, and Armando Razo, "When the Law Does Not Matter: The Rise and Decline of the Mexican Oil Industry," *The Journal of Economic History* 63, no. 1 (2003): 1–32.

62 Bucheli and Salvaj, "Multinational Corporations' Obsolescing Political"; Marcelo Bucheli, "Multinational Corporations, Totalitarian Regimes and Economic Nationalism: United Fruit Company in Central America, 1899–1975," *Business History* 50, no. 4 (2008): 433–54, http://www.informaworld.com/10.1080/00076790802106315.

63 Bucheli and Decker, "Expropriations."

64 Shakila Yacob, "Model of Welfare Capitalism? The United States Rubber Company in Southeast Asia, 1910–1942," *Enterprise and Society* 8, no. 1 (2007): 136–74, https://doi.org/10.1093/es/khl071; Shakila Yacob, "Ford's Investment in Colonial Malaya, 1926–1957," *Business History Review* 83, no. 4 (2009): 789–812; Shakila Yacob and Nicholas J. White, "The 'Unfinished Business' of Malaysia's Decolonisation: The Origins of the Guthrie 'Dawn Raid,'" *Modern Asian Studies* 44, no. 5 (2010): 919–60, https://doi.org/10.1017/S0026749X09990308; White, "The Survival, Revival and Decline of British Econo."

65 Christina Lubinski, "Liability of Foreignness in Historical Context: German Business in Preindependence India (1880–1940)," *Enterprise and Society* 15, no. 4 (2014): 722–58, https://doi.org/10.1093/es/khu045; Lubinski and Wadhwani, "Geopolitical Jockeying: Economic Nationalism and Multinational Strategy in Historical Perspective"; Christina Lubinski, "From 'History as Told' to 'History as Experienced': Contextualizing the Uses of the Past," *Organization Studies* 39, no. 12 (2018): 1785–809, https://doi.org/10.1177/0170840618800116.

List of References

Anderson, Benedict. *Imagined Communities: Reflections on the Origin and Spread of Nationalism*. London and New York: Verso, 1993. 10.2307/2056089.

Austin, Dennis. *Politics in Ghana*. Oxford: Oxford University Press, 1964.

Bates, Robert H. *Markets and States in Tropical Africa: The Political Basis of Agricultural Policies*. Berkeley, Los Angeles, CA, and London: University of California Press, 1981.

Bernecker, WL, and T Fischer. "Rise and Decline of Latin American Dependency Theories." *Itinerario* 22, no. 4 (1998): 25–45.

Biersteker, Thomas J. *Multinationals, the State, and the Control of the Nigerian Economy*. Princeton, NJ: Princeton University Press, 1987.

Bourret, F.M. *Ghana: The Road to Independence 1919–1957*. Stanford CA: Stanford University Press, 1969.

Breton, Albert. "The Economics of Nationalism." *The Journal of Political Economy* 72, no. 4 (1964): 376–386.

Bucheli, Marcelo. "Canadian Multinational Corporations and Economic Nationalism: The Case of Imperial Oil Limited in Alberta (Canada) and Colombia, 1899–1938." *Entreprises et Histoire* 54, no. April (2010): 67–85.

Bucheli, Marcelo. "Multinational Corporations, Totalitarian Regimes and Economic Nationalism: United Fruit Company in Central America, 1899–1975." *Business History* 50, no. 4 (2008): 433–454. http://www.informaworld.com/10.1080/00076790802106315.

Bucheli, Marcelo, and Ruth V. Aguilera. "Political Survival, Energy Policies, and Multinational Corporations: A Historical Study for Standard Oil of New Jersey in Colombia, Mexico, and Venezuela in the Twentieth Century." *Management International Review* 50, no. 3 (2010): 347–378. 10.1007/s11575-010-0036-1.

Bucheli, Marcelo, and Stephanie Decker. "Expropriations of Foreign Property and Political Alliances: A Business Historical Approach." *Enterprise & Society* 22, no. 1 (February 28, 2021): 247–284. 10.1017/eso.2019.66.

Bucheli, Marcelo, and E Salvaj. "Multinational Corporations' Obsolescing Political Legitimacy: ITT in Chile, 1920–1972." *Business History Review* 87, no. 3 (2013): 729–755. 10.1017/S0007680513001116.

Bucheli, Marcelo, and Gonzalo Romero Sommer. "Multinational Corporations, Property Rights, and Legitimization Strategies: US Investors in the Argentine and Peruvian Oil Industries in the Twentieth Century." *Australian Economic History Review* 54, no. 2 (2014): 145–163. 10.1111/aehr.12042.

Burawoy, Michael. *The Colour of Class on the Copper Mines: From African Advancement to Zambianization*. Manchester: Manchester University Press, 1972.

Burke, FG, and PL French. "Bureaucracy and Africanization." In *Frontiers of Development Administration*, edited by Fred W. Riggs, 538–555. Durham, NC: Duke University Press, 1970.

Butler, Larry J. "Business and British Decolonisation: Sir Ronald Prain, the Mining Industry and the Central African Federation." *Journal of Imperial and Commonwealth History* 35, no. 3 (2007): 459–484. 10.1080/03086530701523455.

Butler, Larry J. *Copper Empire: Mining and the Colonial State in Northern Rhodesia, c. 1930–64. Cambridge Imperial and Post-Colonial Studies*. Houndmill: Palgrave Macmillan, 2007.

Coleman, J.S. *Nigeria: Background to Nationalism*. Berkeley, CA: University of California Press, 1971.

Collins, Paul. "The Political Economy of Indigenization: The Case of the Nigerian Enterprises Promotion Decree." *African Review* 4, no. 4 (1974): 491–508.

Cooper, Frederick. *Africa since 1940: The Past of the Present*. Cambridge, UK, and New York, NY: Cambridge University Press, 2002.

Cooper, Frederick. *Decolonization and African Society: The Labour Question in French and British Africa. Africa: Journal of the International African Institute*. Cambridge, UK: Cambridge University Press, 1996. 10.2307/1161082.

Cooper, Frederick, and Randall M Packard. *International Development and the Social Sciences: Essays on the History and Politics of Knowledge*. Berkeley, CA, London: University of California Press, 1997.

Decker, Stephanie. "Africanization in British Multinationals in Ghana and Nigeria, 1945–1970." *Business History Review* 92, no. 4 (December 1, 2018): 691–718. 10.1017/S0007680518001034.

Decker, Stephanie. "Corporate Legitimacy and Advertising: British Companies and the Rhetoric of Development in West Africa, 1950–1970." *Business History Review* 81, no. 1 (March 2007): 59–86. 10.2307/25097298.

Decker, Stephanie. "Less than an Empire and More than British: Foreign Investor Competition in Ghana and Nigeria in the 1960s." In *Imagining Britain's Economic Future, c.1800–1975: Trade, Consumerism and Global Markets*, edited by David Thackeray, Andrew Thompson, and Richard Toye, 183–203. London: Palgrave, 2018. https://www.palgrave.com/gb/book/9783319712963.

Decker, Stephanie. "Postcolonial Transitions in Africa: Decolonization in West Africa and Present Day South Africa." *Journal of Management Studies* 47, no. 5 (July 2010): 791–813. 10.1111/j.1467-6486.2010.00924.x.

Decker, Stephanie. "Return to Imperial Trade? John Holt & Co (Liverpool) Ltd. as a Contemporary Free-Standing Company, 1945-2006." In *The Empire in One City? Liverpool's Inconvenient Imperial Past*, edited by Sheryllynne Haggerty, Anthony Webster, and Nicholas J. Whte. 300–335. Studies in Imperialism. Liverpool: Liverpool University Press, 2008.

Deutsch, Jan-Georg. *Educating the Middlemen: Political and Economic History of Statutory Cocoa Marketing in Nigeria, 1936–1947*. Berlin: Das Arabische Buch, 1995.

Fieldhouse, David Kenneth. "'A New Imperial System?' The Role of the Multinational Reconsidered." In *Imperialism and After*, edited by Wolfgang J. Mommsen and J Osterhammel, 225–240. London: Allen & Unwin for the German Historical Institute, 1986.

Fieldhouse, David Kenneth. *Black Africa 1945–1980: Economic Decolonisation and Arrested Development*. London: Allen & Unwin, 1986. 10.4324/9780203838525.

Fieldhouse, David Kenneth. *Merchant Capital and Economic Decolonisation: The United Africa Company 1929–1987*. Oxford: Clarendon, 1994.

Gallagher, John, and Ronald Robinson. "The Imperialism of Free Trade." *Economic History Review* 6, no. 1 (1953): 1–15.

Glover, Nikolas. "Between Order and Justice: Investments in Africa and Corporate International Responsibility in Swedish Media in the 1960s." *Enterprise and Society* 20, no. 2 (2019): 401–444. 10.1017/eso.2018.87.

Haber, Stephen, Noel Maurer, and Armando Razo. "When the Law Does Not Matter: The Rise and Decline of the Mexican Oil Industry." *The Journal of Economic History* 63, no. 1 (2003): 1–32.

Harneit-Sievers, Axel. "African Business, 'Economic Nationalism', and British Colonial Policy: Southern Nigeria, 1935–1954." *African Economic History* 24 (1996): 25–68.

Henisz, Witold J. "The Dynamic Capability of Corporate Diplomacy." *Global Strategy Journal* 6, no. 3 (2016): 183–196. 10.1002/gsj.1121.

Hodgkin, Thomas L. *Nationalism in Colonial Africa*. London: Frederick Mueller, 1956.

Hoogvelt, Ankie. "Indigenisation and Foreign Capital: Industrialisation in Nigeria." *Review of African Political Economy* 14 (1979): 56–68.

Hoogvelt, Ankie. "Indigenization and Technological Dependency." *Development and Change* 11, no. 2 (1980): 257–272.

Hymer, Stephen. *On Multinational Corporations and Foreign Direct Investment: The Theory of Transnational Corporations*. London: Routledge for the United Nations, 1960.

Johnson, Harry Gordon. *Economic Nationalism in Old and New States. A Publication of the Committee for the Comparative Study of New Nations, University of Chicago*. London: Allen & Unwin, 1968.

Jones, Geoffrey. *British Multinational Banking, 1830–1990*. New York: OUP, 1993.

Jones, Geoffrey. *Merchants to Multinationals: British Trading Companies in the Nineteenth and Twentieth Centuries*. Oxford: Oxford University Press, 2000.

Jones, Geoffrey. *Renewing Unilever. Transformation and Tradition*. Oxford: Oxford University Press, 2005.

Kay, C *Latin American Theories of Development and Underdevelopment*. London: Routlede, 1989.

Killick, Tony. *Development Economics in Action: A Study of Economic Policies in Ghana. Studies in the Economics of Africa*. London i.a.: Heinemann Educational, 1978.

Kobrin, Stephen J. "Expropriation as an Attempt to Control Foreign Firms in LDCs: Trends from 1960 to 1979." *International Studies Quarterly* 28, no. 3 (September 1984): 329–48. 10.2307/2600634.

Leys, Colin. *The Rise and Fall of Development Theory*. London UK: James Currey, 1996.

Lipson, Charles. *Standing Guard: Protecting Foreign Capitalism in the Nineteenth and Twentieth Century*. Berkeley and London: University of California Press, 1985.

Loison, Marie Claire, Celine Berrier-Lucas, and Anne Pezet. "Corporate Social Responsibility before CSR: Practices at Aluminium Du Cameroun (Alucam) from the 1950s to the 1980s." *Business History* 62, no. 2 (2020): 292–342. 10.1080/00076791.2018.1427070.

Lubinski, Christina. "From 'History as Told' to 'History as Experienced': Contextualizing the Uses of the Past." *Organization Studies* 39, no. 12 (2018): 1785–809. 10.1177/0170840618800116.

Lubinski, Christina. "Liability of Foreignness in Historical Context: German Business in Preindependence India (1880–1940)." *Enterprise and Society* 15, no. 4 (2014): 722–58. 10.1093/es/khu045.

Lubinski, Christina, and R. Daniel Wadhwani. "Geopolitical Jockeying: Economic Nationalism and Multinational Strategy in Historical Perspective." *Strategic Management Journal* 41, no. 3 (2020): 400–21. 10.1002/smj.3022.

M Adejugbe. "The Myths and Realities of Nigeria Business Indigenization." *Development and Change* 15, no. 4 (1984): 577–92.

Milburn, Josephine F. *British Business and Ghanaian Independence*. London: C. Hurst, 1977.

Minefee, Ishva, and Marcelo Bucheli. "MNC Responses to International NGO Activist Campaigns: Evidence from Royal Dutch/Shell in Apartheid South Africa." *Journal of International Business Studies* 52, no. 5 (2021): 971–98. 10.1057/s41267-021-00422-5.

Nicolson, I.F. *The Administration of Nigeria 1900–60: Men, Methods, and Myths*. Oxford: Clarendon, 1969.

Nkrumah, Kwame. *Neo-Colonialism: The Last Stage of Imperialism*. New York: International Publishers, 1965.

Nwankwo, G.O. "British Overseas Banks in the Developing Countries." *Journal of the Institute of Bankers*, no. June–October (1972): 148–58, 253–61, 329–39.

Olusanya, G.O. *The Evolution of the Nigerian Civil Service, 1861–1960: The Problem of Nigerianization*. Yaba and Lagos, Nigeria: University of Lagos, 1975.

Perlmutter, Howard V. "The Tortuous Evolution of the Multinational Corporation." *Columbia Journal of World Business* 4, no. 1 (1969): 9–18. https://doi.org/Article.

Phimister, Ian. "Corporate Profit and Race in Central African Copper Mining, 1946–1958." *Business History Review* 85, no. 4 (2011): 749–74. 10.1017/S0007680511001188.

Rothstein, R.L. *Global Bargaining: Unctad and the Quest for a New International Economic Order*. Princeton, NJ: Princeton University Press, 1979.

Sigmund, Paul E. *Multinationals in Latin America: The Politics of Nationalization. A Twentieth Century Fund Study*. Madison, WI, and London: University of Wisconsin Press, 1980.

Stockwell, Sarah E. "Political Strategies of British Business during Decolonization – the Case of the Gold-Coast Ghana, 1945–57." *Journal of Imperial and Commonwealth History* 23, no. 2 (1995): 277–300.

Stockwell, Sarah E. *The Business of Decolonization: British Business Strategies in the Gold Coast*. Oxford: Clarendon Press, 2000.

Suchman, Mark C. "Managing Legitimacy: Strategic and Institutional Approaches." *Academy of Management Review* 20, no. 3 (1995): 571–610.

Tignor, Robert L. *Capitalism and Nationalism at the End of Empire: State and Business in Decolonizing Egypt, Nigeria, and Kenya, 1945–1963*. Princeton, N.J.: Princeton University Press, 1998.

Uche, Chibuike. "Oil, British Interests and the Nigerian Civil War." *Journal of African History* 49, no. 1 (2008): 111–35. 10.1017/S0021853708003393.

Uche, Chibuike Ugochukwu. "British Government, British Businesses, and the Indigenization Exercise in Post-Independence Nigeria." *Business History Review* 86, no. 4 (2013): 745–71. 10.1017/S000768051200181X.

UN Commission on Transnational Corporations. "Transnational Corporations in World Development – Third Survey." 1983.

United Nations Report by a Group of Eminent Persons. *The Impact of Multinational Corporations on Development and in International Relations*. New York NY: UN Department of Economic and Social Affairs, 1974.

Vernon, Raymond. *Sovereignty at Bay: The Multinational Spread of US Enterprises*. New York: Basic Books, 1971.

White, Nicholas J. *British Business in Post-Colonial Malaysia, 1957–70: Neo-Colonialism or Disengagement? RoutledgeCurzon Studies in the Modern History of Asia 21*. London: RoutledgeCurzon, 2004.

White, Nicholas J. "The Business and the Politics of Decolonization: The British Experience in the Twentieth Century." *Economic History Review* 53, no. 3 (2000): 544–64.

White, Nicholas J. "The Survival, Revival and Decline of British Economic Influence in Malaysia, 1957–70." *Twentieth Century British History* 14, no. 3 (2003): 222–42.

White, Nicholas John. "Imperial Business Interests, Decolonization and Post-Colonial Diversification." In *The Oxford Handbook of the Ends of Empire*, edited by Martin Thomas and Andrew Thompson, 1–27. Oxford and New York: Oxford University Press, 2017. 10.1093/oxfordhb/9780198713197.013.35.

Wilkins, Mira. "The Free-Standing Company, 1870–1914: An Important Type of British Foreign Direct Investment." *The Economic History Review* 41, no. 2 (1988): 259–82. http://onlinelibrary.wiley.com/doi/10.1111/j.1468-0289.1988.tb00465.x/full.

Yacob, Shakila. "Ford's Investment in Colonial Malaya, 1926–1957." *Business History Review* 83, no. 4 (2009): 789–812.

Yacob, Shakila. "Model of Welfare Capitalism? The United States Rubber Company in Southeast Asia, 1910–1942." *Enterprise and Society* 8, no. 1 (2007): 136–74. 10.1093/es/khl071.

Yacob, Shakila, and Nicholas J. White. "The 'Unfinished Business' of Malaysia's Decolonisation: The Origins of the Guthrie 'Dawn Raid.'" *Modern Asian Studies* 44, no. 5 (2010): 919–60. 10.1017/S0026749X09990308.

2 Organizational Legitimacy and the Development Discourse

Development ideologies have been central to the relationship between international business and African states, as successive governments in Nigeria and Ghana have experimented with different approaches to economic progress. The economy's needs were almost exclusively seen through the filter of the then-current ideology, and the role of foreign investment was dependent on these trends. The ideas of early development economists dominated the scene until the 1960s and exerted a significant influence on government policy. What has not been considered in the literature is the role that foreign business played in shaping and exploiting these ideas about development. While companies' attempts to find a new role in decolonizing countries have been researched, this has obscured the fact that the strategies of representation that British business developed were not only a response to the end of empire but also an essential feature of corporate political activity in independent states.[1] Thus decolonization was only the beginning of a commercial and political reorientation to the conditions in developing countries. The development framework that dominated economic policies determined the options that businesses had.

In contrast to other studies, like Stockwell's book on the Gold Coast, the first section of this chapter argues that these strategies went beyond mere representation and that executives began to consider their companies' role in terms of the development discourse. This was part of broader goodwill policies to gain and maintain legitimacy and was most noticeable in their corporate political activities. Still, companies endorsed these ideas beyond mere public relations. The final section addresses how businesses responded when the post-war development discourse underwent a crisis in the late 1960s and 1970s, becoming more hostile towards foreign business. To show how conceptions of African development changed through the decades, the following section opens with a brief overview of the dominant post-war development ideology.

DOI: 10.4324/9781003001058-2

2.1 Development ideology and British business

From 1940 to the 1970s has been referred to as the 'development era' for Africa.[2] This had a lasting impact on foreign private investment on the continent as the emerging development theories began to determine colonial economic policies. Post-war development thinking was not monolithic, but most authors agree that several features were broadly accepted. The most important features, especially in the context of this study, were:

- The state as the key instrument of development
- Industrialization, especially import substitution industrialization for domestic markets
- Knowledge transfer through education and training
- Creating growth by raising the investment ratio
- Focus on savings-pushed growth (and, under Nkrumah, deficit financing)
- Development projects were to be financed domestically, supplemented by foreign capital (although conditions and restrictions were defined)

This approach to development can create distortions in markets and prices, one of the most important criticisms levelled against the development orthodoxy by neo-classical critics, as dependency and autarky-inspired policies in Africa and Latin America showed signs of failure. By the late 1970s, the International Monetary Fund (IMF) began to make its assistance conditional on so-called structural adjustment measures, which evolved in the following decade into a more structured set of market-oriented policies. As a result of the Latin American debt crisis, the IMF and the World Bank moved closer together in their policies, which laid the ground for John Williamson's Washington Consensus label in 1989. This framework advocated macroeconomic discipline, a market-based economy and openness to world trade and investment. Although the label referred to a set of policies responding to the economic situation in Latin America, similar measures had been advocated for African countries throughout the 1980s, where they became known as Structural Adjustment Programmes.[3]

The distortions in prices and competition have been mainly criticized for creating windfall profits for favoured elites long after this was necessary to protect infant industries.[4] Robert Bates has commented on 'development coalitions', consisting of owners and workers in industrial firms, economic and political elites, privileged farmers and bureaucrats, who reap the benefits of the policy choices made in the name of development.[5] Harry G Johnson described a similar situation as a type of economic nationalism considerably earlier, in the 1960s. His argument was partly based on an earlier study by Albert Breton on Canada. Both authors highlighted that while such economic nationalism favoured a narrow middle class in developing countries, it undermined wider economic development.[6] In his study of development policies and Nkrumah's government, Tony Killick pointed out that nationalism and development economics in the 1950s and 1960s were mutually reinforcing.[7]

Whether the subject is the economic nationalism of West African states or their commitment to a specific vision of development economics, the outcome, particularly from the perspective of business, was similar. The British colonial administration committed to the idea of 'development' in 1940, but the development framework was only fully developed by the early 1950s.[8] British business was highly unpopular in West Africa and became the target of anti-colonial protests alongside the Gold Coast and Nigeria governments between 1948 and 1951. It became paramount for corporate principals to gain local goodwill and build a new basis for a legitimate presence in Africa. As colonial reform and later decolonization increased the importance of African political and popular opinion, colonial governments did not want to be perceived as collaborating with British companies. Companies had shown themselves to be responsive to governments' economic vision during World War II, having cooperated in the organization of West African trade reaping significant benefits in the process. Based on this, company managers followed the lead of colonial officials, and later nationalist politicians, to integrate their firms' activities into the development framework. The role that emerged for foreign investment was closely linked to these considerations:

- Welfare and the training and promotion of staff
- Industrialization
- Investing in and developing new areas that local capital failed to exploit
- Redeployment – this referred specifically to the merchant companies, which left areas to African competitors that required low levels of capital, technology and skills
- Mobilizing capital, especially savings, for local enterprises – creating new opportunities for banks

Mining companies were to reinvest, like other businesses, more of their profits locally, making attempts to refine more raw materials in the country and develop by-product recovery. However, mines such as the AGC argued that they provided important exports, which earned foreign exchange to pay for development projects and the imports they required.

Commercial strategies aligned with this development discourse will be discussed in the second section of this chapter. In addition, corporate leaders began to make public statements about their companies' commitment to improving West Africa's economic situation. However, and maybe more surprising, they also debated their companies' roles in development in internal memos and correspondence, showing that they sought to participate in the overall discourse on 'development'.

Ideas of development, first endorsed by British colonial governments in 1940, reverberated in local contexts, ultimately beyond the control of officials and later of national politicians.[9] Appealing to these ideas offered a robust base for corporate legitimacy. All the companies in this study emphasized to a greater or lesser degree their role in the seminal process of developing West Africa, and this became one of the dominant tropes in companies' advertising and public relations.[10] Archival records suggest that company managers agreed with many development ideas. Such comments were common in external relations, but company manager and agents often did not see their profit and that of the host country as distinct; indeed, they were considered complementary:

> [...] the first plank in our platform in the future is to take our full share of the colonial Development policy that is now being planned at home. The profit motive is, of course not only legitimate but necessary to our existence as a Company. [...] however [...] it should not be permitted to interfere with the main reason for the existence of the Company – that of helping to improve the lot and well being of West Africa and its peoples. [...] the firm with such a policy will prosper, and [...] the profit motive will thus be indirectly served. I have no doubt that this is already the policy of the Company [...][11]

The view of John Holt's agent in Ibadan was not deemed to be too exotic, as his quarterly report was filed with policy-related correspondence, which is unusual and indicates that it merited special attention.

Companies strove to remain informed about these conceptualizations of development. A report entitled 'Developing a Middle Class in Nigeria' was circulated to Barclays Bank's management in 1961. Its authors suggested that in the absence of a middle class from which indigenous entrepreneurs were to emerge, the state had to step into the gap but act to enable the growth of a middle class in the long term. The absence of a middle class was considered a feature of economic backwardness. Progress would depend on modernizing social structures and creating a productive, politically moderate and stable class at the centre of society. However, in their absence, the newly created states were the most powerful and most promising economic actors. This raised the question of how far the encouragement of indigenous enterprise and the emergent middle class should go. During decolonization and early independence, the attitude appears to have been that this should occur naturally.

How can these corporate efforts at sharing the development discourse be interpreted? Frederick Cooper and Randall Packard criticize the shortcomings of traditional discourse analysis and its attempts to 'deconstruct discursive power': 'It is much harder to discover how discourse operates within institutions.'[12] Instead, they prefer to analyse ideology in a way that connects it to the different sources of support and opposition:

> The point is not to decide whether or not development discourse is truly hegemonic, but to examine the project of building and fracturing hegemonies: how financial, political and discursive power was deployed [...][13]

Discursive power is far from dominant in this trinity, particularly regarding politics, which changes although the language employed remains the same. Firms in West Africa were influential financially and did not hesitate to convert some of this into political influence (for companies' political strategies, see chapter 3). However, their understanding of the political process could also impose limits on this behaviour, as the UAC's careful avoidance of taking the side of political candidates in the Gold Coast shows.[14] How far they influenced discourse or were themselves influenced by it is a more complex issue. Still, Frederick Cooper and Randall Packard have pointed out how powerful development ideas became in the local context, almost taking on a life of their own.[15]

Business was just one of many groups that sought to justify their presence by finding a role in the development framework. The post-war focus on industrialization, capital investment, provision of finance and skills transfer offered ample space. In return, companies accepted the economic leadership of the state. In 1944 the UAC sought close alignment with the new governor of Nigeria, Sir Arthur Richards: '[...] Mr Samuel [...] hoped he had been able [...] to make clear in government circles that the Company's aspiration was to help West Africa'.[16] Two years later, Frank Samuel, one of UAC's managing directors, advised waiting for an official lead on development:

> Referring to new projects he said that although the government appeared to be anxious to encourage the secondary industries they had not yet formed a consistent economic policy and until they had done this he did not consider it was sound to proceed with any extensive new projects.[17]

By the late 1950s, their commercial strategy had been decided. The UAC sought to maintain its commitment to West Africa and plough back profits in an area with a promising economic outlook. Hence, by 1959, their experience of cooperating with the Colonial Development Corporation (CDC), widely considered in West Africa as a form of economic imperialism, was rather negative:

> [...] their preference was for drawing dividends where we would wish to see the profits ploughed back into the venture; and commercially they had no technical skill or local goodwill to contribute.[18]

Their arguments against the corporation indeed seemed to question the development value of the CDC's involvement. The CDC had been set up in the 1940s to earn dollars to alleviate the pressure on sterling, which probably contributed to its poor local image.[19] The merchant companies' more permanent economic interests were based on a different rationale, which also received official blessing in 1948, a point that was reiterated frequently:

> [...] the long term policy of many of the firms which policy has been endorsed by government of confining themselves more and more to wholesale marketing and leaving the retail business to the local small men [...][20]

Especially after the Gold Coast riots, the colonial governments put increasing pressure on the firms to extend their commitment to West Africa in acceptable ways, and they encountered little resistance from UAC's principals, as this letter from DD Jones, the Nigerian General Manager, shows:

> [...] it would be most desirable if the large importing firms kept the African in mind as a possible partner when launching out into new ventures. [...] [Hugh Foot] considered that from a long-term point of view the only solution to racial feelings was to take the African into partnership. I must say that I wholeheartedly concurred with his remarks. I have felt for some time that as a European firm only, our future is uncertain. That picked Africans should be invited to be members of the Boards of the new Companies we are now launching. For some years yet, this would be a political gesture, but in time such Africans might perform useful offices. [...] From now on, I do not think there is any doubt that government will discriminate in favour of the African, and in all our future planning I consider we should be guided by this thought.[21]

Localization and African directorships only became a reality in the 1950s. This positive attitude towards the state's economic leadership was also extended to the newly independent countries, as Holt's chairman publicly announced in 1960:

> [...] in pursuing these enterprises [new manufacturing companies] we are greatly influenced by the statesmanship shown by Ministers in Nigeria and Ghana and are confident that the Governments of these countries will continue to develop their natural resources of materials, manpower and ideas. The tempo of development and expansion will be accentuated when Nigeria attains independence in October this year, and we look forward to participating actively in the economic development of West Africa.[22]

As this statement from the year of Nigeria's independence shows, the development concerns first voiced by their Ibadan agent in 1944 (cited earlier in this section) had become part of the company's official representation.

Advertising was one area where the development discourse featured most noticeably, and Anandi Ramamurthy shows that issues such as industrialization, complementarity and the emergence of a new middle class became familiar tropes in corporate adverts.[23] Barclays Bank showed particular interest in this. Its chairman, Julian Crossley, the chairman of Barclays Bank DCO, even had a report prepared on this topic for Nigeria in 1961. The bank canvassed six 'authorities' with a 'wide field of opinions'.[24] There was broad agreement that the country needed a land-owning educated class with not too high a level of consumption and some savings. The three suggestions that appeared to be most immediately relevant to the bank were commercial education, encouragement of savings and financial assistance to small businesses in retail and manufacturing. Hence Barclays expected the emerging middle class to be a pool for potential staff and customers. Crossley commented explicitly on the involvement of his bank in the development project at the bank's annual meeting in 1957:

> From the primitive tribal Africa of Lord Lugard's time, based on an agriculture at a bare subsistence level, was developing an Africa where education of all grades was very widely available, and where the levels of diet, health services, housing and general well-being were improved out of all recognition. This process had had to be achieved [...] alongside a still surviving background of tribalism, and the evolution of the 'economic man' in Africa – an individual earning his living by a money wage – involved a revolutionary change in status and outlook. To help along this movement merited the goodwill and co-operation of all. This was 'Colonialism' on the British model, and our Bank – by opening offices in remote areas, by educating the African in the way of thrift and encouraging savings accounts by specially produced films and otherwise – was playing its full part in the economic and social development involved.[25]

The BWA justified their use of advertising to increase their savings business in similar terms.[26] The two imperial banks were keen to see further economic growth, and their financial services were presented as enabling this development. Barclays associated itself with post-war initiatives by forming the Barclays Overseas Development Corporation.[27] BWA also tended to count on 'a great revolution whose final pattern is not yet discernible' but which 'deeply affected agriculture, industry and social and political relationships'.[28] The general attitude of British business was summed up by the bank in 1961:

> Wherever one looks in Africa one finds territories, mostly now independent, which, whatever their local problems, have one thing

> in common – a tremendous need for development that only foreign capital can provide.[29]

The AGC was also apt to argue along those lines, emphasizing the importance of the taxes and mineral duties that gold mining generated and social advancement through its labour welfare programme. But overall, the mine's management appeared not to be too aware of the further implications of Ghana's drive for industrialization. When they debated with the British High Commissioner in 1963 why the Consolidated African Selection Trust (CAST) had a better image in the country than themselves, they also mooted a tentative proposal for further by-product recovery from gold mining.

> The High Commissioner jumped at this suggestion and said that any such possibility should be given the highest priority as development along these lines would do more to improve the Corporation's position in Ghana than anything else. He was so enthusiastic about this that I had to remind him that no such project was even under consideration but that the possibility had merely been cited as an example. [...] Complete endorsement of the High Commissioner's views regarding the importance of developing or assisting in the development of an indigenous manufacture or processing industry. Lever Brothers were developing along these lines, apparently most successfully.[30]

AGC's relatively remote operations in Obuasi, away from the hub of power in Accra, might have been the cause of their relative ignorance of Nkrumah's approach to industrialization. Still, CAST, operating in several African countries, was more astute.

Businesses sought to publicly emphasize their commitment to the economic development of West Africa, as they believed it to further both the cause of the African people and its profitability. This appears to have been more deeply rooted than just a publicity measure, as internal correspondence also indicates that principals privately believed in this justification. Development ideas permeated not only the rhetoric of British business but also took shape in its architecture. African politicians promised their voters that development would allow their countries to take part in the way of the modern world and all its amenities, a hope that British companies shared as this would transform Africa into a new market for their goods and services.

2.2 Redeployment and expansion

The 1950s witnessed significant changes in West African trade, referred to by companies as redeployment. This, however, is more relevant to the experience of the merchant companies, whereas the banking sector experienced a phase of expansion until about 1960. Both policies were as much commercially motivated as they were political. Eventually, however, they were successful because they tied in with the understanding of development that dominated West Africa.

2.2.1 Redeployment

The merchant companies' redeployment strategy has been extensively debated in the literature.[31] Sarah Stockwell, for example, has been more interested in how far commercial changes were also influenced by political considerations. In contrast, older research has focused on the contribution of merchant firms to development.[32] To understand the significance of redeployment, it is important to know that merchant companies in the 1920s were general importers and exporters, which ran a network of small trading stations as far as railways and river transport reached inland; further, distribution was undertaken by small African traders via the road network.[33] This organization had its disadvantages: administration of such a vast network was complicated, stock deteriorated, agents were hard to control, and companies engaged in both retail and wholesale in effect competed with their reseller customers. When the competition was suspended during World War II, maintaining such a large network was even more difficult and less profitable. Hence the UAC's retail outlets in Nigeria and Ghana decreased from 1,382 in 1939 to 926 in 1952.[34]

Holt also began to centralize its operations during the war, reducing its merchandise sales points from 525 immediately before the war to 330 in 1940/41 (a reduction of almost 40 per cent), falling to 168 and 156 in the following two years.[35] This 'compression policy', according to Holt's chairman in 1942, was only partly forced upon the company by the shortage of British staff:

> Apart from this, however, it is a settled policy of the Company gradually to withdraw its sales organization to Main Trading Centres and, except for our European Provision Departments, to leave the retail trade to the African.[36]

Holt and UAC, both closely cooperating with the colonial governments under the auspices of the Association of West African Merchants (AWAM) in a controlled war economy, must have been aware of the new commitment to African development and welfare since 1940 and were prepared to give up some of their business to African interests. In 1942, the post-war boom for tropical commodities could not have been foreseen. Still, problems of supervision and a bad public image made it attractive to firms to contract their operations. As their trade in a controlled war economy was also highly profitable, they had little to lose by experimenting with contraction, a policy that could be undone quickly if not successful, according to Holt's chairman.

Why did merchants redeploy in the 1950s, moving into manufacturing and technical services, for example, automobiles in the case of Holt and wholesale and specialized retail, and away from general trading? This entailed a significant break from their previous mode of operations. Such 'extra-territorial' companies (i.e., merchants) had no reason to invest in manufacturing, as it would undermine the productivity of their import and export trade and shipping. Furthermore, it would unsettle domestic supplier arrangements. Kilby argues that distribution mainly in an enlarged and increasingly sophisticated market changed, leading to new competitors' entrance and direct sales by manufacturers. He dates the beginning of merchant companies' withdrawal from general importing to 1958–1959. Still, it is important to note that they had already diminished, if not given up entirely, other traditional areas such as produce and small-scale retail trade.[37] Produce buying, such as cocoa, decreased in profitability due to the introduction of marketing boards, which also meant that it became increasingly politicized.[38] Marketing boards were among the most influential institutions in West African post-war economies. They controlled the price differential between the world market price for commodities and the farm gate prices. During the 1950s, large balances accumulated, which came under the control of African politicians and gave them significant financial and political leverage.

As a result of the increased involvement of the state in the rural economy, merchants became at first licensed buying agents or abandoned the produce trade altogether. UAC withdrew from cocoa in 1959, but two of its subsidiaries, most notably GB Ollivants, continued. Two years later, the CPP reserved cocoa buying exclusively for Africans.[39] There were persuasive commercial reasons for the companies to shift their capital away from traditional trade into more specialized goods, wholesale and manufacturing (and in the case of many merchants, but not John Holt, into department stores). Political reasons were equally important: African retailers and cooperatives were to participate more in the economy, while foreign business was to create new areas of commercial activity.[40] Economic opportunities suited political rationale, but this was partly due to the changes in the economy brought about by a specific vision of development, which became accepted by political actors.

Merchant companies such as Holt and UAC began to embrace industrialization policies in the 1940s and 1950s. This move was facilitated by the declining profitability of their core activities, mainly produce buying and general retailing. The trading companies began to specialize in wholesale and retail, like department stores and chemists, abandoning their traditional activities by the early 1960s. Both UAC and Holt diversified into motor distribution and UAC later into local assembly because of host government pressure and increased competition. Other investments in local manufacturing were brewing and textiles, which Holt and UAC mostly undertook in joint ventures with technical partners.[41] As the existing foreign companies appeared more likely to invest than newcomers, their importance in the eyes of nationalist politicians rose.[42]

2.2.2 Bank expansion

Redeployment became a central feature of commercial operations in West Africa, and the banking boom of the 1950s, which is less frequently recounted, was connected to this change.[43] While Tignor claims that banking was always a specific focus of nationalist aspirations, the expatriate banks encountered public and political pressure later than the commercial companies, which had been targeted since the 1940s.[44] Although nationalists might have considered the financial system as essential to economic sovereignty in later years, in the late 1940s, mobilization was based on consumer grievances, as in the 1948 Gold Coast riots. As the banks did not have many African customers, they were not targeted like the highly visible merchants associated with the much-maligned AWAM.

The early 1950s saw the 'mushrooming' of indigenous banks in Nigeria, halted by the banking ordinance of 1952. The Gold Coast, however, was too small to support a similar development. Still, nationalist pressure led to the establishment of the state-sponsored Bank of the Gold Coast in 1953, renamed Ghana Commercial Bank after the introduction of a Central Bank in 1957.[45]

Barclays and the Bank of British West Africa increased their branch network in both countries significantly throughout the 1950s and remained each other's only serious rivals, despite the entrance of African and other foreign competitors. This geographical expansion went hand in hand with extending banking services, notably savings and lending to African customers. This expansion was prompted by the growth of West African markets and the withdrawal from direct up-country retail by the merchant companies. While merchant companies continued to give advances, their gradual withdrawal opened new opportunities for the banks. Both banks increased their branches rapidly in the 1950s, especially in Nigeria, which experienced a second, smaller boom in the 1960s (Figure 2.1).

Like the commercial companies, this new strategy was not a purely commercial decision but also prompted by political considerations. Development theory proclaimed that local savings should be channelled into industrial and commercial investments instead of being used for consumption. This provided a necessary political impetus to the imperial banks to extend their services to more African customers, finally trying to address obstacles such as illiteracy and insufficient security for credit (Figure 2.2).

Savings and deposits increased during these years, and there is ample evidence that the savings business was booming. RH Oakley visited Barclays' branches in Nigeria in 1963 and, after seeing Ijebu-Ode's dilapidated buildings, remarked on the good savings business of the branch, which had total balances of £500,000 spread over 8,550 accounts (of which 1,600 were dormant), averaging around £72 per active account.[48]

The sharp increase in politically motivated credit that followed failed spectacularly. While this has been researched particularly for Barclays in

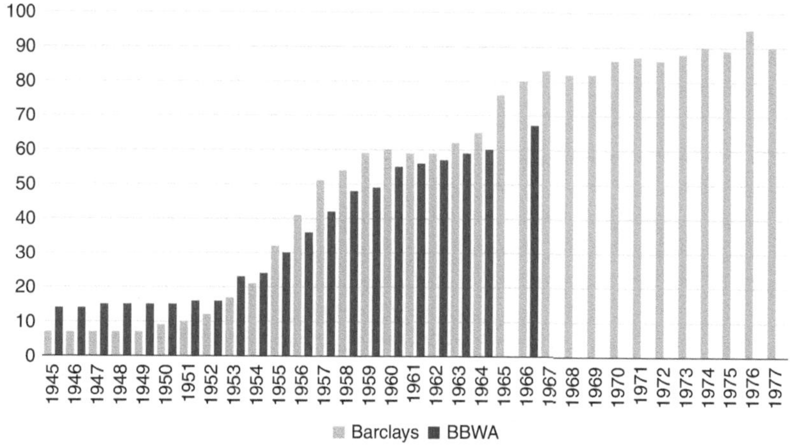

Figure 2.1 Barclays and BBWA branch expansion in Ghana, 1947–1977.

Notes: Figures refer to full branches, sub-branches and agencies. For Barclays for the years 1954, 1957, 1959–1960, and 1963, figures are based on half-yearly branch reviews, which appear to have only been completed by full branches at least until 1960, explaining the inconsistent numbers for the late 1950s. Reproduced with the kind permission of Barclays Group Archives.[46]

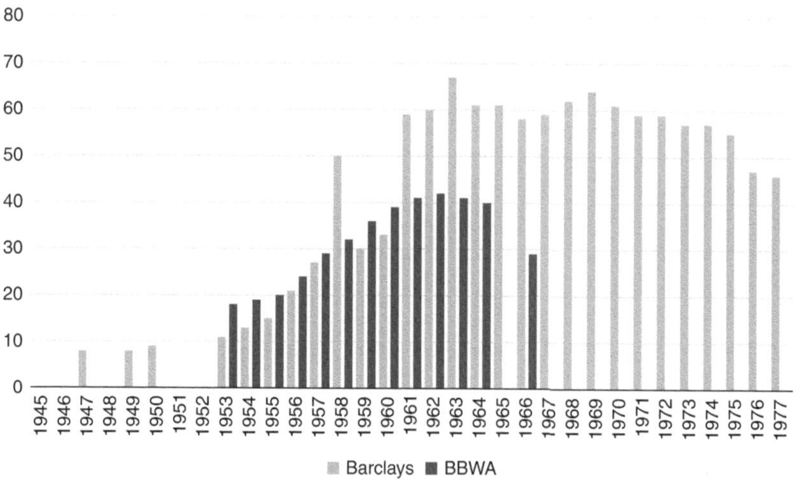

Figure 2.2 Barclays and BBWA branch expansion in Nigeria, 1947–1977.

Note: Data collected from Barclays Group Archives and London Metropolitan Archives. Reproduced with the kind permission of Barclays Group Archives.[47]

Nigeria, it also affected the BWA and the trading company Holt.[49] Barclays was warned by their 'old friend', the Emir of Kano, that they had been lending to the wrong people in mid-1959. In a subsequent enquiry, £2.5m worth of bad and doubtful debts were discovered.[50] This episode went beyond questions of failing managerial controls because of the symbolic importance of extending services to new customers:

> [...] there was a very heavy Bad and Doubtful Debt position, especially with regard to African borrowers. It was clear that the Manager had to be removed [...] it was a matter that would have to be handled carefully if we were to preserve any goodwill.[51]

The extension of credit to Nigerian customers was driven by the desire to create a favourable impression with both African commercial and political leaders.

As independence loomed, banks and commercial companies gave credit in order to create local goodwill, which was in itself a cause for rising bad debts. However, the early 1950s were also a time of rising prices and economic growth, and by the late 1950s, the national governments were committed to a large amount of public expenditure on development projects. Nevertheless, by the late 1950s and early 1960s, growth slowed down, which explained some bad debts. It has also been argued that refusing to honour debts to British imperial business was a form of resistance to colonialism.[52] Bankers also showed a lack of understanding of local attitudes to credit and its recovery: personal contact and persistent hassling were often beyond the capacity of acutely understaffed branches (due to the rapid expansion in those years), and rotating branch management undermined long-term commercial relations.[53] None of this solved the fundamental problem of giving security for a loan: African titles to land were inalienable outside the colony of Lagos and the southern Gold Coast, and the colonial protection of peasant economies had prevented the emergence of unambiguous personal property rights. Even beyond bankers' complaints about African corruption and lack of creditworthiness and the racism that sometimes went with it, making advances to African businesspeople remained a problem for banks.[54] The predominantly political commitment to development thus came at some cost to the banks.

Commercial strategies were, at one level, obviously commercially motivated. But redeployment and the extension of services to African customers had been a course of action open to companies earlier. The 1950s especially were a time of rapid economic growth, which improved the prospects of any new investment and created a more competitive environment through new international and local entrants. While there were good economic reasons for this change in corporate strategies, companies tended to present these decisions in the light of their contribution to development. Hence, they form part of the goodwill policies adopted by businesses. Especially when these policies failed, as in the case of the banks' lending to Africans, the importance of the political motivations behind them became apparent.

2.3 Losing goodwill and corporate legitimacy

In 1966, the independence leaders were deposed in military coups, and in the wake of political instability, their economic policies were questioned. Internationally, the old development orthodoxy also faced criticism from neo-classical scholars like Bauer, a long-time critic of post-war development economics, and more radical academics. They based their approaches on the Latin American ideas of dependency and underdevelopment, Marxism, or both. The failure of previous development efforts to deliver promises of growth, prosperity and opportunities undermined the old development discourse and thus threatened the basis of foreign companies' legitimacy.

How had international businesses suddenly become so vulnerable when they had been accepted as organizations that brought much-needed skills and capital in the previous decade? Other ideas about development gained currency as the old orthodox paradigm failed to deliver its promises in the 'decade of development'. Just as classical development theory before had done, these ideas influenced public policy and found support from local stakeholders who stood to gain from limiting the influence of foreign investment. These trends were not exclusive to West Africa, as a sudden rise in expropriations worldwide shows (Figure 2.3). The majority of these occurred in Africa, followed by the Middle East, mostly in extractive industries, followed by financial services.[55]

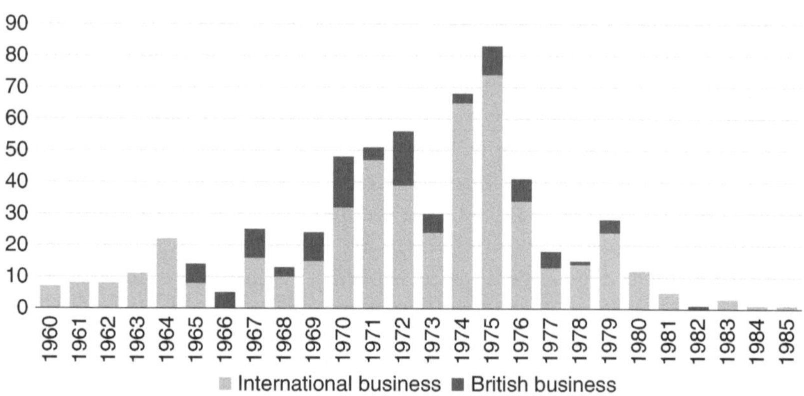

Figure 2.3 Instances of expropriation of International Business worldwide (total) and British Companies affected (from 1965), 1960–1985.

Note: Decker, "Corporate Legitimacy and Advertising," 78. Reproduced with kind permission of Cambridge University Press.

The new development paradigm partially inverted the old understanding of the term. Exchange between rich and developing countries was now viewed more critically as a form of extraction fostering underdevelopment.[56] International business, once considered agents that provided skills, technology and capital under the guidance of a developmental state, now drew criticism as neo-colonial exploiters, providing imperial control via economic means.

These ideas gained some traction in West African politics.[57] The subtitle of Nkrumah's *Neo-Colonialism: The Last Stage of Imperialism* shows that radical writers sought to position themselves as part of the ideological heritage of Marxist-Leninist ideas.[58] Scholars such as Samir Amin argued that outward-directed growth was beyond the capacity and control of states and that only indigenous development, once an economy was 'de-linked' from the international system, held the key to true advancement.[59] The Latin American 'dependencia' school had its roots in the work of the less radical economist Raúl Prebisch, who worked on the UN's Economic Commission for Latin America (ECLA), publishing an influential report in 1950.[60] In it, he suggested import substitution industrialization policies to allow Latin American countries to develop more independently. His ideas became the foundation of the more politically radical dependency school developed a decade later.

Dependency or underdevelopment theories challenged the post-war development framework by challenging its fundamental assumptions. The exchange between rich and developing countries, which had previously been considered potentially beneficial if conditions were suitable, was now perceived as a relation of exploitation. The high level of development in Western countries was based on either the underdevelopment or the similarly detrimental dependent development of the periphery. Latin American dependency writers created a large and varied body of work on the basic assumption that development in the global periphery is linked to that of the centres in such a way as to obstruct sustainable and appropriate progress in these countries. Within the school, different camps exist, which are not directly relevant to this study and have been debated in detail elsewhere.[61] In its most simple and most dramatic incarnation, dependency theory reached Africa through Walter Rodney's famous book *How Europe Underdeveloped Africa* in 1972.[62]

This new understanding of development became politically influential in the 1970s. Within the international community, the Group of 77 began to voice the demands of developing countries. International organizations did not necessarily follow the analysis of dependency and underdevelopment scholars but accepted that global inequality needed to be addressed by improving countries' access to capital, technology and skills and that greater local control of the economy was essential.

Hence underdevelopment constituted a crisis of the old development framework, which it took to more radical forms, but the eventual break occurred with the introduction of structural adjustment programmes, which followed neo-liberal, market-based economic policies. Many of these academic arguments were not received in their full intellectual complexity but rather as a set of methods and policy options, shaping political and social discourse.

2.3.1 The crisis of development

Did the changing discourse in development economics affect policymaking in West Africa? While Busia in Ghana was known to be business-friendly and cooperated with international institutions in economic reforms, his support for liberal policies was limited by vested interests and his precarious political position. For example, he extended the National Liberation Council's (NLC) first Ghanaianization decree to gain the support of local businesspeople. His successor Ignatius Acheampong had a poor grasp of economic issues, which he sought to mask by warlike rhetoric. He declared 'war on the economy', first in 1972 against extractive industries, which had experienced national participation or expropriation all over the world: OPEC countries mostly took control of their oil production facilities in the 1970s, and Chile and then Zambia nationalized their copper industries in 1970 and 1971 respectively. This was justified, according to Acheampong, to end foreign exploitation:

> Our cocoa, our gold, our diamonds, our manganese, our timber, and the energies of our people have for too long been utilized for the benefit of foreigners. [...] those who seek to resist us will only provoke their own destruction.[63]

Acheampong's approach to foreign investment was not unusual in 1972 when localization measures became commonplace.[64]

The subsequent Ghanaian Investment Policy Decree of 1975 bore a greater resemblance to the Nigerian Indigenization Decree, as it combined the previous Ghanaianization Decrees with the part-nationalizations of timber and mining by establishing different schedules of varying degrees of national participation, either private or public. That the Ghanaian administration was monitoring events in Nigeria is certain, as an article about Nigeria's indigenization plans was filed in a folder on the implementation of the Ghanaian Business (Promotion) Act.[65] Acheampong's policies were, however, aimed at autarky, hence in line with a whole host of radical underdevelopment theories from Marxism to dependency. The most common notion was that 'de-linking' a country from the negative, underdeveloping influence of the international economic system would kick-start autonomous growth. While Douglas Rimmer sees such a de-linking occurring in Ghana in the 1970s, he argues that it was a 'reaction to the country's economic decline, not a platform for its development'.[66]

Rimmer's claim that countries became further marginalized is supported by calculations of Africa's share of world trade, which fell from 5 per cent at the time of colonialism to 2 per cent now.[67]

In Nigeria, the military government under Gowon had to deal with more pressing issues than the economy after its takeover in 1966, as the Biafran secession led to the civil war in 1967. Once the federation had effectively defeated the insurgents by 1969, it turned its attention to the better regulation of foreign investment in the country, probably partly provoked on the one hand by the cost of military engagement and on the other by the continued operation of the oil companies, the UAC and the banks on both sides of the front. This legislation was, however, quite mild in comparison, requiring only the local incorporation of foreign firms. For international branch banks, this meant nevertheless that a larger proportion of their funds became tied up in one area, and Barclays, in particular, perceived a threat of nationalization on the horizon. The bank had only recently lost its operations in Tanzania, and management in Nigeria was so nervous that they requested a nationalization checklist that was drafted after events there. When appealing to the World Bank to intervene, they, however, only received the laconic answer that 'worse things had happened elsewhere'.[68] Corporate power appeared curiously muted when not even the World Bank was prepared to make a statement on behalf of international business.[69]

By 1972, the first Nigerian Enterprise Promotion Decree was announced, and its formulation was determined to a large extent by the interests of local businesspeople, who had made similar claims ever since decolonization, and showed little knowledge of international events.[70] In 1976, the Adeosun Commission reported on the implementation of the first decree and criticized its shortcomings thoroughly. As a result, the state took a greater degree of control in the formulation of the second decree and reserved areas not only for nationals but also for state participation. This, however, did not mean that all foreign investors lost control (although the banks and insurance companies did), as not all recommendations of the panel were acted upon by the Obasanjo government. Greater knowledge of international events seems to have played a role in the more radical second decree, as some officials visited Brazil in 1976.[71]

Hence international trends in economic policies had clearly arrived in West Africa but were adapted locally in the form of indigenization programmes, as opposed to Tanzanian and Zambian nationalizations. While globally on the defensive, international business faced volatile political conditions locally, and this determined their responses.

2.3.2 Defending organizational legitimacy

As Cooper and Packard argued, power has several dimensions, political, financial and discursive. In the 1970s, international business was faced with challenges on all these fronts. Discursively, developing countries in Africa had mostly chosen to follow the business-hostile underdevelopment theories, and the rising number of expropriations was an attempt to undermine their financial power (although most countries accepted the payment of compensation).

In a surprisingly weak position, companies had several options, which ranged in a spectrum from outright resistance to taking the initiative. By the 1970s, most companies carefully avoided being seen resisting government policies, and in practice, their responses vacillated between delaying and compromising. On occasion, some corporate principals sought to regain the initiative, and, for example, 'Tiny' Rowland's good personal image in Africa indicates that he might have appeared more considerate of African considerations.

British business remained well-connected politically, although they found it harder to build up contacts with the new military governments of Obasanjo in Nigeria and Acheampong in Ghana (see chapter 4). British business seemed very successful in gaining exemptions from full indigenization of parts of their operations. Their internal perception of African policymaking was often rather cynical. In 1976 UAC's observers commented on the ideological and practical motivations behind Nigerian indigenization:

> As far as it was possible to tell the sole motivation was money and although many statements were made which sounded socialist or even communist they probably arose for the most part from nationalism.[72]

Publicly, however, the company sought to underline its own commitment to development in 1970:

> From a position of absolute political neutrality, the [UAC] Group shares in the life of the community. Matters of social welfare, the youth of the Land and the affairs of the needy are of concern. It strives to help by deploying its resources at the broadest possible level. [...] In manufacturing, marketing, distraction, product quality and administration, the benefits achieved are shared with the Land and set new levels for industrial aspiration.[73]

During the implementation of further indigenization legislation in 1976, UAC, however, assumed a more aggressive stance:

> The Special Committee accepted that in time we would be forced to reduce our shareholding but hoped that we would continue only to part with equity reluctantly and when it was inevitable, either legally or to protect our business. [...] Mr Sedcole stressed the fact that the company was not frightened of its size and importance in Nigeria but

> on the contrary proud of its strength there and anxious to protect it as far as possible. They felt that the question for the future was not whether there were going to be any profits in Nigeria, but who was going to own them and they were conscious of the fact that we would almost certainly be forced to divest a further 10 per cent within the next few years.[74]

The UAC and the other large trading companies were the only foreign firms that were successful in gaining a concession through Article 7 of the second Nigerian Enterprise Promotion Decree, which overrode the enterprise classification and allowed any established company with a turnover of over 25m Naira, and which operated in ten Nigerian states or more, to keep 40 per cent of the equity. This became known as the 'UAC clause' in Nigeria.[75] UAC's files show few reactions to Ghanaian legislation. This had several reasons. While the Gold Coast had been the company's most profitable region in the 1950s, foreign exchange restrictions had been in place since 1961, and no dividends or profits accumulated there had been remitted since then. Internally, Ghana became classified as a political risk country, and profits were written out of the overall company accounts. Since Ghana's decline, Nigeria had succeeded it as UAC's most important base, and by the 1970s, this position was reinforced by Unilever's overall dependence on UAC's profits.

In 1970, the incumbent chairman of Barclays International, Anthony F Tuke, clearly expected further local participation, and on a visit to Nigeria, Ghana and Sierra Leone, he took the view that:

> [...] sooner or later we would have to make a deal, all experience in Africa proved that the sooner you make the deal the better the deal will be. [...] The rate at which we sell shares to local interest is difficult to gauge but it seems more than likely that we will be obliged to move towards a 51 per cent or possibly 60 per cent Nigerian shareholding during the next four or five years. [...] So far we have, on the whole, taken the view that whereas we would keep in line with the pressures from the government, we would not go any faster than we need. It may well be that we should now think in terms of changing this policy and plan for more rapid Nigerianisation accompanied by publicity for our proposals and by our taking the initiative in any discussions that may arise.[76]

Hence it seems that Barclays considered extending its participation in the nationalist discourse and, in this way, gaining greater acceptance and 'a better deal'. Both banks, however, failed to capitalize on this, as the state was intent on taking over the financial sector in Nigeria and Ghana. While they lost control over their investment in Nigeria, the Ghanaian state held 80 per cent of the banks' equity only for a few years before the new military government introduced structural adjustment measures in 1983.

AGC and John Holt were bought by the multinational Lonrho, which mainly operated in Africa, and which expanded rapidly during the 1960s and 1970s under the chairmanship of Rowland 'Tiny' Rowland. While incredibly successful in dealing with African and Arabian heads of state, his business methods drew criticism in Britain, and his dealings were investigated by the Department of Trade.[77] In the inspectors' report in 1976, Rowland was quoted speaking

> of all his personal interests in helping free Africa, whether black or Arab, to develop [...] he thought that as a result of securing a political solution to the problem of Africa, Lonrho could develop into a company earning profits of £50 to £100 million a year! [...] He said that he had two basic interests. One was personal and predominated over the other. The first was his interest in the political evolution of Africa and the generation of better relations between emergent Africa on the one hand and Europe and America on the other. The second was Lonrho. If there was a clash between the two, he would choose the first and willingly give up any participation in Lonrho.[78]

The authors of a highly critical study of Lonrho in the 1970s chose to end their book on this quotation, remarking that it underlined 'the indivisibility of these two facets of the Rowland philosophy which has moulded Lonrho'.[79] Despite their criticisms, apparently, they did not doubt that Rowland believed in Africa's development. He was, of course, by no means representative of businesspeople in Africa, but his success in a decade that was difficult for international business in Africa can be attributed either to his acute business acumen or to the fact that Lonrho, as one of the few newcomers on the scene, was able to get a substantially better deal than the established, formerly imperial, firms.

Whether the commitment to development was just paying lip service or not, British business had changed fundamentally in character and was, by the 1970s, no longer extra-territorial in nature. As most companies now provided goods and services for an African market, they stood to gain from economic growth and a higher standard of living. Development was a central issue for their commercial success, but whether they would be permitted to participate in and profit from the local economy had become a key issue by the 1970s.

2.4 Conclusion

While this study does not suggest that the ideological battleground between development and underdevelopment theory was the exclusive reason for friction between foreign investment and host states, it is certainly a factor that has been largely overlooked in the history of international business. Despite a growing body of recent research into the history of development, the importance of development theory for the continued presence of British investment in West Africa, and indeed international business in the developing world in general has not been sufficiently addressed. This chapter has illustrated how ideas about development began to be reflected in companies' internal and external communications and in the architectural designs they chose. Their commercial policies were also in tune with official visions of economic development, which left sufficient scope for businesses to work profitably in the new framework. By the late 1960s, political instability and international criticism of the post-war development orthodoxy undermined this framework, and as a result, organizational legitimacy in less developed countries declined, leading to a drastic rise in expropriations worldwide. Businesses adopted varying strategies, normally trying to avert or delay the impact of any legislation, but their eventual success or failure was also dependent on other factors, such as the political differences between countries, the type of investment, the quality of informal networks, the economic situation, the age of a business and the probability of future investment from the same source.

Changing theories of development provided an international framework for the encounter between British business and West African states from the 1950s to the 1970s. At a local level, the formation of postcolonial states and businesses' attempts to create wide political networks were based on a common understanding of development. The next chapter deals with the emergence of this discourse in the 1950s and 1960s. Chapter 4 addresses the breakdown of this understanding of development in the 1970s. The expropriations and local participation programmes in Ghana and Nigeria should be seen as a crisis of legitimacy for British and, ultimately, all foreign business.

Notes

1 Sarah E Stockwell, *The Business of Decolonization: British Business Strategies in the Gold Coast* (Oxford: Clarendon Press, 2000), 68–237; Robert L Tignor, *Capitalism and Nationalism at the End of Empire: State and Business in Decolonizing Egypt, Nigeria, and Kenya, 1945–1963* (Princeton, N.J.: Princeton University Press, 1998), 3–24, 195–289, 387–400.

2 Frederick Cooper, *Africa since 1940: The Past of the Present* (Cambridge, UK, and New York, NY: Cambridge University Press, 2002), 85.

3 J Williamson, "Speeches, Testimony, Papers: Did the Washington Consensus Fail?," *Institute for International Economics* (2002), http://www2.econ.iastate.edu/classes/econ502/tesfatsion/WashingtonConsensus.JWilliamson2002.pdf [accesssed 25 April 2022].

4 G Ranis, "The Evolution of Development Thinking: Theory and Policy," in *Annual World Bank Conference on Development Economics 2005: Lessons of Experience*, ed. François Bourguignon and Boris Pleskovic (Washington, D.C.: World Bank, 2004), 126.

5 Robert H Bates, *Markets and States in Tropical Africa: The Political Basis of Agricultural Policies* (Berkeley, Los Angeles, CA, and London: University of California Press, 1981), 121.

6 Harry Gordon Johnson, *Economic Nationalism in Old and New States, A Publication of the Committee for the Comparative Study of New Nations, University of Chicago* (London: Allen & Unwin, 1968), 1–16; Albert Breton, "The Economics of Nationalism," *The Journal of Political Economy* 72, no. 4 (1964): 376–86.

7 Tony Killick, *Development Economics in Action: A Study of Economic Policies in Ghana, Studies in the Economics of Africa* (London i.a.: Heinemann Educational, 1978), 11–32, 53–4.

8 W Arthur Lewis, "Report on the Industrialisation and the Gold Coast" (Accra, Ghana, 1953); Dudley Seers and C Ross, "Report on the Financial and Physical Problems of Development in the Gold Coast" (Accra, Ghana, 1952).

9 Frederick Cooper, *Decolonization and African Society: The Labour Question in French and British Africa, Africa: Journal of the International African Institute* (Cambridge, UK: Cambridge University Press, 1996), https://doi.org/10.2307/1161082; Frederick Cooper and Randall M Packard, "International Development and the Social Sciences: Essays on the History and Politics of Knowledge" (Berkeley, CA, London: University of California Press, 1997), 4, 12, 18, 30.

10 Stephanie Decker, "Corporate Legitimacy and Advertising: British Companies and the Rhetoric of Development in West Africa, 1950–1970," *Business History Review* 81, no. 1 (March 2007): 59–86, https://doi.org/10.2307/25097298.

11 Ibadan agent to John Holt Liverpool, "Quarterly report," 18 September 1944, p. 3, Rhodes House Oxford (RHO) Mss Afr. 825, 232 (ii).

12 Cooper and Packard, "International Development," 28.

13 Cooper and Packard, "International Development," 13, 23.

14 Stockwell, *The Business of Decolonization*, 149–52, 192–93, fn131.

15 Cooper and Packard, "International Development," 4, 12, 18, 30.

16 Directors' Committee, 41. West Africa, 27 January 1944, Unilever Historical Archives (UHA) UNI/BD/DC.

17 Directors' Committee, 137. Mr. Samuel's tour, 28 February 1946, UHA UNI/BD/DC.

18 Directors' Committee, 360. CDC, 5.6.59, UHA UNI/BD/DC. On the CDC, see Butler, *Industrialisation*, p. 215.

19 L J Butler, *Industrialisation and the British Colonial State, West Africa 1939–1951* (London & New York: Routledge, 1997), 193.

20 Cable to General Manager Lagos [UAC], 2 April 1948, RHO Mss Afr. 825, 232 (ii); see also UAC advert, "Colonial Customer," *West Africa*, 23 July 1955.

21 DD Jones (General Manager Lagos) to GJ Cole (UAC London), 31 March 1948, RHO Mss Afr. 825, 232 (ii).

22 Chairman's Statement at Annual General Meeting of John Holt & Co., 4.3.60, Liverpool Records Office (LRO) 380 HOL II.

23 Anandi Ramamurthy, *Imperial Persuaders: Images of Africa and Asia in British Advertising* (Manchester, UK: Manchester University Press, 2003), 175–92.

24 "Developing a middle class in Nigeria," 20 October 1961 and 30 October 1961, Barclays Group Archives (BGA) 80/3468.

25 Summary of a speech given by Sir Julian Crossley at the Annual Meeting in 1957, LA Borer, "Unpublished DCO Story," BGA not catalogued.

26 Report of the Directors and Statement of Accounts, 8 June 1961, p. 8, London Metropolitan Archives (LMA) CLC/B/207/Ms 28,517.

27 Frances Bostock, "The British Overseas Banks and Development Finance in Africa after 1945," *Business History* 33, no. 3 (1991): 157–76, https://doi.org/10.1080/00076799100000106.

28 Report of the Directors and Statement of Accounts, 8 June 1961, p. 9, LMA CLC/B/207/MS28,517.

29 Report of the Directors and Statement of Accounts, 8 June 1961, p. 13, LMA CLC/B/207/Ms 28,517.
30 R D Power, AGC Obuasi, to EL Spears, Chairman of Directors, London, Cc. to EW Morgan, 28 September 1963, LMA CLC/B/015/MS24665.
31 Peter Kilby, *Industrialisation in an Open Economy: Nigeria 1945–66* (Cambridge, UK: Cambridge University Press, 1969), 53–80; David Kenneth Fieldhouse, *Merchant Capital and Economic Decolonisation: The United Africa Company 1929–1987* (Oxford: Clarendon, 1994), 679–715.
32 Stockwell, *The Business of Decolonization*, 152–7.
33 Tignor, *Capitalism and Nationalism*, 205.
34 Frederick J Pedler, *Economic Geography of West Africa* (London,UK: Longmans, 1954), 145.
35 Holt, [chairman's speech at the Annual General Meeting], for year ending 30 September 1941, 27 July 1942, p. 2; Chairman's speech, Ordinary General Meeting, for year ending 30 September 1943, 16 August 1944, p. 1; LRO 380 HOL II.
36 Holt, [chairman's speech at the Annual General Meeting], for year ending 30 September 1941, 27 July 1942, p. 2; LRO 380 HOL II.
37 Kilby, *Industrialisation in an Open Economy: Nigeria 1945–66*, 61–2.
38 Stockwell, *The Business of Decolonization*, 153–4.
39 Stockwell, *The Business of Decolonization*, 155; B Beckman, *Organising the Farmers: Cocoa Politics and National Development in Ghana* (Uppsala, Sweden: Scandinavian Institute of African Studies, 1976), 77–85.
40 The enquiry into the Accra riots of 1948 endorsed merchants' redeployment strategy in its report. A Watson, "Report of the Commission of Enquiry into Disturbances in the Gold Coast" (London, UK, 1948).
41 Geoffrey Jones, *Merchants to Multinationals: British Trading Companies in the Nineteenth and Twentieth Centuries* (Oxford University Press: Oxford, 2000), 141–5.
42 For example, in the case of a soap factory for Eastern Nigeria, see Directors' Committee, 190. West Africa, 24 March 1955, UHA UNI/BD/DC.
43 Richard Fry, *Bankers in West Africa: The History of the British Bank of West Africa* (London: Hutchinson Benham, 1976), 184–6.
44 Tignor, *Capitalism and Nationalism*, 276.
45 DC Rowan, "Native Banking Boom in Nigeria," *The Banker*, October 1951; Stockwell, *The Business of Decolonization*, 61, 104.
46 Barclays Bank DCO branch directories, several years; *The Bankers Almanac & Yearbook 1946–1947, 1956–57, 1962–1963* (London: Thomas Skinner & Co., several years); Barclays Bank DCO half-yearly reviews BGA 29/23, 29/119 (2), 29/34 (7), 29/34 (2); LMA CLC/B/207/MS28517; CLC/B/207/MS28779.
47 Barclays Bank DCO branch directories, several years; LMA CLC/B/207/MS28517; CLC/B/207/MS28644; CLC/B/207/MS28779.
48 RH Oakley, "Report on Visit to Nigeria," 20 January–11 February 1963, p. 2, BGA 29/667.
49 Chibuike Ugochukwu Uche, "Accounting and Control in Barclays Bank (DCO): The Lending to Africans Episode," *Accounting, Business & Financial History* 8, no. 3 (1998): 239–60, https://doi.org/10.1080/095852098330404. Chairman's statement at the AGM of John Holt & Co, 20 April 1956, 3 April 1959, LRO 380 HOL II.
50 Sir E Machtig and J Rodway "Visit to the Emir of Kano," 12 May 1959, BGA 80/4351. The largest single item was a loan of nearly £900,000 to the London & Kano Trading Co., a long-established expatriate commercial firm, which casts doubt on the bank's assessment that most bad debts were to Africans, although true in customer numbers. In 1961 Barclays' accounts board still held a 24 per cent provision against Nigerian debts, the highest percentage of all territories. Barclays Bank DCO board minutes, 25 February 1960, pp. 241–2, ledger No. 10, BGA 38/512.

51 Barclays Bank DCO Board Minutes, "Nigeria – Broad Street Branch, Lagos – Management Bad and Doubtful Debts," No. 10, 25 February 1960, pp. 241–2, BGA 38/512.

52 Gustav Jahoda, *White Man: A Study of Attitudes of Africans to Europeans in Ghana before Independence* (London, UK: Oxford University Press, 1961), 73–4.

53 Interview with Hugh Norris, Reg Dines, Hugh Norris, John Woodcock (former Barclays Bank DCO expatriate managers who worked in West Africa), 17 August 2001; M Fafchamp, "The Enforcement of Commercial Contracts in Ghana," *World Development* 24, no. 3 (1996): 427, 445.

54 See for example the exchange of letters at Barclays, in which the Ghanaian management explains to London Head Office why securities for mortgages are difficult to obtain: Local Director, Accra, to General Managers, London, 23 January 1962; Assistant General Manager PAH van Heerden, London, to Ghana Directors, 23 February 1962; Local Director, Accra, to General Managers, London, 9 March 1962; BGA 11/2390 (1). For African traders' grievances see Jan-Georg Deutsch, *Educating the Middlemen: Political and Economic History of Statutory Cocoa Marketing in Nigeria, 1936–1947* (Berlin: Das Arabische Buch, 1995), 74 fn65. Peter Bauer acknowledges that there is some substance to African grievances against the British banks, see Peter Tamas Bauer, *West African Trade: A Study of Competition, Oligopoly and Monopoly in a Changing Economy* (London, UK: Routledge, 1954), 183–8, https://doi.org/10.4324/9780203838556/WEST-AFRICAN-TRADE-BAUER.

55 Fiona Beveridge (nee Boyd) researched instances of expropriation of British investment between 1965 and 1985, and her sample indicates that 49 per cent of expropriations occurred in Africa, 19 per cent in the Middle East and only 8 per cent in Latin America. Her sample indicates that 30 per cent were extractive companies, 20 per cent financial, 15 per cent in manufacturing and 13 per cent in agriculture. Fiona C Boyd, "Expropriation of Alien Property in International Law: A Study of Recent State Practice Concerning British Nationals" (University of Nottingham, 1988), 37, 43; see also Charles R Kennedy, "Relations between Transnational Corporations and Governments in Host Countries: A Look into the Future," *Transnational Corporations* 1 (1992): 67–91.

56 Walter Rodney, *How Europe Underdeveloped Africa* (London, UK, and Dar-Es-Salaam, Tanzania: Bogle-L'Overture And Tanzania Publishing House, 1972), https://doi.org/10.2307/484037.

57 Obafemi Awolowo, *The Path to Economic Freedom in Developing Countries: A Lecture Delivered at the University of Lagos on 15 March 1968, Annual Lectures 1* (Ibadan, Nigeria: University of Lagos, 1968), 4–5.

58 Kwame Nkrumah, *Neo-Colonialism: The Last Stage of Imperialism* (London: Heinemann, 1968).

59 Samir Amin, "Unequal Development: An Essay on the Social Formations of Peripheral Capitalism," *Science & Society* 42, no. 2 (1978): 219–22, https://doi.org/10.2307/532256; Samir Amin, *Neo-Colonialism in West Africa* (New York, NY: Monthly Review Press, 1973).

60 Raúl Prebisch and United Nations Economic Commission for Latin America, "The Economic Development of Latin America and Its Principal Problems" (New York, NY, 1950).

61 WL Bernecker and T Fischer, "Rise and Decline of Latin American Dependency Theories," *Itinerario* 22, no. 4 (1998): 25–45; Colin Leys, *The Rise and Fall of Development Theory* (London UK: James Currey, 1996); C Kay, *Latin American Theories of Development and Underdevelopment* (London: Routlede, 1989).

62 Rodney, *How Europe Underdeveloped Africa.*

63 *West Africa*, 18 August 1972, p. 1102.

64 "As Frank Dolling says, you can see the political/economic changes in Swaziland following the normal pattern we've so often seen elsewhere and it is not a question of 'if' we have to go local but 'when'." See "Swaziland – Note of discussion with Mr. R Stephens, Minister of Finance, Johannesburg," 8 November 1972, p. 4, BGA 80/5666.
65 "Nigeria: Nigerianising Business," *West Africa,* 2 July 1971, p. 765, in Public Records Administration and Archives Department, Accra, Ghana, (PRAAD) RG 6/1/190 ('Ghanaian Business Promotion, 1970–1971').
66 Douglas Rimmer, *Staying Poor: Ghana's Political Economy, 1950–1990*, ed. World Bank (Oxford: Pergamon, 1992), 147.
67 J Quinn, "W(h)Ither the State (System)?," *International Politics* 38 (2001): 439.
68 AE Ambrose to W Duncan, 17 December 1968, BGA 11/947. On nationalization checklist: AE Ambrose to John Rodway, 8 February 1968; "Draft Check List: Instructions to Branches in Tanzania on Nationalisation," pp. 1–6, BGA 80/5356 (2).
69 Noel Maurer, *The Empire Trap: The Rise and Fall of U.S. Intervention to Protect American Property Overseas, 1893–1976* (Princeton: Princeton University Press, 2013).
70 Thomas J Biersteker, *Multinationals, the State, and the Control of the Nigerian Economy* (Princeton, NJ: Princeton University Press, 1987), 285.
71 Biersteker, *Multinationals*, 164, 266, 280.
72 Minutes of Special Committee, No. U. A. 121, Mr Judd's Visit to Nigeria, 3 May 1976, UHA UNI/SC with UAC International.
73 UAC Nigeria, "The LAND, the GROUP and the ROLE," *Nigeria*, 107–9 (December 1970–August 1971), p. i.
74 Minutes of Special Committee, No. U. A. 122, 14 June 1976, UHA UNI/SC with UAC International.
75 Biersteker, *Multinationals*, 192–3, 197.
76 F. A. Tuke, "Mr. F. A. Tuke's Visit to Nigeria, Ghana and Sierra Leone," 23 November–4 December 1970, pp. 1–2, BGA 80/4292.
77 Chibuike Ugochukwu Uche, "Lonrho in Africa: The Unacceptable Face of Capitalism or the Ugly Face of Neo-Colonialism?," Enterprise and Society 16, no. 2 (2015): 354–80, https://doi.org/10.1017/eso.2014.31.
78 S Cronjé, M Ling, and G Cronjé, *Lonrho: Portrait of a Multinational* (Harmondsworth, UK: Penguin, 1976), 261–2.
79 Cronjé, Ling, and Cronjé, *Lonrho,* 262.

List of References

Amin, Samir. *Neo-Colonialism in West Africa.* New York, NY: Monthly Review Press, 1973.

Amin, Samir. "Unequal Development: An Essay on the Social Formations of Peripheral Capitalism." *Science & Society* 42, no. 2 (1978): 219–22. 10.2307/532256.

Awolowo, Obafemi. *The Path to Economic Freedom in Developing Countries: A Lecture Delivered at the University of Lagos on 15 March 1968, Annual Lectures 1.* Ibadan, Nigeria: University of Lagos, 1968.

Bates, Robert H. *Markets and States in Tropical Africa: The Political Basis of Agricultural Policies*. Berkeley, Los Angeles, CA, and London: University of California Press, 1981.

Bauer, Peter Tamas. *West African Trade: A Study of Competition, Oligopoly and Monopoly in a Changing Economy*. London, UK: Routledge, 1954.

Beckman, B. *Organising the Farmers: Cocoa Politics and National Development in Ghana.* Uppsala, Sweden: Scandinavian Institute of African Studies, 1976.

Bernecker, WL, and T Fischer. "Rise and Decline of Latin American Dependency Theories." *Itinerario* 22, no. 4 (1998): 25–45.

Biersteker, Thomas J. *Multinationals, the State, and the Control of the Nigerian Economy.* Princeton, NJ: Princeton University Press, 1987.

Bostock, Frances. "The British Overseas Banks and Development Finance in Africa after 1945." *Business History* 33, no. 3 (1991): 157–76. 10.1080/00076799100000106.

Boyd, Fiona C. *Expropriation of Alien Property in International Law: A Study of Recent State Practice Concerning British Nationals.* University of Nottingham, 1988.

Breton, Albert. "The Economics of Nationalism." *The Journal of Political Economy* 72, no. 4 (1964): 376–86.

Butler, L.J. *Industrialisation and the British Colonial State. West Africa 1939–1951.* London & New York: Routledge, 1997.

Cooper, Frederick. *Africa since 1940: The Past of the Present.* Cambridge, UK, and New York, NY: Cambridge University Press, 2002.

Cooper, Frederick. *Decolonization and African Society: The Labour Question in French and British Africa. Africa: Journal of the International African Institute.* Cambridge, UK: Cambridge University Press, 1996. 10.2307/1161082.

Cooper, Frederick, and Randall M. Packard. *International Development and the Social Sciences: Essays on the History and Politics of Knowledge.* Berkeley, CA, London: University of California Press, 1997.

Cronjé, S, M Ling, and G Cronjé. *Lonrho: Portrait of a Multinational.* Harmondsworth, UK: Penguin, 1976.

Decker, Stephanie. "Corporate Legitimacy and Advertising: British Companies and the Rhetoric of Development in West Africa, 1950–1970." *Business History Review* 81, no. 1 (March 2007): 59–86. 10.2307/25097298.

Deutsch, Jan-Georg. *Educating the Middlemen: Political and Economic History of Statutory Cocoa Marketing in Nigeria, 1936–1947.* Berlin: Das Arabische Buch, 1995.

Fafchamp, M "The Enforcement of Commercial Contracts in Ghana." *World Development* 24, no. 3 (1996): 427–48.

Fieldhouse, David Kenneth. *Merchant Capital and Economic Decolonisation: The United Africa Company 1929–1987.* Oxford: Clarendon, 1994.

Fry, Richard. *Bankers in West Africa: The History of the British Bank of West Africa.* London: Hutchinson Benham, 1976.

Jahoda, Gustav. *White Man: A Study of Attitudes of Africans to Europeans in Ghana before Independence.* London, UK: Oxford University Press, 1961.

Johnson, Harry Gordon. *Economic Nationalism in Old and New States. A Publication of the Committee for the Comparative Study of New Nations, University of Chicago.* London: Allen & Unwin, 1968.

Jones, Geoffrey. *Merchants to Multinationals: British Trading Companies in the Nineteenth and Twentieth Centuries.* Oxford: Oxford University Press, 2000.

Kay, C. *Latin American Theories of Development and Underdevelopment.* London: Routlede, 1989.

Kennedy, Charles R. "Relations between Transnational Corporations and Governments in Host Countries: A Look into the Future." *Transnational Corporations* 1 (1992): 67–91.

Kilby, Peter. *Industrialisation in an Open Economy: Nigeria 1945–66.* Cambridge, UK: Cambridge University Press, 1969.

Killick, Tony. *Development Economics in Action: A Study of Economic Policies in Ghana. Studies in the Economics of Africa*. London i.a.: Heinemann Educational, 1978.
Lewis, W Arthur. "Report on the Industrialisation and the Gold Coast." Accra, Ghana, 1953.
Leys, Colin. *The Rise and Fall of Development Theory*. London, UK: James Currey, 1996.
Maurer, Noel. *The Empire Trap: The Rise and Fall of US Intervention to Protect American Property Overseas, 1893–1976*. Princeton: Princeton University Press, 2013.
Pedler, Frederick J. *Economic Geography of West Africa*. London, UK: Longmans, 1954.
Prebisch, Raúl, and United Nations Economic Commission for Latin America. "The Economic Development of Latin America and Its Principal Problems." New York, NY, 1950.
Quinn, J. "W(h)Ither the State (System)?" *International Politics* 38 (2001): 437–46.
Ramamurthy, Anandi. *Imperial Persuaders: Images of Africa and Asia in British Advertising*. Manchester, UK: Manchester University Press, 2003.
Ranis, G. "The Evolution of Development Thinking: Theory and Policy." In *Annual World Bank Conference on Development Economics 2005: Lessons of Experience*, edited by François Bourguignon and Boris Pleskovic, 119–40. Washington, DC: World Bank, 2004.
Rimmer, Douglas. *Staying Poor: Ghana's Political Economy, 1950–1990*. Edited by World Bank. Oxford: Pergamon, 1992.
Rodney, Walter. *How Europe Underdeveloped Africa*. London, UK, and Dar-Es-Salaam, Tanzania: Bogle-L'Overture And Tanzania Publishing House, 1972. 10.2307/484037.
Rowan, D.C. "Native Banking Boom in Nigeria." *The Banker*, October 1951.
Seers, Dudley, and C Ross. "Report on the Financial and Physical Problems of Development in the Gold Coast." Accra, Ghana, 1952.
Stockwell, Sarah E. *The Business of Decolonization: British Business Strategies in the Gold Coast*. Oxford: Clarendon Press, 2000.
Tignor, Robert L. *Capitalism and Nationalism at the End of Empire: State and Business in Decolonizing Egypt, Nigeria, and Kenya, 1945–1963*. Princeton, NJ: Princeton University Press, 1998.
Uche, Chibuike Ugochukwu. "Accounting and Control in Barclays Bank (DCO): The Lending to Africans Episode." *Accounting, Business & Financial History* 8, no. 3 (1998): 239–60. 10.1080/095852098330404.
Uche, Chibuike Ugochukwu. "Lonrho in Africa: The Unacceptable Face of Capitalism or the Ugly Face of Neo-Colonialism?" *Enterprise and Society* 16, no. 2 (2015): 354–80. 10.1017/eso.2014.31.
Watson, A "Report of the Commission of Enquiry into Disturbances in the Gold Coast." London, UK, 1948.
Williamson, J "Speeches, Testimony, Papers: Did the Washington Consensus Fail?" *Institute for International Economics*, 2002. http://www2.econ.iastate.edu/classes/econ502/tesfatsion/WashingtonConsensus.JWilliamson2002.pdf.

Part I

Managing Postcolonial Transitions Externally

3 Corporate Political Activities before and after Independence

Although foreign companies became targets of African nationalism in the late 1940s, the relations between corporate executives and nationalist politicians were at times surprisingly cordial by the mid-1950s. What had prompted this change of attitude? Colonial governments' post-war policies and decolonization were partly responsible for this change. Still, businesses' local networks continued after independence, establishing firms as partners for the development aspirations of West African countries.

This chapter argues that a mutual understanding of development facilitated cooperation between African politicians and foreign businesspeople. Private enterprises accepted the mixed economy created through the marketing boards, while governments set lenient parameters for (foreign) private economic activity. British business, colonial governments and African politicians all had a stake in creating workable states and economies. The following sections are organized roughly chronologically. During the late 1940s and early 1950s, economic nationalism in West Africa was widespread and influential. The beginning of political devolution meant businesses had to engage with African opinions more than before.

For Ghana, Sarah Stockwell has analysed the political strategies of British business during decolonization, which the section on business representation reflects.[1] However, evidence from Nigeria shows that there were other considerations about representation than those mentioned in her study. Political strategies to position the companies for independence were complemented by commercial considerations, which underline how pervasive notions of development and modernization were in the 1950s and how much businesses subscribed to them in practice. Hence this chapter reframes Stockwell's concern with business responses to decolonization in favour of articulating corporate presence as essential to a development framework that continued to be relevant beyond independence. Stockwell's study of the Gold Coast not only concludes with independence, despite the continued presence of British business in the former colonies but also focuses on institutional representation.

In contrast, the present chapter emphasizes the many personal contacts that businesses established and utilized in different ways. This is significantly

DOI: 10.4324/9781003001058-4

more low-key than policy formation. Still, it is evident from business files that social networks were perceived as crucial in canvassing opinion, gaining local intelligence and eventual decision-making. Once independence arrived, businesses profited from this political and administrative network developed during the 1950s. This was most noticeable in Nigeria, but even in Ghana, the relationship with Nkrumah after 1962 was surprisingly cordial. It is necessary to begin by examining the roots of the economic nationalism which undermined the wartime links between the imperial authorities and British business to see how this contributed to the subsequent corporate attitude during decolonization and in the post-independence state.

3.1 Organizing business and political representation during decolonization

During World War II, it was already becoming clear that imperial rule of Britain's tropical colonies would substantially change once hostilities ceased. Britain's commitment to its empire was reinforced by post-war shortages and increased reliance on tropical commodities and export earning power.[2] In the mid to late 1940s, consumer protests and economic nationalism were ripe and foreign business became the target of intense criticism. Far from being perceived as agents of development, companies were criticized for exploiting Africans, and the close alliance of government and merchants during the war made both intensely vulnerable to anti-colonial mobilization. The situation only calmed down in the early 1950s, when decolonization had gained momentum. By the late 1940s, however, colonial governments were less inclined to champion the cause of companies which were universally decried as discriminating against Africans and exploiting the country because this might have undermined the credibility of their commitment to economic development. As traditional channels for influencing politics increasingly failed, British business turned towards other forms of official representation, which began to reflect the political changes and the necessity to gain the goodwill of the West African public.

3.1.1 Commercial protests and colonial reform

During World War II, West African trade was controlled by statutory produce boards for export commodities and trade was managed by the Association of West African Merchants (AWAM), which was formed by large merchant companies. Their individual share of the trade was frozen at pre-war levels, according to the so-called past performance principle. Smaller African and Lebanese traders were designated B shippers (as opposed to the European merchants, who were A shippers) and given significantly smaller quotas.[3] Local buying power rose during the war because of the enhanced terms of trade that producer countries enjoyed and the effective protection for local industrialization. Scarce imports not only caused inflation and a higher cost of living but also offered lucrative opportunities in import and export, from which Africans were effectively excluded due to the collusion of the colonial state and the large European merchants. Consumers also voiced their discontent at high prices and scarce goods, for which they held the AWAM companies responsible, in particular, its largest member, the United Africa Company (UAC). Early nationalist movements such as the Nigerian Youth Movement (NYM) and the United Gold Coast Convention capitalized on these public protests. The NYM's criticism of AWAM highlights how closely intertwined political and economic grievances were at this early stage of colonial resistance:

> If in truth political power has no practical meaning without economic control the AWAM with its limitless ramifications and formidable array of influential combines is undoubtedly the uncrowned king of British West Africa.[4]

Consumer protests culminated in the Gold Coast consumer riots of 1948, which prompted a change in business strategies.[5] The central role that is given to a consumer riot in the history of West African decolonization, a process normally seen as dominated by politics, emphasizes that initially, the lines of conflict had not been limited to constitutional questions. However, the focus on 1948 has often obscured the fact that conflicts with British business and the use of economic nationalism in political propaganda not only predated 1948 but also continued until the early 1950s. It noticeably diminished around the time when African politicians gained access to political power as well as the marketing boards and their associated stabilization funds. The reason that the events of February 1948 became so momentous was due to their political repercussions. The relationship between merchant companies and the Colonial Office had come under strain before, but only when governments decided publicly to break ranks with business in both Nigeria and the Gold Coast, did the companies change their public relations policy.[6]

The economic nationalism that became apparent in those early years often surprised the firms' leaders – as there had never been a political avenue for African subjects to voice their discontent, their opinions had been immaterial to business. But while merchant companies had been well aware of the unpopularity of AWAM at least since 1943 and feared it might prejudice opinion against them, it had been unthinkable until 1948 that African public opinion would be relayed directly into politics.[7] By 1949 Holt's district agent in Lagos, G Cotgreave was becoming aware of this possibility:

> […] a number of political speeches were made, stressing the need for executive powers being given so that they could ensure that the trade of Nigeria was enjoyed by Nigerians and not by the few big firms.

> I was surprised at this attitude, which was most unexpected, but it is a pointer of how some of our possible future legislators are thinking.[8]

Once in government, most African politicians also agreed that 'a new undertaking in Africa must have an African majority shareholding'.[9] Less than a year later, in November 1952, Unilever's directors rejoiced that ministers in Nigeria encountered some practical constraints: 'Half of them considered that foreign capital meant exploitation; the one thing they all realised was that there was no African capital available.'[10] This was, however, a dubious claim: while there were significant constraints on African capital, the type of large-scale industrial development favoured in those years was indeed often beyond the scope of local businessmen and required outside assistance. Policy choices influenced by the development discourse constrained African participation as much as capital constraints. This opened a new avenue for foreign business to underline its usefulness to politicians, who had publicly committed themselves to rapid economic development and the industrialization of their countries.

The notion of exploitation had surfaced in the political discourse on foreign investment in Britain, in particular in conjunction with the mining industry and the post-war Labour policy of nationalizing the mines and transport industry.[11] In 1946 a white paper on colonial mining policy argued that where private capitalist interests were 'prone to exploit and abuse the labour of the primitive native population [...] for the latter's protection [...] the State should take over and run the business'.[12] Furthermore, there were suggestions from the Colonial Office and the Fabian Colonial Bureau about nationalizing the UAC, which were eventually abandoned in favour of a less radical solution of a cooperative movement.[13]

Although the Labour Party gave up any attempts to nationalize the industry outside the United Kingdom, as well as any further metropolitan companies by the late 1940s, the emerging Gold Coast politicians did not. In a speech in 1950, Gbedemah criticized the mining companies for removing the natural wealth of the country. He promised that the CPP would nationalize the gold mines once in power, 'thus preserving the wealth of Africa for Africans'.[14]

A year later, in 1951, however, the position of a new Conservative government in Britain on the decolonization process made such promises seem rather hollow, and the more radical voices in the Gold Coast became more muted. Holt's Accra manager was relieved and admitted that he hoped for 'saner debates and fewer wild statements about nationalization'.[15] In 1953, Hugh Thomas, the secretary of the Gold Coast Chamber of Mines, sent an angry letter to Nkrumah advising him that claims about the mines' nationalization, made by another CPP functionary, were damaging 'at a time when the Gold Coast wants friendly relations with all foreign capitals'.[16]

This change in official policy, both in Britain and in West Africa, was not exclusively due to political change in the metropolis but also to the reconfiguration of economic organization, which became framed by the development consensus. All parties – the colonial state, business and nationalist politicians – had become content to administer the economy as part of development and modernization efforts and to reduce decolonization correspondingly to a political process of constitutional development. For nationalists in Nigeria and the Gold Coast, control of marketing board funds largely relieved them of the need to mobilize public and financial support through economic issues. With the opening of political avenues for Africans, the importance of the firms' image with the population rose. However, only after the Gold Coast riots of 1948 did companies realize that connections to the colonial government were no longer sufficient political insurance. Both UAC and Cadbury assumed that the Colonial Office would be central to any post-war representation, and in 1945 Holt refused to join a UK-based or even European lobby group as it would undermine the direct contacts of Liverpool-based firms to the government. However, the events of February 1948 would change this.[17]

3.1.2 The debate over public relations policy and the Gold Coast riots

Commercial protests before 1948 already show that corporate agents in West Africa considered different strategies from their metropolitan leadership. Internal debates at John Holt during the Kojo Thompson trial in 1944 explored the possibility of an active and independent corporate public relations policy. Thompson, a lawyer, had, according to Richard Barrow, a leading manager of the Unilever Group in the colony, offered to withhold press attacks on AWAM in return for a bribe. Without witnesses, the trial was based on one man's word against the other's, and the court sided with the expatriate. However, the case focused on criticism of AWAM and coincided with a wave of criticism by the NYM.[18] At Holt's, the district agent in Accra, Goddard, argued that a proactive public relations strategy was necessary to deflect criticism against the AWAM firms, particularly as government support was not forthcoming. Barrow, the GB Ollivants' manager implicated in the Kojo Thompson case, agreed with him, but Goddard's managers in Liverpool considered the legal proceedings and the anti-AWAM protests as directed mainly against the UAC and remained convinced they would not affect Holt. These internal arguments did not influence business strategy until the late 1940s, when AWAM's unpopularity, scarce supply and disputes over distribution formed a potent political mix. In March 1947, the Martindale commission reported on irregularities in the customs department in the Gold Coast, which sparked a new bout of anti-AWAM protests.[19] In Nigeria, an African traders dispute had erupted in Ibadan in the same year, objecting to restrictions on sales and the allocation of textiles between Lebanese and African customers by the European merchants.[20] Here, the UAC was again singled out for criticism, while Holt was excluded from many of the allegations.

In the Gold Coast, the Ga businessman Nii Kwabena Bonne III organized a consumer boycott over the high prices of imported goods, which forced the trading companies and the government to negotiate a reduction in profit.[21] Press reports had, however, given the impression that the overall prices, and not the profits, were to be cut by almost half.[22] The majority of the population also did not buy directly from expatriate company stores but from middlemen, small traders and hawkers, who set their own prices according to the level of demand. Thus, the reduction in prices did not remotely meet public expectations. On 28 February, riots broke out, company shops were looted, and at an ex-servicemen's demonstration, the police opened fire on the crowd, killing one person and injuring another. The UAC in particular, but also other merchants, including John Holt, sustained a lot of damage to their shops, and looting spread beyond the capital. Lebanese and Indian stores were also attacked, with the exception of AG Leventis, who had publicly supported the nationalist cause. The two banks were not affected, but the diary of a visiting manager from Barclays' London head office conveys the sense of panic of the expatriate community. Many managers were sworn into the police as special constables, and women and children were evacuated to safe houses and guarded.[23] The disturbances did not spread to Obuasi, AGC's place of operations, where high unemployment had followed a strike in 1947 and industrial action was more likely to mobilize people than consumer protests.[24]

The Watson commission of enquiry into the disturbances was accompanied by the appointment of a further committee of enquiry into the distribution of scarce cargo in Nigeria.[25] In the face of public condemnation, AWAM was disbanded in the Gold Coast before the first meeting of the Watson commission. Although the expatriates considered the political situation in the Gold Coast more volatile, in Nigeria, firms were also blamed for high prices and the black market. Hugh Foot, the chief secretary in Nigeria, informed AWAM that 'Government can deal with riots if they should occur, but [the AWAM firms] must restore the African's confidence in the merchant firms'.[26] WTG Gates of Holt commented: 'You can take it that we are agreed that AWAM [...] must disappear without delay, but if possible, we want to give it a decent burial.'[27] As neither government nor business wanted to lose face over the incident, a great deal of blame-shifting ensued. The government refused to state that AWAM had been formed at their request because they did not want to be associated with the firms.[28] Government intransigence led the firms to reassess their public relations policy:

> I am not sure that we were right when we refused to reply to the Press criticism which started four or five years ago. We took the view that our propaganda would appear only in a garbled form if it were printed at all; that, if we ignored the Press campaign it would, in time, die out [...] we have never attempted to deny the fantastic accusations which have appeared in print from time to time. Admittedly, we probably

> should not have been believed had we done so, but I think intelligent and skilful counterpropaganda might have had good results, and the bitterness which exists today might have been less harmful.[29]

The AWAM firms also implicated other traders. Holt argued that 'large unreasonable profits' were made by African and Lebanese middlemen, over whom the firms had no control.[30] The UAC's general manager in Lagos blamed high prices on the existence of a black market, the consequence of the scarce supply of goods and hence the government's responsibility. WTG Gates, one of Holt's top managers, however, admitted that all firms had, on occasion, made conditional sales, but he was certain that his own company had little to fear.[31] Conditional sales, a highly controversial issue at the time, meant that traders were forced to buy products that sold very poorly if they wanted to obtain any scarce and highly desirable goods.[32] UAC, however, found itself the target of popular dissatisfaction, with even the colonial government and moderate African politicians being intensely suspicious of its power. The company recognized the need to 'appease public suspicion' and expanded its public relations activities in the aftermath of the riots.[33]

As a result, after the Gold Coast riots in February 1948, British companies changed their public relations strategy and sought to influence popular opinion in their favour. While cooperation with the colonial administration did not entirely break down, relations deteriorated markedly, and collaboration through vehicles such as AWAM became impossible. Businesses nevertheless continued to seek other less criticized and better-suited forms of organized political representation.

3.1.3 Alternative forms of business representation

When AWAM was disbanded in both the Gold Coast and Nigeria in 1948, businesses had to find an alternative form of representation. There had been no lack of thinking about possibilities, as most merchants had expected that the Association would decline after the war.[34] Hence most AWAM firms intended to withdraw the employees they had seconded to the Association in 1945, but the Colonial Office insisted on negotiating with one body that could represent the commercial sector. Holt's district agent in Lagos, JF Winter, had anticipated this response in Nigeria where the government wanted to deal with the merchant interests in such a large and varied territory through one coordinated 'mouthpiece'.[35] This overwhelming concern to work with a joint commercial sector remained an issue once AWAM had been abandoned. While racially-biased organizations became a liability, other forms of representation had to be found. The most obvious choice was the existing chambers of commerce in West Africa. This did not mean that other forms of metropolitan-based organizations were entirely abandoned, but they were not as important as long as business interests were represented in the new political institutions in West Africa.

The changes to the West African chambers of commerce have already been researched by Stockwell for the Gold Coast and by Harneit-Sievers and Tignor for the Lagos chamber.[36] Tignor's account, however, finishes in 1949, although Holt's files show that individual efforts to propose non-European firms for membership of the Chamber were only beginning at this time. Harneit-Sievers only gives an overview of the motivations of European firms and focuses more on the activities of African traders. In May 1949, the Lagos chamber still only counted eight African firms among its 60 members, despite the efforts of Holt, British American Tobacco (BAT) and APEX to reduce the membership fee and diversify the composition of the Chamber.[37] Already in 1948, Holt's district agent had written disappointedly about the lack of foresight of the other European members, who failed to see the advantages of being 'fully representative of all persons and firms engaged in trade and industry [...] particularly the African traders and African firms'.[38] A year after AWAM had been disbanded, the Nigerian government regularly asked for representation from the Lagos chamber and the African Importers and Exporters Association.[39]

Although Holt's and BAT failed in a proposal to halve the membership fee of £20, the UAC group companies agreed to reduce it to £15, and the African Importers and Exporters Association eventually became defunct as their most important members joined the Chamber.[40] Other firms increasingly supported their efforts to find African businessmen interested in membership.[41] In subsequent years, the membership of smaller African and Lebanese firms was regularly proposed and seconded, and by 1952 the Lagos chamber had a membership of 124, of which 74 were European, 19 African, 18 partly African, five Lebanese, five Indian and three American.[42] A year later, numbers had increased to 156, 'predominantly African and British [...] and the growth of our African membership is keeping pace with the progress which is being made towards self-government'.[43] While the Chamber continued to be dominated by European concerns and the high membership fee prevented too radical a change in composition, the organization became more concerned with promoting its role as representing the interests of commerce, particularly of small traders.[44] This was in contrast to Ghana, where a rival chamber was formed by indigenous businessmen in 1953.[45]

The Chambers of Commerce were not the only form of organized representation that British businesses used. Until the early 1950s in the Gold Coast and in southern Nigeria, they were in the favourable position that special representatives from business sat in the legislatures. Stockwell gives a detailed account of business efforts in the Gold Coast, in particular the role of Edward Spears, who attempted to exert political pressure when most other mining and commercial companies were distancing themselves from his position, as not all were convinced of the necessity of special members. The firms had successfully campaigned to retain special representation in the 1951 constitution, but the CPP abolished it in 1953.[46]

The situation regarding business representation in Nigeria differed from the Gold Coast, as companies appeared more uncertain whether it was worth the effort. Holt's management advised avoiding making any claims for representation out of tactical considerations:

> I think we shall do better to be unrepresented either as Europeans (for we are a very small numerical community) or as business interests. If we are specifically represented we shall be submerged in Council voting and shall weaken the moral right to appeal to the Governor for consideration as a prejudiced unrepresented interest.[47]

However, this did not mean that Holt had completely given up the issue because they expected that government would insist on special members anyway, leaving businesses to accept the invitation gracefully. In 1951 the Governor Sir John Macpherson of Nigeria made his intentions clear to a select group of British company managers (representatives from BBWA, Barclays, GB Ollivants, UAC, Holt, Elder Dempster, BAT and Mr Irving). Due to the federal structure of the colony, 22 special members were to be appointed, and the commercial firms expected that they would be asked to provide a large proportion.[48] Holt's agent RWT Bateson doubted the undertaking that the firms' head offices had given to the government that, firstly, the senior representatives would be supported by additional staff and, secondly, local agents would be allowed sufficient discretionary authority.[49]

The role that special representation played for business has been described by Stockwell as a means of correcting false information, defending their interest and working on draft legislation, but Holt's files on Nigeria suggest another motive: generating African contacts.[50] Holt's manager EW Pearce became a special member in the Northern Assembly and regularly reported back to head office on the various ministers, including Tafawa Balewa, 'who is obviously going to be the outstanding Central Minister from this region':

> [...] the most interesting part [...] is in getting to know the other members and to watch the assembly shaping itself. Much of this contacting has to be done outside the House [...][51]

Frederick Pedler remarked in his memoirs that Patrick Fitzgerald used his seat in the Gold Coast parliament to gain access to the members' bar and restaurant, making sure 'he knew them all personally on drinking terms'. When special members were abolished in 1953 (or in 1951, according to his memoirs), the House passed a resolution that former members were still entitled to use these amenities, enabling Fitzgerald to make further contacts, especially with Kwame Nkrumah.[52] Holt and UAC's approach shows that business began to adapt its strategies in the early 1950s, but when special representation was discontinued in 1953, a flurry of activity ensued to find another vehicle like AWAM that could serve metropolitan corporate interests. One possibility was a federation of all chambers of commerce in Nigeria:

> [...] there would be considerable merit in having one central body speaking on behalf of commerce for the whole of Nigeria which would be in a position to advise Government on general policy.[53]

The rivalry between the different regional chambers, particularly between Kano and Lagos, had prevented such an organization previously. In 1954 there were even suggestions to revive AWAM under a different name and with a wider constituency, as a representation of a sectional interest group of UK-based West African merchants.[54] Eventually, an employers' organization was set up in 1955 in Nigeria, and a year later, the old Joint West Africa Committee reconstituted itself as the West Africa Committee (WAC), a representation of West African corporate interests that liaised with the British, Nigerian and Ghanaian governments.[55]

3.2 Legitimization strategies at the end of empire

By the mid-1950s, animosity towards foreign firms had declined. A report to Unilever's board stated that 'the attitude towards the WAC [West Africa Committee] and foreigners [had] generally greatly improved [...] In the Gold Coast, as in Nigeria, the company's reputation was very high'.[56] Since 1953/54, both Ghana and Nigeria had achieved a degree of internal self-government, and as African politicians were co-opted into the late colonial state, they relied noticeably less on nationalist protest politics that had brought them to power.[57] Mobilizing consumer and labour unrest against colonial rule and imperial business was dropped in favour of the 'political kingdom', according to Nkrumah's dictum, now that the new parties had access to political power and, increasingly, to sterling balances and marketing board funds. Their economic programme became subsumed by development orthodoxy, and buoyant producer prices, particularly those of cocoa before 1955, seemed to validate the assumption that low levels of economic achievement had previously been due to foreign political domination. Once this was removed, West Africa would prosper.

British business showed its willingness to accept this new status quo by adapting its commercial strategies to the development plans: leaving small-scale retail to Africans, investing in wholesale and manufacturing, extending modern financial institutions, localizing business and selling shares locally. Since the mid-1950s, British principals also appear to have understood that lobbying the Colonial Office and governors was no longer appropriate and focused their political networking on the future political leaders in Africa. While Stockwell mentions in her study that the Colonial Office had to remind firms of this as late as 1954, Maria Misra has claimed that for British businessmen in India, personal contacts with politicians were more effective than they had been with colonial officials.[58] Although the seeds for post-war economic cooperation were laid during late decolonization, there were also political and economic crises that threatened this process. While business was wary of instability, new internal rivalries had the positive side effect that they 'tended to divert attention away from the big trading companies'.[59] The three different strands of commercial strategies that can be distinguished are redeployment (already discussed in chapter 2), localization and political networking.

3.2.1 Localization

Localization has been described by Stockwell as a further aspect of public relations policies, but she does not give further details as to which companies followed this course and how far. She also does not distinguish between the establishment of local boards and local registration of a company, which were separate.[60] Some companies, mainly in commerce, voluntarily incorporated locally and even offered shares, but the banks, for example, resisted this step and only established local boards. AGC did neither.

Localization was mainly motivated by political considerations. In 1960 Unilever's directors' committee commented on

> [...] the importance of approaching the question of public relations in a positive and constructive way; and the need to avoid giving the outward impression that the business was controlled ultimately from London.[61]

The first company to incorporate a local subsidiary was John Holt in 1954, but no assets were transferred to it initially. Its main function was that 'African directors could be appointed if the Government insisted'.[62] In 1953, Unilever's management remained dubious over whether localization was really successful as a public relations exercise after their experience in India, where subsidiaries were locally known as 'the foreign Limiteds'.[63] Cadburys decided a year later not to incorporate locally as the management doubted whether the benefits would outweigh the costs, while UAC formed only local companies in both Nigeria and the Gold Coast in response to changing regulations. In Nigeria, companies were now required to file a balance sheet for their local operations. For tax reasons, however, assets were transferred only gradually to the newly registered subsidiaries. As a safeguard against similar events in the Gold Coast, the UAC increased the capital of a dormant local subsidiary.[64] When Unilever announced it would create new local companies in 1955, this 'aroused considerable interest' but no demands for local participation.[65] Holt also used imminent Ghanaian independence in 1957 to highlight their localization strategy:

> As a sign of our confidence in the future of these new nationals we have strengthened the authority of our locally registered companies in Nigeria and the Gold Coast, to enable them to play their full part when self-government is attained. I believe that the good relations which exist between Africans and Britons in the Gulf of Guinea are favourable omens for future prosperity.[66]

This statement also illustrates the common belief of the complementarity of British and African interests in economic development. In 1960, both commercial firms were actively preparing to offer shares in their local subsidiaries to West African residents, of which Holt's chairman said they were intended to be 'a true partnership between the Company and the national interests in West Africa'.[67] Holt had also invested in industrial ventures under the Pioneer Industry Ordinance, which granted tax relief for development capital, and later entered joint ventures with the West African governments and other companies. In 1961 one of their subsidiaries had over 1,000 Nigerian shareholders, and when, in 1962, all trading activities were transferred to a wholly-owned company, further equity issues were planned. The UAC also decided to invite public participation in 1960, but initially only in their subsidiary Kingsway Stores of Ghana.[68] While the local subsidiaries were still controlled by their parents abroad, localization meant that more capital was retained in West Africa and it made the firms' accounts more transparent. However, some firms were opposed to forming local subsidiaries.

The banks did not consider local subsidiaries because, as international branch bankers, they relied on shifting funds between territories. Nevertheless, they aimed to create goodwill by other means, for example, by sanitizing their imperial names. Barclays Bank Dominion, Colonial and Overseas was officially abbreviated to DCO in 1954.[69] The Bank of British West Africa changed its name to Bank of West Africa (BWA) for similar reasons in 1957. It also created local boards to which non-executive African directors were appointed. The bank intended that the African members would keep the board informed of political developments and bring in new business but not take any commercial decisions. In 1961, Barclays' Nigerian management was careful to represent all three major ethnic groups which corresponded to the administrative regions: Yoruba, Igbo and Hausa.

Some African politicians, however, saw the move as window-dressing, maintaining that a company could not be called Nigerian just because 'one foolish man, who is usually given a big salary' but who 'has nothing to do with the company' was appointed as a director.[70] Nevertheless, the need for positive publicity made it necessary for the bank to repeat this in Ghana as well. Having done so, the contributions of Sir Edward Asafu Adjaye, the retiring high commissioner for Ghana in London, and his fellow director Sir Charles Tachie Menson, formerly the chairman of the Civil Service Commission, were, however, sparse to non-existent. An exception to this was Robert Mensah, one of Barclays' most senior Ghanaian managers, who was appointed to the board on retirement in 1964 and who took an active interest in business affairs. In an interview with Stockwell, he commented that the others were little more than 'figureheads', an assessment also found in contemporary archival files.[71] While Barclays had hoped to use its African directors for political and commercial intelligence, the bank only succeeded with its primary intention – improving its local image.

3.2.2 Political networking

Commercial policies during decolonization were often employed to a greater or lesser degree with an eye to gaining political goodwill. But British business also sought direct personal contacts with leading politicians and civil servants, something that both UAC and Holt considered important.[72] But companies such as the UAC adapted more quickly to the new political realities than colonial officials realised.

Barclays' managers, for example, such as colonial officials, preferred the Northern Nigerian leaders, and visiting managers routinely called on Hausa-Fulani leaders, particularly their 'old friend', the Emir of Kano (Figure 3.1). In the Gold Coast, the bank's influence was such that when Barclays hosted a cocktail party in 1958, the Prime Minister, the Minister of Finance and the Minister of State all appeared. Both Barclays and the UAC found access to Nkrumah easy.[73] One of Barclays' managers was friends with Erica Powell, Nkrumah's personal secretary, who controlled access to the President. Sir Patrick Fitzgerald of the UAC was appointed as the first head of the Ghana National Trading Corporation (GNTC) in 1961.[74] The UAC and other Unilever subsidiaries did not consider their political connections in the Gold Coast threatened by imminent independence:

> The grant of independence would not mean any great shift of power because the Ministers would be the same people as those who had been in office for the past several years [...][75]

On visits to West Africa, managers would routinely meet the Governor and Regional Premiers in Nigeria and the Prime Minister and the Asantehene in the Gold Coast.[77] Since the mid-1950s, nationalist sentiment appeared less relevant, and UAC's management attributed this to financial considerations:

> [...] funds were running low [...] and the more responsible members of the Government were beginning to realise how much the economy depended upon the great companies and in particular the UAC. [...] reference had been made to the contribution which the UAC had made in the past towards the economy, and the wise counsel which her representatives had always given. It had been emphasised that in times

Figure 3.1 Julian Crossley, chairman of Barclays Bank DCO, with the Emir of Kano in February 1952.

Note: Reproduced with kind permission of Barclays Group Archives.[76]

> of stress like the present, it was only right to turn to one's old friends like the UAC. Indeed, there had been no adverse criticism, and the company had been pressed to continue with its policy of investment.[78]

The necessity of cultivating political contacts increased with independence, and most firms considered political and public relations as an essential management function. 'By strengthening the management at all levels, it was possible to leave the men at the top more free to establish good public relations, a vitally important function in the present political situation', concluded Unilever's Directors' Committee in 1959.[79] Barclays' local chairman in Nigeria, Leonard Daldry, was even a member of the independent legislative assembly until December 1961.[80] John Holt's chairman also publicly commented on the close relationship between new governments and businessmen in 1957:

> [...] African ministers and officials are quick to seek the advice of merchants and industrialists and they have earned our respect and trust by their ability to pick the brains of experienced and specialist knowledge.[81]

This was an area in which African managers became useful to British business, as many of them had good professional or even personal relationships with politicians; for example, in Ghana, Cato at the UAC, who was acquainted with Gbedemah and Nkrumah, and Mensah at Barclays, who often visited Ghanaian ministerial offices on behalf of the bank, both before and after Mensah had been appointed director in 1962.[82] By 1958, WTG Gates, Holt's new chairman, reflected positively on Ghanaian independence so far and also showed confidence in a smooth transition in Nigeria.[83] The African politicians in both Ghana and Nigeria had held important posts before the transfer of power, and companies had learned, by the late 1950s, to shift their attention to the new African elites. While the relationship between the West African governments and British business was improving, the Suez crisis raised anxieties internationally.

> Some foreign powers [...] view the approach of self-government by Colonial nationals with distrust and doubt when considering the advisability of industrial investment. The high-handed conduct of Nasser will undoubtedly have caused apprehension in the minds of those who may intend to make investments in West Africa.[84]

Holt's chairman, however, opined in 1957 that the situation in Nigeria and the Gold Coast was different due to the support of successive British governments and the extensive training of Africans by both official and commercial interests.

Of course, the transition was not as smooth as Holt's managers would have liked people to believe. In Nigeria, the regional autonomy within the federation was proving problematic as early as 1952, and by 1955 the system was considered 'unworkable' by the UAC.[85] In the Gold Coast, it was also a dissenting region, Ashanti, under its traditional leader, the Asantehene, and the National Liberation Movement party (NLM), which opposed Nkrumah's CPP. In November 1956, Ashanti and the Northern Territories requested independence separately from the Gold Coast. The struggle between the NLM and CPP affected the AGC in particular due to its location in Ashanti. Stockwell recounted Edward Spears' involvement with the opposition politician Kofi Busia and his attempts to influence the course of decolonization in the Gold Coast. Crisp, however, notes that in 1955 Nkrumah and Spears were acquainted and that the former tried to moderate the position of Daniel Foevie, who was at the time leading a strike at the AGC.[86] By early 1957, Spears changed his political attitude and thought it better not to take sides in the political conflict.[87] During decolonization,

British business had learnt to live with the prospect of being left behind while the empire withdrew, and even imperial enthusiasts such as Spears showed some cautious optimism:

> [...] independence [...] would be a very serious turning point in the history of the Corporation, as after the 6 March there would be no appeal other than to a Native Government, and we would be [...] guests in an African country. [...] The Corporation should keep on good terms with the Government and the Union. The Chairman concluded by saying that this Corporation was a major asset in the Country, and he knew that the people of Ghana were well aware of this.[88]

Nkrumah eventually defeated the NLM, and by 1959 Pedler of the UAC concluded that the opposition was on its knees. The stance of business towards the ascent of Nkrumah was ambiguous, but they realized it had advantages:

> [...] the Government was moving steadily towards elimination of an effective opposition and establishment of a one-party state so as to avoid the possibility of interrupting economic progress by political disturbances. The general feeling of expatriates in Ghana was that, although they disliked the movement towards a one-party state and the harsh measures that went with it, nevertheless the Government was effective, and was bringing the country a desirable degree of stability. It was interesting that the attitude of the leading Africans towards Europeans was one of positive friendship.[89]

While this book does not address the question of corruption in greater depth, there are some indications that the good relations between foreign businessmen and nationalist politicians were helped by gifts and questionable services.[90] In Nigeria, a political and commercial scandal surrounded the Eastern Premier, Nnamdi Azikiwe, and his involvement in the African Continental Bank (ACB). During the proceedings, Azikiwe alleged unfair treatment of Africans by the BWA. Subsequent research by Martin Lynn demonstrated that his party used Barclays Bank in the United Kingdom as to launder funds transferred from the regional government via the ACB. In the Gold Coast, BWA organized a loan for Kofi Busia to build a house, for which he had previously received money from the UAC as well. While the Foster Sutton commission explicitly criticized the close connection between politics and politicians' business interests that had come to light in the ACB's case, it was already a common feature not only for African business but also for British business in Nigeria and Ghana.[91]

A distinction must be made between political contacts and corporate influence on politics, and many connections do not mean that business had a great influence on the course of decolonization and subsequent policies.[92]

Stockwell addresses the networking of corporate principals with African politicians; but she is more interested in how far this translated into direct influence in the political arena and less about what this meant for the firms themselves.[93] Companies became accustomed to a specific type of corporate-political organization that relied on personal contacts, goodwill, favours and even bribes or generous loan arrangements. Despite being pervasive, these contacts were not necessarily influential but ensured that businessmen could voice their concerns, even discuss issues, and get intelligence directly from political and administrative decision-makers, which were central to the emerging polities in West Africa. Despite some political crises, nationalist leaders remained in place after independence: Nkrumah in Ghana, Tafawa Balewa as prime minister and Nnamdi Azikiwe as president and governor-general in Nigeria. The personal continuity went hand in hand with a basically similar understanding of economic development, even in Nkrumah's case, which became the basis for the post-independence consensus.

3.3 The development discourse after independence

The relationships between British businessmen and West African politicians continued to be well-maintained after independence, and developmental economic policies that needed foreign investment to come to fruition were the engine of this cooperation. In this, there was surprisingly little difference between Ghana and Nigeria, although they are commonly perceived to have followed very different political trajectories.[94] In the early 1960s, both governments experienced a challenge from radical left-wing elements, which in Nigeria did not gain influence, while Kwame Nkrumah shifted to the left. Although his policies were hostile to African private business, this made him ironically more dependent on foreign investment, as Trevor Jones has pointed out.[95] In both countries, British businesses continued to find access to politicians easy, whether privately or professionally, and positioned themselves as broadly supportive: 'our own course must be to conduct our affairs in such a way that we help the Government to succeed.'[96]

3.3.1 Ghana

While Nkrumah's reorientation from pro-Western politics to African socialism is well-known, this did not translate directly into policies against foreign business. Trevor Jones commented on Nkrumah's admiration for 'captains of industry' and his friendships with some, most notably Edgar Kaiser and AG Leventis.[97] The Capital Investments Act of 1962 offered relatively generous terms to foreign investment. Although it worried the UAC board, Frederick Pedler remained optimistic about conditions in Ghana, probably as a result of his political connections.[98]

In the early 1960s, however, a radical left-wing economic nationalism resurged. When Frederick Pedler of the UAC attended the celebrations of Ghana becoming a republic in 1960, he remarked that:

> [...] he was particularly encouraged by the high reputation which our local company appears to enjoy with the authorities [...] The only incident marring the occasion was a function arranged by communist sympathisers after the official celebrations were over, at which a direct attack was made against enterprises such as our own.[99]

He was, however, soon appeased because President Nkrumah encouraged the UAC to extend their activities in Ghana and maintained in a speech on economic and foreign policy a few months later that cooperative trade organizations would be 'developed side by side with private enterprise in a freely competitive manner'.[100] The company surmised that this was a struggle between moderates and left-wing elements, with

> [...] the moderates under President Nkrumah being mainly the revolutionaries of 1951 who had grown in responsibility and maturity since they had been called upon to exercise power.[101]

Pedler assumed that Nkrumah reasserted his authority, despite being now committed to a course of economic development 'along cooperatives and State trading lines rather than private enterprise'.[102] In talks with the West Africa Committee, the President nevertheless offered to see personally to any infringement of employers' interests; he also clarified that there was no policy to restrict remittances from Ghana.[103] Under these conditions, businesses could accommodate the change in economic policy.

> [...] the Ghana Government intended to create powerful state cooperative organizations. It was desirable that we should avoid giving the impression that we were irreconcilably hostile to such a development and that we should in fact actively plan for the inevitable changes in our business which would result.[104]

By the summer of 1961, the president made allegations about transfer pricing in big companies, as the revenues from tax were not as high as anticipated. Purchase tax on vehicles, for example, was sharply increased and, according to Holt, which had redeployed into this area, practically halted sales.[105] Later in the year, exchange control regulations were enforced, contrary to previous assurances.

> It was quite clear from this and from other indications that no privileges whatsoever would be granted to large expatriate firms and that trading in Ghana would be extremely difficult in the future.[106]

This assessment proved to be correct, and the remaining years of Nkrumah's tenure were marked by import restrictions, blocked remittances, lack of sterling and spiralling debt.[107] Shortly afterwards, import licensing restrictions were introduced 'which appeared to be aimed at reducing the turnover of companies'.[108] Late in 1961, the chairman of UAC Ghana and Andrew Knox of Unilever's Overseas Committee met the President in a friendly atmosphere, where he indicated that he would curb the socialist influence.[109] Unilever and UAC considered pulling out of the country over the new tax regulations, but whether that was really an option even in the early 1960s is doubtful, as the UAC alone still had £20m worth of investment tied up in Ghana as late as 1972.[110] During the negotiations over the government's purchase of Leventis in 1961, it transpired that the government 'would never buy an existing foreign-owned business out, although they would not prevent withdrawal'.[111]

In the Seven Year Plan in 1961/62, the government clarified that it would plan broad aspects of the economy but continue to allow foreign investment. While this was better than business had come to expect in the preceding months, the UAC concluded that there were no 'quick opportunities for making easy profits' but thought that the framework would allow them to work reasonably.[112] Of particular concern was the compulsory reinvestment of 60 per cent of pre-tax profits. This, it was feared, could potentially lead to investors not having a free choice in where to invest and could become a precedent internationally.[113] Despite disagreeing with the principle of compulsory reinvestment, Unilever's directors were careful how to criticize it because their own publicity proclaimed that they aided the economic development of West Africa through the investment that the company provided.[114]

However, any extreme measures against enterprises were unlikely, as about half of the £1,000m to be spent under the Seven Year Plan was supposed to come from private investors. In May, Frederick Pedler visited Ghana to discuss UAC's relationship with the government with civil servants, ministers and finally, the president. For the UAC, its Ghanaian business was problematic, as directors considered it the best run of all the African subsidiaries they had ever had but thought that it was 'hampered by unsatisfactory relations with the authorities, as there was no steady Government policy and many of those in authority seemed to be frightened of the hard core of party zealots on the left wing'.[115] Thus preliminary discussions had been inconclusive, but during talks with Nkrumah, Pedler pointed out that the formula to retain 60 per cent of profits would discourage further foreign investment, and it seemed Nkrumah was prepared to reconsider it. However, the formula was subsequently extended, and the dividend that could be remitted was further reduced to 24 per cent of profits a few months later.[116]

Pedler continued to meet Nkrumah and tried in 1965 to persuade the president to accept a repayment scheme on outstanding debts to the company and get information about possible government monopolies in distribution. While Nkrumah maintained that it was his policy to 'create a feeling of confidence in the Western world' and instructed his ministers to arrange the payment scheme, according to Pedler, however, they blocked the execution of his instructions.[117] He also urged companies to 'abandon their suspicions and accept reassurances [...] he had repeatedly given [...] that the companies should continue to have a substantial share in distribution'.[118] By January 1966, Ghana's economic crisis had finally reached its climax, the British Export Credit Guarantee Department (ECDG) stopped its guarantees, and the World Bank refused to cooperate.[119]

In the light of Nkrumah's *Neo-colonialism*, his cordial relations with foreign businessmen seem surprising, but his treatise was also perceived by some as an attempt to shift the blame for Ghana's economic failure and his subsequent downfall to the international economy.[120] It reiterated the NYM's criticism that the company was the 'uncrowned king of West Africa', but also referred to a recent description of the UAC as the 'gentle giant' to argue how much more subtle its methods had become. The author claims that the company's redeployment strategy was an attempt to prevent developing countries from industrializing because

> [...] the exploitation of the indigenous expanding market is now the prime objective. If the attempts to prevent industrialisation fail, then at all costs the Trust must secure a participation in a development it cannot prevent.[121]

By siphoning off profits, it argued, UAC's participation nevertheless thwarted further progress and moreover tried to deceive customers by packaging goods under the 'false labels of indigenous concerns' (an attack on the company's localization strategy). Why foreign firms should have an interest in destroying the expanding markets that they wanted to exploit remained unresolved beyond a general statement that UAC's interests were essentially part of British economic imperialism. Interestingly, Pedler recalls in his memoirs that Nkrumah made a similar statement for a factory opening in 1963: 'The foreign investor has a further interest in common with the people of Africa. His profit is directly proportional to their prosperity. If the economy of any African state gets out of hand, if, for example, there is balance of payments crisis, then not only will the investor be unable to export his earnings but the market on which he depends for the sale of his product will be endangered.'[122] By 1965, the year *Neo-Colonialism* was published, Nkrumah's economic policies had failed to deliver the development successes promised. Blaming foreign companies was an obvious strategy, which had been successful in the rise of nationalist parties in West Africa, even though shifts in global commodities prices and terms of trade clearly indicated a bigger issue. How far Nkrumah himself believed in this (and there are questions about the authorship of his publications) seems dubious in the light of his friendly relationship with foreign businessmen, most notably Edgar Kaiser from the US, Edward Spears (AGC) and the UAC's Patrick Fitzgerald. Fitzgerald was even appointed as the head of the GNTC.[123] While Nkrumah was in power, his view of development policies was predominantly technocratic and pragmatic. Many restrictive economic policies were the result, not necessarily of deliberate planning or antagonism towards foreign firms, but of the foreign-exchange crisis.[124]

It was noteworthy, however, that *Neo-Colonialism* represented a disavowal of his famous dictum, 'Seek ye first the political kingdom, and everything else shall be added onto thee.' To quote from the first chapter of *Neo-colonialism*: 'The essence of neo-colonialism is that the state which is subject to it is, in theory, independent and has all the outward trappings of international sovereignty. [...] Neo-colonialism is also the worst form of imperialism. For those who practise it, it means power without responsibility and for those who suffer from it, it means exploitation without redress.'[125] The political kingdom had become worthless (although the book left it somewhat unclear whether Ghana was subject to neo-colonialism or indeed free from it due to its non-aligned status).

3.3.2 Nigeria

Nigeria's conservative economic policies were also challenged by left-wing politicians in the Action Group (AG), led by Obafemi Awolowo. In the parliamentary session 1961–1962, a motion to nationalize basic industries was debated. Awolowo, the leader of the AG opposition in the federal parliament, proposed in a speech to reserve the retail trade for Nigerians, leaving wholesaling to foreign firms. He claimed that, while the fight for political independence had been concluded, the struggle for economic freedom was far from complete. Some members of the federal government seemed to share this view, in particular the Minister of Economic Development, Ibrahim Waziri:

> Over 70 per cent of our overseas trade is controlled by forces over which we have no control. [...] the expatriate firms and individuals who engage in our country's distributive trade and road transport business are extremely powerful, influential, and virtually control the economy of our country [...][126]

Waziri continued to be a vocal critic after the parliamentary motion had failed, as Barclays was to discover in 1964:

> [...] instead of a courtesy call we soon found ourselves listening to a harangue on the necessity for expatriate banks to lend more to small African business men. I told him that we had tried this and lost a lot of

> money […] The Minister's views were very naïve and further argument would obviously have been unprofitable.[127]

Despite being a federal minister, Waziri's opinions could safely be disregarded by the expatriate banks, as the general consensus remained in favour of foreign capital: 'private enterprise is respectable and, indeed, popular […] you hear no talk about neo-colonialism', Pedler reported in 1965, probably referring to neighbouring Ghana.[128] Within the AG, Awolowo had lost a leadership conflict with Samuel Ladoke Akintola, the Western Premier, who was closely associated with many Yoruba businessmen who supported the party.[129] Barclays' manager Richard Dyson met him on a trip in 1964, and the picture below illustrates how keen British executives were to remain in close touch with local politicians (Figure 3.2).

UAC and Unilever perceived these occasional resurgences of economic nationalism as struggles between the extremists and moderates. They

Figure 3.2 Richard Dyson meeting Samuel Akintola, 1964.

Note: Reproduced with kind permission of Barclays Group Archives.[130]

considered Nigeria as 'essentially conservative', but with some radical elements, who exhibited 'an attitude of recrimination expressed as a feeling that the reason why Nigeria was backward in comparison with many other African countries was its exploitation by foreigners, and if this was firmly brought to an end the standard of living would automatically adjust itself'.[131] Government and business clearly had a mutual interest in the view of Unilever's directors:

> Thus the position of the Government was basically the same as that of the Company, but they had certain handicaps of their own: there were individual ministers and officials who had to be classed in the recrimination school; the opposition found the recrimination school a much more attractive one than the Government; and thirdly the moderates in the Government, in order to match the outbursts of nationalists and the opposition, had themselves to indulge in a certain amount of criticism of the old regime.[132]

Due to the good relations between leading politicians and businessmen, these internal pressures were well-known to British executives, who were informed on occasion 'to ignore certain hostile speeches made by Nigerian Ministers recently, the tone of which had been dictated by local political considerations'.[133] Unilever's directors' committee agreed with the Nigerian economic policy of suppressing standards of living to create internal savings and attract investment. This policy for long-term prosperity was predictably unpopular, but foreign businesses believed it merited their support to avoid polarization between the government and opposition.

Cultivating political contacts was a common strategy for international business, but in West Africa, the connections of British business still appeared close. Nationalists, such as Nkrumah, Azikiwe and Akintola, met foreign business representatives and debated development plans and policies, despite their otherwise hostile statements about business.[134] Others, such as Ibrahim Waziri in Nigeria and the more radical left-wing of the CPP in Ghana, were more openly committed to economic nationalism but generally less influential. The cooperation between the leaders of the newly independent states and international business went deeper. Both relied on the successful economic development of West Africa, and both subscribed to the same orthodox framework in the 1950s and 1960s: industrialization, mixed economy, limited import substitution and sterling parity.

Most British firms expanded and increased profitability after the war when the West African colonies were economically successful because of the commodities boom, and per capita income was on the rise. This confirmed the belief in the development discourse that imperial companies and the economic development of their area of operation were closely entwined. Economic nationalism, which had been successful for the first wave of African nationalists in the 1940s and early 1950s, was subsequently resurrected at specific junctures during and after decolonization to legitimize the demands of groups that had been side-lined politically and economically. In the first few years of independence, however, politicians in power exhibited pragmatic and accommodating behaviour towards British businessmen.

3.4 Conclusion

Early economic nationalism finally convinced firms to commit to an active public relations policy after 1948. This was clearly connected with imminent independence because the opinions of people who had no political voice could mostly be ignored by business. Firms realized that the accelerating devolution of power made it necessary for them to lobby for their special interests, which was achieved through a variety of vehicles. With AWAM discredited, Holt, for example, hoped to build the power of local Chambers of Commerce. Edward Spears (AGC), however, preferred special representation in the new legislative bodies. These representatives, although abolished in the Gold Coast in 1951 and Nigeria in 1953, were particularly useful in forming the first links to emerging African politicians. These connections were maintained and extended, and it was common for visiting officials from UK head offices to call on African politicians. Businesses also developed several legitimization strategies in the late 1950s, such as the extension of business links and credit to Africans and different forms of localization. The cooperation of business and African leaders was based on a mutual understanding of development that both were eager to see in West Africa. This consensus grew out of the continued interaction between foreign business and African politicians.

Economic nationalism was a recurring phenomenon during the twentieth century and had been an essential part of African nationalism before rapid constitutional devolution focused attention on the political programme. During these early years, the nationalist movement constituted itself through its opposition to AWAM and what was viewed as the domination of large foreign firms. The 1948 Gold Coast riots gained special significance because they were co-opted by nationalist politicians such as Kwame Nkrumah; their origin in a commercial boycott was soon obscured when the event led to greater acceptance of political decolonization in West Africa.

Notes

1 Sarah E Stockwell, "Political Strategies of British Business during Decolonization – the Case of the Gold-Coast Ghana, 1945–57," *Journal of Imperial and Commonwealth History* 23, no. 2 (1995): 277–300; Sarah E Stockwell, *The Business of Decolonization: British Business Strategies in the Gold Coast* (Oxford: Clarendon Press, 2000).

2 J Darwin, *Britain and Decolonisation: The Retreat from Empire in the Post-War World* (Basingstoke: Macmillan, 1988).

3 Axel Harneit-Sievers, *Zwischen Depression Und Dekolonisation: Afrikanische Händler Und Politik in Süd-Nigeria, 1935–1954* (Saarbrücken and Fort Lauderdale: Breitenbach, 1991), 220–1.
4 "AWAM must go!," article by the Nigerian Youth Movement, Daily Service, 11 May 1944, RHO Mss Afr. s 825, 232 (i).
5 Stockwell, *The Business of Decolonization*, 145, 162.
6 Jan-Georg Deutsch, *Educating the Middlemen: Political and Economic History of Statutory Cocoa Marketing in Nigeria, 1936–1947* (Berlin: Das Arabische Buch, 1995), 234–5.
7 Stockwell, *The Business of Decolonization*, 113.
8 G Cotgreave, District Agent Lagos, to Gates, Liverpool, 9 Novemebr 1949, RHO Mss Afr. s 825, 232 (ii).
9 Directors' Committee, 13. Nigeria, 3 January 1952, Unilever Historical Archives (UHA) UNI/BD/DC.
10 Directors' Committee, 611. West Africa, 6 November 1952, UHA UNI/BD/DC.
11 Stockwell, *The Business of Decolonization*, 87–8.
12 This was quoted in Duncan Sandys, "General Outlook – Report," n.d., presumably 1947, p. 13, Churchill College Cambridge (CCC) SPRS 1/112.
13 Stockwell, *The Business of Decolonization*, 86–90.
14 G Sealy, Security Officer AGC, "Intelligence Report No. 104," 17 November 1950, London Metropolitan Archives (LMA) CLC/B/015/MS14171 v. 108, Jul–Dec 1950.
15 JAR Williams to WTG Gates, General Manager Liverpool, 23 February 1951, RHO Mss Afr. s 825, 421 (v).
16 Hugh Thomas to Kwame Nkrumah, 4 August 1953, LMA CLC/B/015/MS14171, v. 114, July–Dec 1953.
17 Stockwell, *The Business of Decolonization*, 114–15.
18 Mr Rawlings to Mr Goddard, District Agent Accra, 26.7.44, RHO Mss Afr. S.825, 232 (ii); Article: "Kojo Thompson is said to be fighting the case of all African merchants," no newspaper name, n. d., RHO Mss Afr. s 825, 232 (i).
19 EW Pearce to Mr Rawlings, 31 March 1947, RHO Mss Afr. s 825, 421 A (iii).
20 Robert L Tignor, *Capitalism and Nationalism at the End of Empire: State and Business in Decolonizing Egypt, Nigeria, and Kenya, 1945–1963* (Princeton, N.J.: Princeton University Press, 1998), 227–8; Harneit-Sievers, *Zwischen Depression Und Dekolonisation*, 310–15.
21 FM Bourret, *Ghana: The Road to Independence 1919–1957* (Stanford CA: Stanford University Press, 1969), 169–74; Dennis Austin, *Politics in Ghana* (Oxford: Oxford University Press, 1964), 69–77; Stockwell, *The Business of Decolonization*, 70–90.
22 A Watson, "Report of the Commission of Enquiry into Disturbances in the Gold Coast" (London, UK, 1948), paras 174–5.
23 One of Barclays' General Managers happened to be visiting West Africa at the time of the riots and documented his experiences in his diaries, a board report and letter: Barclays Group Archives (BGA) 38/906; Holt deposited an entire folder on the Accra riots at Rhodes House Oxford (RHO) Mss Afr. s 825, 549.
24 Gale to Secretary, 10 March 1948, LMA CLC/B/015/MS14171, v. 103, Jan–Jun 1948.
25 UAC cable from General Manager, Lagos, 30 March 48, and DD Jones to GJ Cole, UAC, 31 March 1948, RHO Mss Afr. S.825, 232 (ii).
26 Memo 'AWAM', n.d., presumably March/April 1948, RHO Mss Afr. S.825, 232 (ii) [hereafter Memo 'AWAM'].
27 WTG Gates to Cotgreave, 2 April 1948, RHO Mss Afr. s 825, 232 (ii).
28 This information, as all concerned seemed to have forgotten, was already in the public domain since Barrow's witness statement in the Kojo Thompson trial. The

Nigerian Youth Movement had subsequently published it in an article series calling for the end of AWAM. 'AWAM must go!', article in three parts by the Nigerian Youth Movement, Daily Service, 11 May 1944, RHO Mss Afr. s 825, 232 (i). The Nigerian government had begun to distance itself from foreign companies since about 1940, see Deutsch, *Educating the Middlemen*, 234–5.

29 Memo 'AWAM'.

30 WTG Gates to Cotgreave, 2 April 1948, RHO Mss Afr. s825, 232 (ii). Harneit-Sievers, *Zwischen Depression Und Dekolonisation*, 159–61, 313–14, 317.

31 Cable to General Manager Lagos, 2 April 1948; WTG Gates to Cotgreave, 2 April 1948, RHO Mss Afr. s825, 232 (ii).

32 Dudley Seers and C Ross, "Report on the Financial and Physical Problems of Development in the Gold Coast" (Accra, Ghana, 1952), 85.

33 Cable from General Manager, Lagos, UAC, 26 March 1948, RHO Mss Afr. s 825, 232 (ii).

34 Stockwell, *The Business of Decolonization*, 114.

35 J F Winter, District Agent Lagos, to Liverpool, 11 October. 1945; AWAM also constituted a manpower drain on commercial companies that began to jockey for position toward the end of World War II and wanted their staff back: JF Winter, Senior District Agent to Mr Rawlings, Liverpool, 25 April 1945; RHO Mss Afr. S.825, 232 (ii). A different story is told by Deutsch, *Educating the Middlemen: Political and Economic History of Statutory Cocoa Marketing in Nigeria, 1936–1947*, 250. He presents evidence that AWAM firms threatened to use their financial power to oust smaller firms from the trade as soon as the quota system ended.

36 Stockwell, *The Business of Decolonization*, 112–13, 116, 128; Tignor, *Capitalism and Nationalism*, 201; Harneit-Sievers, *Zwischen Depression Und Dekolonisation: Afrikanische Händler Und Politik in Süd-Nigeria, 1935–1954*, 382–6.

37 G Cotgreave, Lagos, to WTG Gates, Liverpool, 25 May 1949, RHO Mss Afr. s 825, 232 (ii).

38 Winter, district agent Lagos, to Coast Administration Department, 30 September 1948, RHO Mss Afr. s 825, 232 (ii).

39 G Cotgreave, Lagos, to WTG Gates, Liverpool, 25 May 1949, RHO Mss Afr. s 825, 232 (ii).

40 Deutsch, *Educating the Middlemen: Political and Economic History of Statutory Cocoa Marketing in Nigeria, 1936–1947*, 60; Tignor, *Capitalism and Nationalism*, 201.

41 RC Irving to WTG Gates, 22 June 1949; WTG Gates to RC Irving, 4 July 1949, RHO Mss Afr. s 825, 232 (ii); on African Importers and Exporters Association: RA Norman, general manager Lagos area, to Mr. Walker, Coast Administration Department, Liverpool, 21 May 1952, RHO Mss Afr. s 825, 232 (iv).

42 CM Booth, President of Lagos Chamber of Commerce Inc., 8 October 1952, RHO Mss Afr. s 825, 232 (iv).

43 Lagos Chamber of Commerce, Minutes of Annual General Meeting, 7 October 1953, RHO Mss Afr. s 825, 232 (v).

44 Lagos Chamber of Commerce Inc., Minutes of Council Meeting, 2 September 1953, RHO Mss Afr. s 825, 232 (iv).

45 JD Esseks, "Government and Indigenous Private Enterprise in Ghana," *The Journal of Modern African Studies*, 1971, 18, http://journals.cambridge.org/abstract_S0022278X00024666.

46 Tignor, *Capitalism and Nationalism*, 246–7; Stockwell, *The Business of Decolonization*, 119–228.

47 [Gates] to [Cotgreave], 11 May 1949; RHO Mss Afr. s.825, 232 (iv).

48 Federal House of Representatives: 6, Northern House of Assembly: 10, 3 each in the Eastern and Western houses. RWT Bateson, General Manager, Lagos Area, to AC Walker, Liverpool, 26 August 1951, RHO Mss Afr. s 825, 421 (v).

49 RWT Bateson, General Mananger, Lagos Area, to AC Walker, Liverpool, 26 August 1951, RHO Mss Afr. s 825, 421 (v).

50 Letter WTG Gates, 11 May 1949, RHO Mss Afr. s 825, 421 (v).

51 Balewa became the first Prime Minister of independent Nigeria. EW Pearce, General Manager Kano, to Mr. Walker, 15 February 1952, RHO Mss Afr. s 825, 421 (v).

52 Frederick J Pedler, *Business and Decolonization in West Africa, c.1940–1960: A Personal Memoir by Sir Frederick Pedler* (Oxford: Privately printed, 1989), 30.

53 Lagos Chamber of Commerce, Minutes of council meeting, 4 March 1953; EW Pearce, General Manager Northern area, Kano, to John Holt's Coast Administration Department, Liverpool, 25 March 1953, RHO Mss Afr. s825, 232 (iv).

54 PN Hanney, "Possible re-organization of the Association of West African Merchants," n. d. [February/March 1954]; Geoffrey Bates, Draft Memorandum, n.d. [February/March 1954]; RHO Mss. Afr. s825, 232 (v).

55 The JWAC had been the principal government-business liaison body in the 1930s, dealing with the Colonial Office and drawing its delegates from the three main UK-based chambers of commerce: London, Liverpool and Manchester. For mining the equivalent body was the London Advisory Committee of the Gold Coast Chamber of Mines. Stockwell, *The Business of Decolonization*, 27, 131–2.

56 Directors' Committee, 753. West Africa, 8 December 1955, UHA UNI/BD/DC.

57 Frederick Cooper, *Decolonization and African Society: The Labour Question in French and British Africa, Africa: Journal of the International African Institute* (Cambridge, UK: Cambridge University Press, 1996), 5, 468–9, https://doi.org/10.2307/1161082.

58 Stockwell, *The Business of Decolonization*, 125–6; Maria Misra, *Business, Race and Politics in British India, c.1850–1960* (Oxford: Oxford University Press, 1999), 181.

59 Directors' Committee, 753. West Africa, 8 December 1955, UHA UNI/BD/DC.

60 Stockwell, *The Business of Decolonization*, 145.

61 Directors' Committee, 730. Nigeria and Sierra Leone, 14 October 1960, UHA UNI/BD/DC.

62 Chairman's Statement at AGM of John Holt & Co., 23 April 1954, Liverpool Records Office (LRO) 380 HOL II.

63 Directors' Committee, 368. UAC, 18 June 1953, UHA UNI/BD/DC.

64 Directors' Committee, 536 UAC, 12 August 1954, UHA UNI/BD/DC.

65 Directors' Committee, 190. West Africa, 24 March 1955, UHA UNI/BD/DC.

66 Chairman's Statement at AGM of John Holt & Co, 8 March 1957, LRO 380 HOL II.

67 Chairman's Statement at AGM of John Holt & Co., 4 March 1960, LRO 380 HOL II. Directors' Committee, 729. Ghana, 14 October 1960, UHA UNI/BD/DC.

68 Directors' Committee, West Africa – Local Participation, 11March 1960, UHA UNI/BD/DC; Chairman's Statement at AGM of John Holt & Co., 23 April 1954, 6 May 1955, 3 March 1961, 1962 and 31 August 1964, LRO 380 HOL II.

69 Geoffrey Jones, *British Multinational Banking, 1830–1990* (New York: OUP, 1993), 404.

70 Senator Nwafor Orizu in 1961, Hansard, Senate, 1961–1962 session, 30 March 1961, col. 315, cited in: Henry L Bretton, *Power and Stability in Nigeria: The Politics of Decolonisation* (New York: Praeger, 1962), 191 fn12., p. 191, FN 12.

71 Julian Wathen to GNM Law, 29 September 1961; Memorandum 'CAST' to General Manager, 30 June 1960; Boreham to Crossley, 3 January 1961; Julian Wathen to Julian Crossley, 20 January 1964, BGA 80/3580; Julian Wathen's reminiscences, BGA 1189/1. Stockwell, *The Business of Decolonization*, 145.

72 F. Samuels addressing Directors' Conference, 4. West Africa, 27 January 1944, UHA UNI/BD/DC; EW Pearce, district agent, Accra, to WTG Gates, coast administration department Liverpool, 12 May 1947, RHO Mss Afr. s 825, 421 B (ii).
73 Brian Macdona, "Visit to Sierra Leone and Ghana," February–April 1958, BGA 38/382 (4). Stockwell, *The Business of Decolonization*, p. 152, shows that despite the company's connections to Nkrumah's rival Kofi Busia, Frederick Pedler and Patrick Fitzgerald had amicable relations and easy access to Nkrumah.
74 Julian Wathen, "Reminiscences 1947–1987," p. 16, (revised 2002) BGA 1189/1.
75 Directors' Committee, 592. UAC, 20 September 1956, UHA UNI/BD/DC.
76 Julian Crossley's trip to West Africa, 1951–52, BGA 80/3792.
77 Directors' Committee, 753. West Africa, 8 December 1955; 364 UAC – Discussion with Nigerian Prime Ministers, 14 June 1957; UHA UNI/BD/DC.
78 Directors' Committee, 753. West Africa, 8 December 1955, UHA UNI/BD/DC.
79 Directors' Committee, 153. West Africa – Mr Hartog's Visit, 13 March 1959, UHA UNI/BD/DC.
80 Barclays Bank DCO board minutes, 7 December 1961, p. 53 and 10 October 1963, p. 360, BGA 38/513.
81 Chairman's statement at the annual general meeting John Holt & Company (Liverpool) Ltd., 8 March 1957, LRO 380 HOL II.
82 Ghana Board Members, BGA 80/3580. Stockwell, *The Business of Decolonization*, 144, 146.
83 Directors' Committee, 592 UAC, 20 September 1956, UHA UNI/BD/DC; Chairman's statement at the annual general meeting of John Holt & Company (Liverpool) Ltd., 14 March 1958, LRO 380 HOL II.
84 Chairman's statement at the annual general meeting John Holt & Company (Liverpool) Ltd., 8 March 1957, LRO 380 HOL II.
85 Directors' Committee, 611. West Africa, 6 November 1952; 190. West Africa, 24 March 1955; UHA UNI/BD/DC.
86 Stockwell, *The Business of Decolonization*, 95, 103, 123–7, 191–4; Jeff Crisp, *The Story of an African Working Class: Ghanaian Miners' Struggles 1870–1980* (London: Zed Press, 1984), 119; Richard Rathbone, *Ghana: British Documents on the End of Empire*, Series B (London: Institute of Commonwealth Studies, 1992), lxi–lxiii, lxvi–lxvii, lxxvii fn99.
87 Edward Spears to RTH Fletcher, the Lord/Baron Winster, 2 January 1957, CCC SPRS 1/350.
88 Staff conference minutes, 2 March 1957, LMA CLC/B/015/MS14171, v. 127, Jan–Jun 1957.
89 Directors' Committee, 138 Ghana and Nigeria – Mr Pedler's Visit, 6 March 1959, UHA UNI/BD/DC.
90 Foster Sutton, "Report of the Tribunal Appointed to Inquire into Allegations Reflecting the Official Conduct of the Premier of, and Certain Persons Holding Ministerial and Other Public Offices in the Eastern Region of Nigeria, Cmnd. 51" (London, 1957), 42. Stephanie Decker, "Less than an Empire and More than British: Foreign Investor Competition in Ghana and Nigeria in the 1960s," in *Imagining Britain's Economic Future, c.1800–1975: Trade, Consumerism and Global Markets*, ed. David Thackeray, Andrew Thompson, and Richard Toye (London: Palgrave, 2018), 183–203, https://www.palgrave.com/gb/book/9783319712963.
91 *Imperial and Commonwealth History*, 30 (2002), 91–109 (105);
92 Michael Hadani, Jean Philippe Bonardi, and Nicolas M. Dahan, "Corporate Political Activity, Public Policy Uncertainty, and Firm Outcomes: A Meta-Analysis," *Strategic Organization* 15, no. 3 (2017): 338–66, https://doi.org/10.1177/1476127016651001.
93 Stockwell, *The Business of Decolonization*, 10–18.

94 P Nugent, *Africa since Independence* (Basingstoke: Palgrave Macmillan, 2002), 39–40, 119–24, 166–78, 213–24, 335–47, 414–15, 417–26.
95 T Jones, *Ghana's First Republic, 1960–1966: The Pursuit of the Political Kingdom* (London, UK: Methuen, 1976), 162; Tony Killick, *Development Economics in Action: A Study of Economic Policies in Ghana, Studies in the Economics of Africa* (London i.a.: Heinemann Educational, 1978), 37–8.
96 Directors' Committee, 358. Nigeria, 11 May 1962, UHA UNI/BD/DC.
97 Stephanie Decker, "Corporate Political Activity in Less Developed Countries: The Volta River Project in Ghana, 1959–1966," *Business History* 53, no. 7 (2011): 993–1017, https://doi.org/10.1080/00076791.2011.618223.
98 Jones, *Ghana's First Republic, 1960–1966: The Pursuit of the Political Kingdom*, 161, 167–8; Killick, *Development Economics in Action*, 552–3.
99 Directors' Committee, 497. Ghana, 15 July 1960, UHA UNI/BD/DC.
100 Directors' Committee, 729. Ghana, 14 October 1960, UHA UNI/BD/DC [hereafter Director's Committee, 14 October 1960].
101 Director's Committee, 14. October 1960.
102 Directors' Committee, 497. Ghana, 15 July 1960, UHA UNI/BD/DC.
103 Directors' Committee, 213. Ghana, 17 March 1961, UHA UNI/BD/DC.
104 Directors' Commitee, 109. Ghana – Long Term Policy, 10 February 1961, UHA UNI/BD/DC.
105 Directors' Committee, 504. Ghana – New Financial Policy, 7 July 1961, UHA UNI/BD/DC; Chairman's statement at AGM of John Holt & Co, 1962, LRO 380 HOL II.
106 Exchange controls in Ghana were in effect from 1 October 1961. Directors' Committee, 721. Exchange Controls in Ghana, 22 September 1961, UHA UNI/BD/DC.
107 David Kenneth Fieldhouse, *Merchant Capital and Economic Decolonisation: The United Africa Company 1929–1987* (Oxford: Clarendon, 1994), 593–607; Douglas Rimmer, *Staying Poor: Ghana's Political Economy, 1950–1990*, ed. World Bank (Oxford: Pergamon, 1992), chapter 5.
108 Directors' Committee, 968. Ghana – Import Licences, 8 December 1961, UHA UNI/BD/DC.
109 This episode does not feature in his memoirs: Andrew M Knox, *Coming Clear: A Postscript after Retirement from Unilever* (London, UK: Heinemann, 1976).
110 Fieldhouse, *Merchant Capital and Economic Decolonisation*, 606.
111 Directors' Committee, 1002. Ghana, 22 December 1961, UHA UNI/BD/DC. On the Leventis deal see Jones, *Ghana's First Republic, 1960-1966: The Pursuit of the Political Kingdom*, 187–93.
112 Directors' Committee, 136. Ghana, 16 February 1962, UHA UNI/BD/DC.
113 Directors' Committee, 239. Ghana, 30 March 1962, UHA UNI/BD/DC.
114 See for example the UAC advert: 'Change in West Africa', *West Africa*, 23 April 1960.
115 Directors' Committee, 348. Ghana, 11 May 1962 (hereafter Directors' Committee, 11 April 1962); UHA UNI/BD/DC.
116 Directors'Committee, 11 April 1962; Fieldhouse, *Merchant Capital and Economic Decolonisation*, 595–6.
117 Special Committee meetings, 423. Ghana, a) Talks with President Nkrumah, 18 June 1965, UHA UNI/SC with Tropical Africa Committee (hereafter TAC), (this document hereafter Special Committee, Talks with President Nkrumah, 18 June 1965). Fieldhouse, 596, 600. The ministers in question were Amoaka Atta (Finance) and Djin (Trade); the former had appeared unsympathetic to foreign business in his earlier position as deputy governor of the Bank of Ghana.
118 Special Committee, Talks with President Nkrumah, 18 June 1965.

119 Special Committee, Talks with President Nkrumah, 18 June 1965.
120 Dennis Austin, "Introduction," in *Politicians and Soldiers in Ghana 1966–72*, ed. Dennis Austin and Robin Luckham (London, UK: Frank Cass, 1975), 13; Kwame Nkrumah, *Neo-Colonialism: The Last Stage of Imperialism* (New York: International Publishers, 1965), 178.
121 Nkrumah, *Neo-Colonialism*, 178.
122 Pedler, *Business and Decolonization*, 22.
123 Henry Bretton argues most strongly against Nkrumah's authorship, pointing out that it would have required too much research for a busy head of state, conflicted with policies he was trying to implement at the time and that he often did not appear to be aware of what he supposedly wrote. As for the committee he believes did write the book, he names Professor Willie Abraham, Michael Dei-Anang, Nkrumah's personal secretary Erica Powell, the scholar Thomas Hodgkin and HM Basner, amongst others. Henry L Bretton, *The Rise and Fall of Kwame Nkrumah: A Study in Personal Rule in Africa* (London: Pall Mall Press, 1967), 20, 190 fn2.
124 Nugent, *Africa since Independence*, 168; Killick, *Development Economics in Action*; Decker, "Corporate Political Activity."
125 Nkrumah, *Neo-Colonialism*, ix–xi.
126 Ibrahim Waziri, Federal Minister of Economic Development of Nigeria, *Hansard*, House of Representatives, 1961–62, 16 November 1961, col. 2943 and 22 November 1961, col. 3235–36; cited in Bretton, *Power and Stability in Nigeria*, 190, fn9.
127 Dyson, "Report: Visit to Nigeria – January/February 1964," p. 2, BGA 80/4641.
128 FJ Pedler, "Report to Directors' Conference," 10 December 1965, UHA UNI/SC with TAC.
129 Larry Diamond, *Class, Ethnicity and Democracy in Nigeria* (London: Macmillan, 1988), 93–113.
130 Dyson, "Report: Visit to Nigeria – January/February 1964," BGA 80/4641.
131 Directors' Commitee, 358. Nigeria, 11 May 1962, UHA UNI/BD/DC (hereafter Directors' Committee, 11 May 1962).
132 Directors' Committee, 11 May 1962.
133 Directors' Committee, 11 May 1962.
134 Nkrumah, *Neo-Colonialism*. N Azikiwe, *Banking Monopoly in Nigeria: Statement Made by the Hon. Premier in the Eastern House of Assembly on 8th Aug 1956* (Enugu: 1956).

List of References

Austin, Dennis. "Introduction." In *Politicians and Soldiers in Ghana 1966–72*, edited by Dennis Austin and Robin Luckham. 1–15, London, UK: Frank Cass, 1975.

Austin, Dennis. *Politics in Ghana*. Oxford: Oxford University Press, 1964.

Bourret, F.M. *Ghana: The Road to Independence 1919–1957*. Stanford CA: Stanford University Press, 1969.

Bretton, Henry L. *Power and Stability in Nigeria: The Politics of Decolonisation*. New York: Praeger, 1962.

Bretton, Henry L. *The Rise and Fall of Kwame Nkrumah: A Study in Personal Rule in Africa*. London: Pall Mall Press, 1967.

Cooper, Frederick. *Decolonization and African Society: The Labour Question in French and British Africa. Africa: Journal of the International African Institute*. Cambridge, UK: Cambridge University Press, 1996. 10.2307/1161082.

Crisp, Jeff. *The Story of an African Working Class: Ghanaian Miners' Struggles 1870–1980.* London: Zed Press, 1984.

Darwin, J. *Britain and Decolonisation: The Retreat from Empire in the Post-War World.* Basingstoke: Macmillan, 1988.

Decker, Stephanie. "Corporate Political Activity in Less Developed Countries: The Volta River Project in Ghana, 1959–1966." *Business History* 53, no. 7 (2011): 993–1017. 10.1080/00076791.2011.618223.

Decker, Stephanie. "Less than an Empire and More than British: Foreign Investor Competition in Ghana and Nigeria in the 1960s." In *Imagining Britain's Economic Future, c.1800–1975: Trade, Consumerism and Global Markets*, edited by David Thackeray, Andrew Thompson, and Richard Toye, 183–203. London: Palgrave, 2018. https://www.palgrave.com/gb/book/9783319712963.

Deutsch, Jan-Georg. *Educating the Middlemen: Political and Economic History of Statutory Cocoa Marketing in Nigeria, 1936–1947.* Berlin: Das Arabische Buch, 1995.

Diamond, Larry. *Class, Ethnicity and Democracy in Nigeria.* London: Macmillan, 1988.

Esseks, JD "Government and Indigenous Private Enterprise in Ghana." *The Journal of Modern African Studies*, 1971. http://journals.cambridge.org/abstract_S0022278X00024666.

Fieldhouse, David Kenneth. *Merchant Capital and Economic Decolonisation: The United Africa Company 1929–1987.* Oxford: Clarendon, 1994.

Foster, Sutton. "Report of the Tribunal Appointed to Inquire into Allegations Reflecting the Official Conduct of the Premier of, and Certain Persons Holding Ministerial and Other Public Offices in the Eastern Region of Nigeria, Cmnd. 51." *London*, 1957.

Hadani, Michael, Jean Philippe Bonardi, and Nicolas M. Dahan. "Corporate Political Activity, Public Policy Uncertainty, and Firm Outcomes: A Meta-Analysis." *Strategic Organization* 15, no. 3 (2017): 338–66. 10.1177/1476127016651001.

Harneit-Sievers, Axel. *Zwischen Depression Und Dekolonisation: Afrikanische Händler Und Politik in Süd-Nigeria, 1935–1954.* Saarbrücken and Fort Lauderdale: Breitenbach, 1991.

Jones, Geoffrey. *British Multinational Banking, 1830–1990.* New York: OUP, 1993.

Jones, T. *Ghana's First Republic, 1960–1966: The Pursuit of the Political Kingdom.* London, UK: Methuen, 1976.

Killick, Tony. *Development Economics in Action: A Study of Economic Policies in Ghana. Studies in the Economics of Africa.* London i.a.: Heinemann Educational, 1978.

Knox, Andrew M. *Coming Clear: A Postscript after Retirement from Unilever.* London, UK: Heinemann, 1976.

Misra, Maria. *Business, Race and Politics in British India, c.1850–1960.* Oxford: Oxford University Press, 1999.

Nkrumah, Kwame. *Neo-Colonialism: The Last Stage of Imperialism.* New York: International Publishers, 1965.

Nugent, P. *Africa since Independence.* Basingstoke: Palgrave Macmillan, 2002.

Pedler, Frederick J. *Business and Decolonization in West Africa, c.1940–1960: A Personal Memoir by Sir Frederick Pedler.* Oxford: Privately printed with the assistance of generous grants for UAC, Barclays Bank and Mr John Zochonis, 1989.

Rathbone, Richard. *Ghana: British Documents on the End of Empire.* Series B. London: Institute of Commonwealth Studies, 1992.

Rimmer, Douglas. *Staying Poor: Ghana's Political Economy, 1950–1990.* Edited by World Bank. Oxford: Pergamon, 1992.

Seers, Dudley, and C Ross. "Report on the Financial and Physical Problems of Development in the Gold Coast." Accra, Ghana, 1952.

Stockwell, Sarah E. "Political Strategies of British Business During Decolonization – the Case of the Gold-Coast Ghana, 1945–57." *Journal of Imperial and Commonwealth History* 23, no. 2 (1995): 277–300.

Stockwell, Sarah E. *The Business of Decolonization: British Business Strategies in the Gold Coast.* Oxford: Clarendon Press, 2000.

Tignor, Robert L. *Capitalism and Nationalism at the End of Empire: State and Business in Decolonizing Egypt, Nigeria, and Kenya, 1945–1963.* Princeton, N.J.: Princeton University Press, 1998.

Watson, A "Report of the Commission of Enquiry into Disturbances in the Gold Coast." London, UK, 1948.

4 Indigenization Programmes and Organizational Legitimacy

With the removal of the first independent leaders of Nigeria and Ghana, a period of political instability began that British business viewed ambiguously. In Ghana, the military and the police took over the government with a corrective, reformist agenda, returning power to a relatively liberal, if short-lived, democracy in Ghana, followed by military governments, while Nigeria descended into civil war. In 1968 and 1969, Nigeria legislated the local incorporation of all extraterritorial business and more significant restrictions on banking. In Ghana, the National Liberation Council (NLC) reserved certain small-scale enterprises for Ghanaians, and in 1969 Busia extended this earlier decree, followed by an expulsion of mainly African foreigners. This marked the beginning of so-called indigenization programmes and part-nationalizations, which became a feature of economic policy in the 1970s.

Expropriations in developing countries have been discussed from various positions as set out in the introduction. This chapter argues that domestic and international trends interacted and created a climate that was more hostile to multinationals. The development discourse shifted towards more critical interpretations of the failure to substantially advance the economies of developing countries (see chapter 2.3). This has generally been interpreted as an attempt to take control of Western companies' investments. However, neither the design of the indigenization decrees nor the experience of companies consistently suggested that this was the case. Drawing on the experience of British companies in Ghana and Nigeria, this chapter focuses on the shifting domestic political alliances that were the driving force behind the local content and participation legislation.

The following chapter aims to analyse the response of businesses to this and poses the question of how much this legislation was influenced by expropriations in other countries and by new paradigms in development, as opposed to local conflicts over redistribution and citizenship. Much of the early indigenization legislation was aimed at Lebanese and other African foreigners, whereas the later decrees were more radical in enforcing state participation. Concerns about citizenship and the role of foreigners in the economy meant that measures such as the expulsion of other West African

DOI: 10.4324/9781003001058-5

nationals, and the increasingly restrictive handling of expatriate immigration quotas for Western multinationals, should be considered in the broader context of indigenization legislation. This chapter commences with an overview of the bills and their background in Nigeria and Ghana and continues in the second section by highlighting corporate responses. The final section analyses the role of indigenization programmes in light of the international discourse and a worldwide trend to expropriate foreign nationals and the local pressures during the formation of postcolonial African states.

4.1 Indigenizing business in Nigeria and Ghana

Ghana and Nigeria seemed to develop similar forms of expropriation legislation, specifically partial nationalization and local equity restrictions instead of complete nationalization.[1] They differed in the intensity of regional rivalry, the emergence of large-scale oil production and the influence of African businesspeople, all of which were more critical factors in Nigeria. The country also experienced windfall gains through the export of oil. It joined OPEC in 1971 and profited from the worldwide oil price hikes in 1973–1974 and 1979. Only by the 1980s, when the price for crude oil was reduced, did the bonanza end, but oil remained the primary source of income for the federal government. The adverse effects of the oil fortune have been referred to as 'Dutch disease': local agriculture could not compete with the influx of food imports that were not restricted due to the oil wealth, and a hike in wages unsettled the labour costs in the economy even further, making traditional export staples no longer viable.

These differences in economic fortunes did affect economic policies towards foreign business to a lesser degree than might be expected. Both countries openly pursued policies of Ghanaianization or Nigerianization of their national economies from at least 1968, and legislation frequently coincided (for a chronology, see Table 4.1).

At the same time, a worldwide rise in expropriations occurred, and the academic and public discourse became noticeably more critical of large multinational companies (see chapter 2).[2] The association of foreign, mainly British, business with the empire was a shared historical legacy of postcolonial states. Nkrumah's referred to this as neo-colonialism in his 1965 book. As discussed in the previous chapter, this did not fully translate into his economic policy towards Western business. Nevertheless, the successors of this first generation of African political leaders (Acheampong in Ghana and Gowon in Nigeria) pursued economic nationalism more actively, emphasizing the dynamic economic role of the state.

Similarly, new theories of underdevelopment and dependency emerging in Latin America in the late 1960s and 1970s elevated the state's role through a new form of nationalism, incorporating socialist aims. The break-up of the old development discourse left foreign businesses with no role to

Table 4.1 Chronology of significant restrictions on foreign capital in Ghana and Nigeria

Ghana	*Year*	*Nigeria*
	1966	Expatriate Quota Allocation Board
Ghanaiazation Decree (December)	1968	Companies Act
Ghanaian Business Promotion Act (June)	1969	New banking legislation requiring local incorporation and published statements of accounts
	1970	New credit guidelines for commercial banks published by Central Bank National Development Plan
	1971	Government acquires 40 per cent of the three largest banks (April) Nigeria joins OPEC (July)
Mining Operations (Government Participation) Decree	1972	NEPD 1
Investment Policy Decree Ghanaian Enterprises Development Decree	1975	NEPD 2

play in developing countries. The greater attraction of underdevelopment theories did not mean a clean break with the tenets of the old development framework, as they both shared a belief in the state as the primary economic actor. Instead, it was a radicalization of earlier policies of mercantilist import substitution, state-led investment and autonomous growth. Economic nationalism took different paths in Ghana and Nigeria: the smaller country aimed to achieve an almost autarkic economy under Acheampong's rule. The larger country sought to increase its share of African business internally and its control over exports, mainly crude oil, externally. However, instead of fully nationalizing big business, both countries simultaneously devised what became known as indigenization programmes – economically nationalist legal vehicles that soon became fraught with several different interests and aims.

4.1.1 Ghana

The removal of Kwame Nkrumah hardly caused any upset in British business circles. While personal relations had often been good, businessmen thought that he had bankrupted the country.[3] British companies, especially the UAC, quickly found access to the new rulers. In March 1966, the Special Committee, the interface between Unilever and UAC, decided '[...] that we should do everything possible to support the new regime, even if this involved some risk to ourselves'.[4] The head of UAC Ghana soon after had a 'cordial' interview with General Ankrah 'to define our relationship over a term of years long enough to envisage the new regime getting the country's finances in order and bringing the economy more towards free exchange and private enterprise'.[5]

The management of Holt considered the upheaval in West Africa so great in 1966 that the old top management stepped down to make way for new people, many recruited from outside the firm, to take over the lead.[6] While they worried in particular over Nigeria, the situation in Ghana was of less concern as the investment was smaller and had not remitted dividends and profits for years anyway.

> Our profits and assets in Ghana are still frozen, though I am glad to be able to report that present policies in that country do encourage us to hope that the very great economic problems there will be resolved to a large extent within the next year or two.[7]

This optimistic assessment was not fulfilled, and by 1977 Ghana had still not remitted profits accrued by multinationals some ten years earlier.[8]

AGC's first experience with the new government was less promising when Colonel Akwasi Afrifa, the NLC member for Finance, Trade and Economic Affairs, intervened in an unofficial strike in December 1966, asking for all strikers to be reinstated and paid fully because the 'majority of the workers [were] being totally misled' about the real causes of the strike. The AGC agreed that its cause was political.[9] The colonel explained his personal involvement with his concern for Ghana's financial position:

> He said that a strike in one of the State Mines would not have affected him as they were running at a loss but the loss to the country when the mine was Ashanti Goldfields was serious.[10]

Gold accounted for about 8 per cent of total exports from 1966 to 1971, and AGC was the largest mine in the country.[11] In return for their conciliatory attitude, the corporation gained reassurance that there would be no further government involvement in labour matters. Afrifa recognized that AGC was a private company and that 'he had no right to intervene', and that there was no restriction on employers running their business as they thought best.[12] Government intervention, however, increased again when Colonel Ignatius Acheampong took over in 1972.

While the Nigerian Enterprise Promotion Decrees (NEPDs) have probably been more thoroughly debated in the academic literature, Ghanaian governments also developed a series of similar decrees.[13] When the NLC took over the government in 1966, they began to manage the economy in line with the demands from the International Monetary Fund (IMF), which slightly reduced state-owned enterprises' (SOEs) influence and worked more closely with foreign interests again.[14] However, in the first Ghanaianization decree of 1968, they sought to promote the expansion of local Ghanaian firms, especially in small-scale enterprises in areas such as retail and wholesale trade and simple manufacturing (see appendix 1).[15] This was a departure from the policy of Nkrumah, who had favoured state companies, in particular the GNTC.

Busia's government followed this in 1969 with the Ghanaian Business Promotion Act, which extended the scope to include more enterprises and brought the deadline for compliance with the first decree forward. Although most of the activities of British multinationals were not affected by it, the legislation included some smaller foreign firms, particularly two advertising agencies, Graham and Gilles and LINTAS (a Unilever subsidiary), that handled the accounts of large concerns. Both firms sought relief from the act, which led to rival petitions by a prospective buyer of Graham and Gilles and Ghanaian newspaper editors to the Office of Business Promotion. While the former pointed out his company's ability to take over the enterprise, the newspaper editors argued that they would lose substantial revenue if those companies were indigenized because large multinationals would not work with the smaller, less professional Ghanaian agencies. It appears that they were granted exemptions because only one UK company, a subsidiary of the Guardian Royal Exchange Co., had to divest 40 per cent.[16]

Around 600 small to medium-sized firms were affected, mainly Lebanese, Syrian and Indian, which was the express intention of the legislators for both the 1968 and 1969 decree: 'It is no secret that this legislation was directed against the Lebanese and Indians'.[17] Rivalry with business owners from other African states was also an issue, as the subsequent expulsion of aliens without documents in November 1969 demonstrated.[18] While this affected mainly independent shopkeepers rather than British expatriates, many miners in the Ashanti Goldfields were from other African countries in the area, mainly from Upper Volta/Burkina Faso.[19] Local incorporation of banks followed in 1970. Ghanaianization of the economy was popular but not necessarily successful, despite government financial assistance to business people.[20] In some cases, SOEs took over the business.

Busia's economic policies ultimately failed partly because of the liberalization of imports, which led to a foreign exchange crisis, combined with a drop in cocoa prices. In an austerity budget, the cedi was devalued by 44 per cent, which alienated many and was followed by another army coup in January 1972. Colonel Acheampong benefited from a rise in gold and cocoa prices but also from repudiating debts in the form of four suppliers' (180 days) credits to the tune of US $94m, mostly owed to overseas contractor-financed firms, on the grounds of corruption.[21] This signalled a departure in policy and was quickly followed by the compulsory acquisition of 55 per cent of equity in the AGC and four foreign-owned timber enterprises, one of them owned by the UAC. The Investment Policy decree of 1975 combined previous indigenization legislation with the recent government seizures since 1972/73. It also required a level of public shareholding of 55 per cent in timber or mineral extraction (apart from oil, where participation was at 30 per cent) over a certain annual turnover or level of capital employed or that produced certain goods classed as 'necessities'. It also established two schedules. The first prescribed a minimum of 50 per cent of Ghanaian shareholding in enterprises over a certain size in a series of listed activities. The second schedule included all those areas that had been entirely reserved for Ghanaians in the decrees of the late 1960s. In banking and insurance, 40 per cent of Ghanaian equity was necessary. The number of companies affected was 287, and only 12 made a public offer of shares (among them UAC), and of the C33m offered in this way, the state took up C14m. Additionally, the government acquired all the 40 per cent stakes in the banks and half of those in insurance.[22] Although Ghanaians received loans from the government to enable them to purchase equity and assets, the share issues were sluggish, particularly compared to Nigeria, where the NEPD's issues were oversubscribed.

4.1.2 Nigeria

The overthrow and assassination of key politicians Balewa, Bello and Akintola came as a shock to British business leaders. The death of Balewa was regretted by many businesspeople.[23] Under General Gowon, the administration and, in particular, the permanent secretaries became highly influential in policy formation. By 1968, the attitudes towards foreign investment began to visibly harden, but the first pieces of legislation aimed to regulate large commercial ventures rather than indigenize them. Economic nationalism in Nigeria, as in Ghana, was not a new discovery in the late 1960s, but previous legislation had offered special benefits for Nigerians or firms with 'local content' and participation rather than enforced indigenization.[24]

The first restrictive measure was the creation of the Expatriate Quota Allocation Board in 1966, whose handling of immigration quotas was at first not threatening to foreign firms but which tightened noticeably in 1974. The Companies Decree of 1968, which required 'localization' (i.e., the local incorporation of foreign business in Nigeria), was the first step towards greater control and regulation, as it brought overseas businesses within the remit of existing national legislation. This was followed in 1969 by specific banking legislation which required incorporation and publication of audited statements of accounts. A year later, the Central Bank introduced credit guidelines to ensure that finance was available to Nigerian nationals.[25] This changed outlook on foreign investment developed during the civil war, when the oil companies, the banks and UAC continued to operate in the Eastern region.[26] The attitudes of the oil companies, which cooperated with the Biafran state, had particularly undermined Nigerian trust. Subsequently, Shell-BP and others were excluded from the provisions in the NEPD and instead negotiated government shares separately.[27] While the West African oil industry was not included in this study, the nationalizations in OPEC countries, together with previous expropriations by

Nasser in 1956 and Nyerere in 1968, formed the international backdrop to events in West Africa.

In April 1971, the government acquired 40 per cent of the major foreign banks: Standard Bank of West Africa, Barclays Bank of Nigeria and the British and French Bank, in preparation for the first NEPD in February 1972. The first decree established two schedules: the first listed sectors which were reserved for Nigerians and consisted of small, low-tech enterprises, mainly run by Lebanese; the second encompassed small to medium-sized firms in certain industries where local participation in equity or assets of 40 per cent was compulsory (see appendix 2 for details). In response, Holt and UAC both reorganized and received special dispensation to withdraw all the subsidiaries that fell into Schedule 1 and merge them with the majority of their interests in Schedule 2.[28]

After its implementation, NEPD 1 was criticized for the low rate of compliance, the long time (two years) that companies had to comply with – and circumvent – the legislation and 'fronting', i.e., the formal takeover by a nominal Nigerian owner without executive control. The Adeosun Commission particularly criticized the fact that the highly oversubscribed public issues led to the concentration of wealth with a few already affluent individuals. Biersteker estimates that about 20 individuals or family groups took up the majority of shares.[29]

The second decree, promulgated in 1977 by the Obasanjo government, which had removed Gowon from power two years earlier, aimed to address some of the problems of the first attempt: more foreign firms were affected by the introduction of a third category that now required 40 per cent local equity for the largest, mostly more technology-intensive ventures; some previously unaffected areas were included in Schedule 2 that now prescribed 60 per cent local participation such as chemicals, drugs, metal manufacturing, hotel industry and oil-servicing companies. Some commercial activities were moved from Schedule 2 to Schedule 1, which was still exclusively reserved for nationals. Thus wholly foreign-owned subsidiaries or new investments became impossible in Nigeria. The trading companies and banks all fell into Schedule 2, although the banks had more state participation than UAC or Holt. Overall, there was a greater degree of compliance, and the new share issues limited individual acquisitions to 5 per cent.[30]

4.2 Corporate responses to the indigenization programmes

Economic nationalism in Nigeria and Ghana employed similar techniques to create areas reserved exclusively for nationals, which excluded other African, Lebanese and Western competitors. In Nigeria, many Lebanese decided to naturalize, which allowed them to continue their business under Schedule 1.[31] However, the indigenization programmes have often been presented as measures against Western foreign investment.[32] Others have pointed out that indigenization followed several different goals.[33] Despite their different economic and political development, Ghana and Nigeria almost concurrently introduced localization and indigenization legislation. This suggests that the existence of international discourse on the structure and inequalities of the global economy that increasingly favoured expropriation created options for economic policy in developing countries and a degree of learning from other cases.

This section focuses on companies' perceptions of as well as their responses to the localization and indigenization programmes. Different companies experienced economic nationalism in different ways. This was partly due to the sectors they operated in, especially because legislation differentiated between types of enterprises. Companies also perceived the threat from localization differently, depending on their previous experience with nationalist pressure in other countries. This was particularly the case for Barclays in Nigeria, which is the subject of the first part of this section, followed by the experiences of the UAC and the AGC. The final two parts address the different trajectories of legislation in Ghana and Nigeria.

4.2.1 Nationalism, localization and international banking

Enforced localization occurred in Nigeria in 1968 and had greater repercussions for banking rather than commercial companies. Some of Holt's and UAC's subsidiaries were already locally incorporated, sometimes even with local participation. In the case of Barclays Bank DCO, however, the changes were far-reaching. Previously, funds had been deposited mainly in the more profitable London money markets and profits, and capital requirements were remitted from, to and between territories as necessary. This essentially deprived developing countries of capital for investment, as revenue opportunities were better in developed countries. Globally, these dynamics only changed with the emergence of 'emerging economies' in the 1990s and made developing countries more dependent on the World Bank, the IMF and foreign investors. Due to exchange controls in Ghana since 1961, remittances had been blocked for many years. Local incorporation in Nigeria meant that the new subsidiary required as much as £12m, of which DCO's board estimated £9m would have to be remitted to Nigeria. Suggestions were even made to enter a joint venture with another US or European bank to limit Barclays' expenditure, as the concern was that the money would be inaccessible for some time. Hence, the formation of local companies in Africa was considered sensitive enough to be the subject of a board memorandum and a related poll of DCO's board members, which ascertained '[...] the Board as being in favour of staying in Africa on the best terms we could obtain and that this did not preclude our taking the initiative in incorporating locally if this seemed advisable, and that we should exercise caution in capital expenditure there in the future'.[34]

This decision was the endpoint of a longer internal debate that was held at different levels within DCO's organization, where local incorporation was considered the first step towards nationalization. This had happened to the bank twice before: first in 1956 in Egypt and then in Tanzania in 1969.[35] Local incorporation, which followed in Ghana late in 1970, prompted heated discussions about the future of the bank, particularly in an exchange of letters between the former chairman Sir Julian Crossley, who had presided over much of Barclays' expansion in the 1950s and 1960s, and his successor, Frederick Seebohm. Seebohm believed that Barclays could continue to work with local subsidiaries as they used to, while Crossley maintained that this would weaken the bank's position and even prompt further action.[36]

Earlier in 1969, the general manager for Nigeria, William Duncan, presented the board with a 'Plan for the Future', illustrating that, in his opinion, mere localization did not go far enough. He claimed that soon indigenous banks would outstrip the British overseas banks because they appealed to national sentiment. Therefore, he advised that Barclays should hive off part of the African business and, ideally, forge an agreement with one of the indigenous banks, preferably the National Bank of Nigeria. Ultimately, they would handle the Nigerian end of the business, while Barclays provided the services in the main financial centres outside Nigeria.

This was a highly contentious plan, and while the nationalization in Tanzania still haunted management, Barclays was disinclined to let go of one of its largest, most profitable sections.[37] Moreover, none of the indigenous banks was in a financial position to buy the extensive branch network. There were also reservations about how profits would be split up between the partners and if profitability could have been maintained in such an arrangement anyway. A handwritten aside summed up one board member's feelings on the matter: 'Establish an agreement if you like but no suggestion of withdrawal'.[38] In the end, Duncan's plan was shelved because it seemed 'a policy of despair'.[39] Barclays let the chance of an innovative solution to the problem of localization pass and went public on 30 March 1969 as Barclays Bank of Nigeria Ltd. – a last-minute name change to reflect a greater 'Nigerian' identity.[40]

4.2.2 Responses to local participation at UAC and AGC

The two companies with the largest investment in West Africa, UAC and AGC, were in very different positions because AGC mined gold only in Obuasi, while the merchant company ran many different ventures and had, partly through its parent Unilever, greater international exposure. Consequently, the UAC was in a better position to adapt. AGC's dispersed shareholding meant that the corporation was vulnerable to takeovers, and it was bought by Lonrho in 1968. Even though the gold mine remained relatively independent as part of the conglomerate, it changed corporate policy to a more flexible approach. The takeover improved AGC's access to finance and potentially increased its local political leverage. But Lonrho also represented a unique political approach for a British firm in Africa, and under the leadership of 'Tiny' Rowland, Lonrho's strategies were highly controversial.[41]

The UAC developed a strategy for local participation in London in consultation with Unilever's directors, the importance of which was, however, limited by the understanding that it was 'impossible to generalise on the subject of participation and each country would have to be considered individually'.[42] Like Barclays, UAC struggled with the question of whether it would be better to offer participation voluntarily and pre-empt any legislation or rather do nothing in the hope of being left alone. Another issue was to whom to sell: management feared that government could potentially use even a minority shareholding to exert effective majority control, whereas the association with individuals involved the risk that they might fall from grace. Thus, a broadly based shareholding was the preferred option.[43] However, there were six basic principles on which the committee members agreed:

1 Management of the investment should be sought
2 Disinvested money should be repatriated (described as a pious hope)
3 Regular evaluations of fixed asset values for tax considerations should be implemented
4 The company would seek to negotiate a service fee or any remuneration for management functions
5 To protect the interests of remaining expatriate management
6 To resist double standards with regard to the blocked remittance of dividends to shareholders abroad[44]

The AGC was not affected by the Ghanaianization acts in the late 1960s, as gold mining was not included. Nevertheless, the company had introduced local participation in 1969, when the mine was taken over by Lonrho.[45] A new agreement with the local stool (the chieftaincy) was negotiated, which ensured that the Adansi council, on whose lands the firm operated, now received £100,000 annually instead of £54, a demand backed by the government.

At the same time, in January 1969, the government took a 20 per cent equity participation in AGC. In lieu of payment, it surrendered its mineral royalty. In exchange, the government received the equity, on which it was entitled to a dividend, and Lonrho guaranteed that if the dividend on the 20 per cent should ever fall short of the sum that the government would have received as the royalty, the firm would pay the difference. In return, the AGC's lease, which had only another 17 years to run, was extended for a further 50 years from 1969 onwards. This was important for further investment decisions, as the lead times in mineral extraction were considerable. By giving up the royalty in favour of equity participation, the government effectively became a shareholder of the mine. While the dividend could have potentially been more than the royalty, in the years to come, AGC hardly paid more than what the royalty would have been.[46] In contrast to other shareholders, however, the Ghanaian government was insured against the risk of falling dividends. Hence, in financial terms, this transfer largely maintained the status quo.

Local participation thus seemed to benefit almost everybody – apart from the miners, who, worried about the implications of the takeover for their work conditions and security, went on strike with the argument that they were entitled to three months' severance payment. In contrast to the 1966/67 strike, the government showed no lenience, and in a police shooting, several miners were left wounded or dead. The tragedy finally prompted AGC to pay a three months' 'goodwill award' to the miners.[47]

4.2.3 Acheampong's 'war on the economy'

After Lonrho's takeover of AGC, the noticeably more conciliatory and cooperative attitude towards the government probably sought to create more favourable relations with the new democratic government. However, the coup by Acheampong in 1972 dashed any hopes of having secured the position of the mine. The new military government followed a much more economically nationalist agenda than any of the previous governments. Commissioner Major Kwame Baah invited Lonrho (and the foreign-owned diamond mining company CAST) to enter negotiations with the government about a participation agreement in June 1972 and made the position of the new leadership clear:

> The NRC is committed to a policy of capturing the commanding heights of the economy of this country. […] The Government's position, which is not different from other developing countries, is that the major resources of the sub-soil are part of the public domain, not only de jure but also in practice. […] In a country where the extractive industries play a strategic role in the whole economy, the Government has a duty to assume effective control over the exploitation of the State's mineral resources to ensure that the country realises the maximum economic benefit from these resources.[48]

Lonrho's hopes of having gained some insulation from participation demands through the deal they struck in 1969 were quickly shattered when the negotiating team continued its statement by unravelling the old agreement. The transfer of 20 per cent without charge had realized substantial tax benefit for Lonrho; the royalty payment should have continued regardless of government participation; the new lease was now considered excessively long and would be halved; the dividend paid had hardly exceeded the surrendered royalty for tax reasons; and, last but not least, the tax assessment for the transfer of equity to the government had actually saved the company a substantial amount in payable taxes. All in all, the new government considered the existing agreement a drain on its tax income, concluding: 'The effect of all this is that the Ghana Government has actually financed the AGC's capital expansion programme [...]'.[49]

These criticisms were partly justified, but while the equity transfer might have realized tax benefits, and the dividend payments appear to have been doctored, the company had been paid for their assets through the surrendered royalty, and the lease of mines was usually over long periods to encourage capital-intensive investment. The final criticism – that the government had effectively financed AGC's expansion – was somewhat surprising considering that the government was a co-owner of the company with a vested interest in greater profits. However, if such profits were achieved through lower taxation, this reduced the government's income elsewhere, highlighting a key issue for SOEs in developing countries, particularly in this period.

By December, the breakdown of negotiations between the government and the two foreign mining companies, CAST and AGC, was announced. A government White Paper set out a plan for a mandated joint venture alongside the compensation payable by Ghana's government. Company assets were transferred to a new, locally incorporated company in which the government held 55 per cent but undertook to 'enter into appropriate arrangements for the protection of the interest of the junior partners in the joint venture'.[50] The technical management and direction of the company were also entrusted to the foreign private investors, which 'should insulate the day-to-day management and operation of the undertaking from undue interferences'.[51] Most importantly, joint ownership by state and foreign investors was accepted as sufficient for purposes of control. The government's choice of participation over nationalization was in cognizance of the importance of foreign expertise.[52]

While this was a distinct departure from previous more business-friendly policies, there was no intention to remove foreign investment entirely. This part-nationalization was specific to the extractive industries in minerals and timber, but other sectors were equally affected by the change in economic policy. Holt, which had been bought by Lonrho in 1969, was also required to indigenize and sell at least 50 per cent of its equity to Ghanaians.[53]

In February 1973, the Acheampong government announced its intention to have either state or at least private Ghanaian participation of around 50 per cent in most foreign businesses. UAC's management planned to amalgamate all their interests into one company, as they had done in Nigeria a year before, in response to the first NEPD.[54] In the autumn of 1972, 55 per cent of UAC's timber business was expropriated, and over a year later, no agreement had been reached on the terms of the compensation. UAC considered the government's suggestions as too low, remittances were not guaranteed, and management and technical fees that had been agreed at the time of the takeover had not been paid.[55] By the end of 1975, a government agency took over management control of the timber company, and UAC withdrew all contributions and divested the remaining 45 per cent equity share after they '[...] had received a circular letter saying that we had been weighed in the balance as managers and found wanting and the government was now going to transform the business'.[56]

Despite Acheampong's often extravagant rhetoric (for example, declaring war on the economy), Chazan has argued that by 1975 the government was rapidly losing control over it, as smuggling and the shifting of price-controlled foods into a black market was becoming widespread. Acheampong's lack of interest in and understanding of the economy appears to be encapsulated in his statement that 'despite the needs of the economy, many Ghanaians are only interested in making money'.[57] Overvalued exchange rates raised the cost of Ghanaian exports, making them uncompetitive. As a result, Ghana found it difficult to pay for imports, which became scarce, making it more profitable for economic actors with access to desirable goods to sell them on the black market. The government's fiscal policies combined with an exacerbating economic crisis led to smuggling and the emergence of a black market, ultimately culminating in a series of deep economic crises in the late 1970s and 1980s.[58] In the early 1980s, the government took up to 80 per cent of the banks' equity for a short period of time, but shortly afterwards, a structural adjustment programme was introduced that liberalized economic policies and undid many of the changes from the 1970s. The Ghanaian state nevertheless retained some level of shareholding in foreign business until the 1990s, in the case of the AGC, even longer.

4.2.4 The Nigerian Enterprise Promotion Decrees

In Nigeria, similar policies were being enacted, and the NEPDs would become better known than the Ghanaian programmes by virtue of Nigeria's larger size and better economic outlook. Conservative economic policies and the beginning of oil production in the late 1960s had attracted more foreign investment than Ghana, which had not allowed repatriation of profits since 1961.[59] The West Africa Department of the Foreign and Commonwealth Office commented on the threat of indigenization in 1972:

> Indigenization and nationalization policies are not exclusive to Nigeria. We have encountered them in varying degrees in different parts of the world and it seems likely that developing countries will increasingly deal with expatriate companies in this way. But we recognise that Nigeria which represents such a substantial element of our total investment stake in Africa is of particular importance.[60]

While the Foreign and Commonwealth Office suggested that 'the banks are not attempting to resist the principle of part-nationalization, particularly since they will retain management control', it still surprised officials when Mr Piercy from Standard Bank stated categorically that he was well content with the compensation offered for the 35 to 36 per cent share taken by the government in addition to the 12.9 per cent that had already been issued to Nigerian shareholders.[61] He doubted that the government aimed to gain greater leverage over the bank's lending policies, as Standard already conformed to the lending guidelines issued by the central bank, which could be amended at any time by the government without any participation in the banks. The High Commission and the managing director both agreed 'that there was a difference between what certain Government leaders and politicians said in public about the banks' need to revise their role and what the financial officials were in practice doing'.[62] The Bank's 'many important Nigerian contacts' certainly had a role to play in minimizing the impact of the legislation.[63]

The big trading companies such as Holt and UAC, with their complicated structure of subsidiaries, avoided having some of their more traditional activities placed in Schedule 1 by merging them with their other interests and offering 40 per cent participation in the whole group.[64] The Nigerian government had agreed in principle that it was preferable to amalgamate and offer participation in one single company rather than having individual share issues. UAC intended to try and strip the maximum profits out of these subsidiaries before combining them with UAC Nigeria Ltd., whose capital would rise from N5m to N14m, of which the company wanted to issue N5–6m worth of shares at about par.[65] By 1974 this arrangement had created many enemies, according to UAC's internal discussions, particularly from 'the second echelon of senior civil servants and certain other people with their own business interests in mind'.[66] In the case of the UAC, the uproar over the treatment of their subsidiary LINTAS appeared to have been the reason for the long delay in negotiations and the punitive evaluation of the share price. Even though LINTAS was an advertising and public relations firm that would have fallen into Schedule 1 of the NEPD, it was exempt as a division of UAC(N), which had an overall participation of 40 per cent.[67]

While the Federal Executive Council had agreed to the amalgamation and given an all-clear to proceed, the Federal Ministry of Trade claimed in January 1974 that the merger was illegal, contrary to the Nigerian Attorney General. However, without the clearance from the Ministry of Trade, the issue on the Lagos Stock Exchange could not proceed, which now put UAC in serious danger of not complying with the NEPD at the decreed date of 31 March 1974. This technically entitled the government to take over the entire business if the UAC failed to be granted an extension. At the start of March, the chairman was seeking an interview with the head of state, who, on 15 March, granted the required extension.[68] While the business had not been taken, by July, UAC's management received a further blow when the share price for the UAC Nigeria issue was fixed at 40 kobos (but, according to UAC's files, was worth between 57 and 86 kobos), which was much lower than their own assessment, and 'was considered grossly unjust'.[69] Nevertheless, the decision was not to appeal but to go ahead,

> [...] because an appeal would involve considerable delays and application for further extension which would probably not be granted with a consequent risk of expropriation. In the circumstances it was thought to be better to accept which would at least safeguard our position in Nigeria, comforting ourselves with the thought that it was better to have 60 per cent of £8m or £9m than 100 per cent of possibly nothing at all.[70]

This entailed a loss of about £2m on book value. A few days later, however, it turned out that due to the length of negotiations, the UAC was entitled to receive dividends worth £1.9m, which would not otherwise have accrued to the company – in effect cancelling out the expected loss. Overall the directors were well content that all subsidiaries had been merged into one, as this 'would make them very much easier to control'.[71] David Fieldhouse concludes his account of the episode by stating that the UAC 'swallowed the pill', omitting that the company made up the loss from the share price valuation through dividends. Fieldhouse's account is problematic because he used the first half of the document as evidence for his interpretation, while the second half of the same document clearly outlines the dividend gains and how this offsets the loss. His account thus ignored that UAC viewed the deal as far more positive than he presented it in his history of the firm.[72]

Other companies also found their evaluations corrected downwards when they offered their shares. Barclays, which offered new shares in their Nigerian subsidiary in 1971, a year before the government took a large part of the equity, had had a similar experience with the Ad Hoc Committee on Capital Issues in Lagos, which would not allow their suggested price per share of between 17/- and 18/- and set the price at 16/6. This was considered too low but not greatly unjust. The issue was highly oversubscribed as the UAC issue in 1974.[73] In Ghana, however, the situation was slightly different after the Investment Act, when UAC of Ghana sold 40 per cent of their equity, which totalled C8m or £3.4m. There had been some difficulty before the issue was fully subscribed, which the company attributed to a general disinterest in owning shares among the Ghanaian public, as, on average, Ghanaians were poorer than their Nigerian counterparts. Another reason, however, was that in Ghana, the share price was 'not unreasonable' compared to the net asset value, i.e., shares in UAC (G) were not as relatively cheap as the Nigerian issue.[74]

In 1976 the Nigerian government's White Paper announced the plan to issue a second NEPD. This development was still hugely threatening to UAC International, which was practically dependent on its Nigerian profits – profits from the country translated straight into improved group results, underlining the fact that Nigeria was the only country with a dynamic enough economy to sustain UAC's overall performance.[75] This new decree was, in contrast to NEPD 1, centred around the interests of the state, and foreign investors were clearly one of its main targets.[76] By July 1976, UAC was trying to get many of its subsidiaries reclassified out of Schedule 1, which was successful in the case of Kingsway Stores. While the company had had good relations with the civil service until 1975, after the Mohammed/Obasanjo coup, their old contacts no longer had any authority. Nevertheless, the new NEPD had been leaked in draft form to foreign business people several times, which UAC's management took as a sign that the government was testing their reactions.[77] In the experience of foreign companies, government actions and public opinion diverged noticeably. While 'there was at present a lot of animosity against the British in Nigeria and against big businesses simply because of their size', the West Africa Committee received an 'understanding' reception in a meeting with senior government officials, including the new president of the Enterprises Decree.

> [The West Africa Committee] had been asked to send an aide memoire on the discussions during the visit and had been told that the door was still open and that the authorities were prepared to have some negotiations although they would not specify the method of it.[78]

Eventually, the large trading companies were excluded from the enterprise classification and their operations were summarily assigned to Schedule 2, or 60 per cent local equity ownership, colloquially known as the 'UAC clause'. This was probably the only major concession to foreign capital made in the NEPD 2. The banks, however, lost control of their operations as the government took a majority shareholding, and the Central Bank placed their own people into the companies' top management. In Nigeria, the provisions of the NEPD 2 were also relaxed in the 1980s because the civilian regime had not been involved in the legislation and had to contend with an economic downturn as the oil price declined.[79]

4.3 The political economy of indigenization in Ghana and Nigeria

Both the secondary literature and most corporate sources focus on events in Nigeria, mainly because of the more buoyant economy and the greater importance of the country for company results in the case of UAC, Barclays and Holt. While considerably less interest was directed towards Acheampong's legislation in Ghana, this was partly because the economy was unsettled by several other factors: the deteriorating exchange position, widespread corruption, price controls and black markets, and the exodus of a significant proportion of Ghanaians. In both cases, however, indigenization appears to have followed two distinct phases: the early decrees were affected by local considerations to reserve activities for nationals in the face of competition from other Africans, Lebanese, Indians and a few smaller Western multinationals. An exception to this was the Companies' Act in Nigeria, which aimed squarely at foreign companies but stopped short of expropriation. In the late phase, programmes were initiated that increased the economic clout of the state and showed greater awareness of events in other countries and international debates about the control of foreign investment.

The interpretation of corporate expropriation by governments of developing countries falls roughly into two categories: those who see it as a struggle for control over the economy and those who have focused on the local socio-economic trends that accompanied it. The former view is more dominant in the literature but normally refers to it as an international phenomenon, while the other group has analysed the specific West African cases more closely. This section argues that both approaches have overlooked some major issues because of their overriding concern with the expropriation of Western multinationals.

While scholarship on the subject was far from homogeneous in its opinions, there was a general sense that indigenization constituted an attempt to take charge of foreign investment to increase control over the economy. In particular, Biersteker and Collins's research into the Nigerian indigenization programmes showed that the issue was considerably less clear cut and pointed towards internal reasons for the legislation:

> Nigeria's indigenization program was not exclusively designed to assert the national will against the interests of foreign enterprises. Economic nationalism was used in part as a disguise for a redistributional struggle underway within the country.[80]

However, despite this conclusion, academic research was framed by ideological contests over development issues. Hence, although Collins and Biersteker are among the few scholars who have noted the importance of local conflicts for the policy formation in Nigeria, Biersteker's book nevertheless bears the title *Multinationals, the State and Control of the Nigerian Economy*, thus reflecting the dominant perception of the issue in the 1970s and 1980s.[81] Cooper summarized the dominant intellectual trends of the 1970s in a long article that introduced the theoretical approaches that sought to explain Africa's integration into the world economy: neo-liberal orthodox economics, dependency and underdevelopment theories, and Marxist class analysis.[82] None of these approaches was particularly well equipped to analyse the dynamics of economic nationalism, which were similar in Latin America, and also Canada.[83]

The wave of expropriations that swept across developing countries in the 1970s thus poses questions about how international and local events intertwined. The term expropriation somewhat obscures the multiplicity of approaches employed: local incorporation, reserving enterprises for nationals, local content requirements, enforced participation and nationalization (with or without compensation).[84] They indicated different political goals. For Nigeria and Ghana, two West African countries at once different and similar in their economic policies, this poses several questions. If it was really the state's goal to break the dominance of foreign capital, why not nationalize instead of indigenizing? Who benefited most from indigenization programmes, and who was targeted? Did legislators distinguish between different groups of non-nationals? Moreover, the issue of control has been difficult to assess in practice, and it has often been conflated with ownership. This hardly reflected business practice either then or now – control through ownership depended on the nature of shareholding (dispersed or in blocks) and whether management contracts were in place.

Economic nationalism in West Africa benefited two groups: African businessmen and governments. African entrepreneurs could eliminate competition and elicit joint venture or partnership offers because of indigenization. Governments derived several benefits: the popularity of those in power increased, and additional revenue and resources for increased patronage were created. Whose interests were dominantly expressed differs from programme to programme, but two phases can be made out: an early phase, mainly the late 1960s in Ghana and the early 1970s in Nigeria, and a late phase which began in Ghana with Acheampong's takeover in 1972 and in Nigeria with the Mohammed/Obasanjo coup in 1975.

The early legislation benefited African business and, evidence suggests, was the result of their pressurizing the government. Biersteker has underlined the importance of African businessmen in lobbying for the first NEPD, and similarly for the Ghanaianization decrees, as the Commissioner for Lands and Mineral Resources argued in 1968 that the average Ghanaian wanted economic independence, not 'something abstract like more economic power to the state. He wanted new opportunities for himself, his relatives, and friends to earn a living in trade or other fields'.[85] The main targets were not Western multinationals but specifically Levantine and Indian competitors in the retail trade. Evidence for this is not only the nature of reserved areas in these early indigenization programmes but also long-standing grievances against Lebanese, which were often voiced explicitly during the implementation of the programmes.[86] Unilever's directors were even informed by the Nigerian ambassador in 1974 that:

> [...] the whole exercise had been the result of popular demand but not because of the multi-nationals. The complaints had been against the misbehaviour of the Lebanese and other small traders and nothing but

> praise was heard in respect of the performance throughout the years of Unilever and UACI [UAC International].[87]

While it appears that in Ghana and Nigeria, Levantines and Indians were the main targets, it is also possible that this move against foreigners spilt over into the informal economy, as the expulsion of other Africans, mainly involved in small trade and shops, from Ghana in 1969 and Nigeria in 1983 indicates.

Western multinationals, however, were much more widely affected by the provisions of NEPD 1 in Nigeria than by the Ghanaianization decrees of 1968 and 1969. According to a Foreign and Commonwealth Office source on the Indigenous Businessmen's Seminar held in Lagos in September 1972, '[t]here is a latent disposition to regard expatriate firms as fair game, to be clubbed – with Government assistance – until they render up their assets'.[88] Nigerian businessmen, operating in a far more buoyant economy than their Ghanaian counterparts, could aspire to take over some of the smaller multinationals – LINTAS, for example. Whether they antagonized the interests of foreign companies or cooperated with them depended on the opportunities available: the pressure exerted through NEPD 1 led multinationals to search actively for local joint venture partners from the Nigerian business community. Although those who collaborated were depicted as selling out, one could also argue that they were instead buying into the international system.

The later decrees, under Acheampong in Ghana in 1972 and 1975, and Obasanjo in Nigeria in 1975, favoured state ownership over the transfer of equity to nationals. They nevertheless included previous legislation that reserved areas for domestic activity and investment. There were, however, some noticeable differences. While Acheampong sought to shore up a substantially devalued currency, Obasanjo's government followed a more strategic agenda, concentrating state ownership in the oil and petroleum as well as the financial sector. The greatest difference was the fact that Nigeria's economy was buoyant, and there was a sizeable group of Nigerians who could afford to invest in shares, whereas Ghana suffered from the decline in cocoa prices and an overvalued exchange rate.

The notion of increasing national control was central to the discourse surrounding indigenization. When businesses were indigenized or nationalized 100 per cent, this was not problematic, but in cases of minority and majority shareholding, or indeed service agreements, it was not necessarily evident who was in charge of a company. Political economy authors such as Biersteker and Hoogvelt were not convinced that Nigerian indigenization led to greater national control over the economy. In Nigeria, criticism of NEPD 1 also centred on the concentrated shareholding that resulted from the decree.[89] Hence the second NEPD limited the percentage of shares that could go to an individual, thus further diluting equity which in turn allowed foreign multinationals to maintain control even with a minority holding.

Business records indicate that the governments of Nigeria and Ghana continued to consult and negotiate with firms and that the relationship was not as consistently antagonistic as it was often assumed by contemporaries. Chibuike Uche argued that this reflected the influence that the UK government exerted to protect its commercial interests in the region.[90] He bases his argument on government records in The National Archives, which painted a picture of greater political involvement than company files indicated. By contrast, British companies in West Africa had long-standing complaints about insufficient government assistance, suggesting a fundamental difference in perception between the two groups.[91] Since the late 1960s, the companies in this study were unhappy with the support that they received from the UK government. Firms were gaining experience of local content requirements through their network of subsidiaries, and increasingly felt that they could manage indigenization requirements better.

In terms of gaining control of foreign investment, indigenization programmes were not an ideal solution either – certainly not compared to the nationalization of foreign assets. While this also occurred in some cases, nationalizations were far more targeted to specific industries. In Ghana, Acheampong's government took management control over the timber enterprises. In Nigeria, the banks were effectively state-controlled by the late 1970s. Indigenization, however, focused on the purchase of shares or assets by private individuals or public bodies. In its third survey, the UN Commission on Transnational Corporations applauded the new pragmatism of these programmes: replacing foreign direct investment where possible but continuing to work with it where its absence would leave a gap. On the point of control, however, their assessment was less positive: the commission criticized the idea that ownership and control were equated and concluded that domestic control, 'in the sense of key decisions taken at enterprise level and in accordance with local needs and priorities, not subject to the approval of the parent company', was, despite ownership, still elusive for most developing countries.[92] Yet indigenization programmes, with their focus on the private acquisition of shares and assets, were more likely to lead to dispersed ownership and thus enabled foreign control to persist.

Nevertheless, indigenization programmes were popular precisely because they enabled investors and entrepreneurs to acquire resources with the assistance of governments. Furthering local business through such tangible measures was hardly novel in the late 1960s, as Biersteker points out that 'principal components of the first decree were outlined in documents written prior to independence'.[93] African businessmen themselves were pressing for greater state support, not against Western multinationals, which were considered potential partners, but against the Levantine competition in retail trading. As the discourse in development economics shifted increasingly towards a more invasive state in the mid-to-late 1960s, these new approaches became dominant at international advisory bodies such as

UNCTAD.[94] This formed the intellectual and political basis for a changed interpretation of the post-war development discourse.

These new interpretations of economic development agreed with orthodox theory on the importance of the state as the dominant actor in the economy. Some, for example, the Nigerian politician Obafemi Awolowo, went further and advocated the creation of socialism.[95] Here, only the state had the power to improve the position of the periphery and could only do so by taking control of the economy. This interpretation of economic policy options was evident in West Africa in the later indigenization programmes. While this could be termed an international view of the meaning of indigenization, there is also a local component, which has already been noted by scholars such as Johnson and Breton in the 1960s.[96] The importance of this factor is particularly clear in Nigeria. Just at the point when the state and its agencies increasingly took a share in business interests, political discourse focused on greater redistributive justice. In Ghana, a general tendency existed to increase public supervision over commerce in order to extend the possibilities for political patronage, at least since Nkrumah. Fela Kuti commented on this for Nigeria in a song lampooning the American multinational ITT:

> Multinationals which are established here make great declarations in the press for better swindling us. They have an infallible method for that: they find a corrupted African whom they give a million naira. In his turn he gives some crumbs in his surroundings and thus becomes the chief. [...] he [...] goes up in power because he is friend-friend with the journalists, friend-friend with the Secretary of State, friend-friend with the ministers, friend-friend with the head of state. It is there the beginning of our misfortunes: embezzlement, inflation, confusion, oppression. It is the itinerary which borrowed Obasanjo and Abiola, two members of International Thief Thief.[97]

The alliance of domestic businesspeople and military rulers was a feature of the NEPDs, which was not mirrored in Ghana, where indigenous business was less influential. Economic nationalism created jobs and opportunities for patronage through the greater official supervision of the economy, and this favoured the educated middle class who were able to get a position in the civil service. While manufacturing had been central to all development programmes in West Africa, retail trade was a key activity reserved for nationals. Until 1966, the language of economic nationalism had been employed by those distant from power, but by 1968 changing governments aimed to increase public support through indigenization, for example, by the NLC and Busia in Ghana.[98] However, such indigenization programmes promoted either the purchase of shares by individuals or the takeover of smaller firms, depending on the sector and the size of the companies. In that sense, they were the opposite of classic economic nationalist demands such as controlling the 'commanding heights of the economy'.[99] They were designed and implemented at a time of significant political instability, and changing groups of policy-makers balanced the need for further investments from foreign investors with immediate needs for income. As corporate archives demonstrate, there continued to be communication and consultation from West African governments.

The foreign companies that were targeted were often not Western multinationals but resident Lebanese and Indians, or indeed other Africans, running at times very small enterprises. Where foreign businesses were targeted, then it was in many cases to obtain an economic rent. Bucheli and Decker compared the nature of expropriation drives across Latin America and Africa during this period and concluded that both the timing and the form of expropriations (nationalizations vs indigenization) were driven by political alliances which optimized the interests of different groups of supporters. This shifted dynamically over time and benefitted from a more permissive international environment and high prices for petroleum and other commodities.[100]

The emergence of new political alliances required additional resources for political patronage. African states have been described as 'gatekeeper states', funding elites through their connection with the international system, regulating access to their territory and extracting payment for this in the form of tariffs, taxes, development aid and bribes. By extending their control over this nexus, they extended their power internally, and for Nigeria, it has been argued that the state-owned and controlled all sources of income.[101]

> As things stand now, the Nigerian state appears to intervene everywhere and to own virtually everything including access to status and wealth. Inevitably a desperate struggle to win control of state power ensues since this control means for all practical purposes being all powerful and owning everything. Politics becomes warfare, a matter of life and death.[102]

While it was indeed possible to capture already sunk investment, the stranglehold on the 'gate', however, risked stopping the further influx of funds. When cocoa and petroleum prices were high, this could be sustained for a time, but as economic growth failed to materialize, the cost of these policies was ultimately too high. States seemed to have overstretched themselves, and the high level of regulation, the political rationale behind the allocation of resources and the ambitious nature of development programmes left most African economies, including Ghana and even oil-rich Nigeria, in a precarious situation by the 1980s. Yet throughout the 1970s, scholars such as Walter Rodney and Samir Amin contested whether development initiatives based on integrating developing countries into the international economy could lead to anything other than dependent development that retained economic subservience to old and new imperial powers. Such dependent development, they argued, engendered entrenched elites who supported the demands of foreign capital and did not defend the national interest.[103]

Alternative interpretations challenged whether indigenization programmes should be understood as global struggles over control of foreign investment or instead as domestic struggles over redistribution, citizenship and indigeneity.[104] The postcolonial transition in Ghana and Nigeria centred on contestations of who was entitled to the resources of postcolonial gatekeeper states. British companies sought to negotiate the best deal for local content requirements, and where domestic shareholding allowed them to repatriate dividends and profits, these deals were often considered reasonable. The British government similarly noted that businesspeople rarely complained about the impact of the indigenization programmes but frequently about foreign exchange controls and expatriate quotas.[105] The latter particularly was a major concern to businesses and even led Barclays to remove its corporate spread eagle logo from its minority-owned Nigerian subsidiary in 1979.[106] Arguably, in situations where foreign investments are no longer wholly-owned subsidiaries and subject to local content legislation, management is central to the issue of control.

4.4 Conclusion

The crisis of legitimacy that theories of economic development experienced had clear consequences for British business. As dependency and neo-colonialism undermined the standing of foreign companies as potential agents of development, economic policies became less favourable in response. In West Africa, this generally took the form of indigenization programmes, which combined forced sales and part-nationalizations. Behind this legislation were, on the one hand, the interests of African businessmen, who sought to have sections of the economy reserved for themselves, and on the other hand, the African governments, which sought to maintain political alliances through redistributive measures tied to economic nationalism.[107]

British companies in Nigeria and Ghana mostly did not interpret indigenization programmes as attempts to take control of their subsidiaries, also because the government showed some leniency to companies (except for banking and oil industry in Nigeria and timber in Ghana, which were singled out for nationalization). Firms were generally more concerned by mounting pressure to speed up the Africanization of subsidiary management. British companies viewed this as a greater challenge to their control over their subsidiaries. This appeared to have been motivated to some extent by the desire to create jobs and career opportunities for supporters. Like economic nationalism elsewhere, the popularity of these policies lays in the direct economic benefits they provided to their political supporters.

What has received significantly less attention in the literature on economic nationalism and expropriation was how adapting to postcolonial transitions required companies to open managerial posts and responsibilities to Africans.

Notes

1 Marcelo Bucheli and Stephanie Decker, "Expropriations of Foreign Property and Political Alliances: A Business Historical Approach," *Enterprise & Society* 22, no. 1 (February 28, 2021): 247–84, https://doi.org/10.1017/eso.2019.66
2 Charles Lipson, *Standing Guard: Protecting Foreign Capitalism in the Nineteenth and Twentieth Century* (Berkeley and London: University of California Press, 1985); Michael Minor, "The Demise of Expropriation as an Instrument of LDC Policy 1980–1992," *Journal of International Business Studies* 25, no. 1 (1994): 177–88, https://doi.org/10.1057/palgrave.jibs.8490850; Stephen J Kobrin, "Testing the Bargaining Hypothesis in the Manufacturing Sector in Developing Countries," *International Organization* 41, no. 4 (1987): 609–38, https://doi.org/10.1017/S0020818300027624; Stephen J Kobrin, "Expropriation as an Attempt to Control Foreign Firms in LDCs: Trends from 1960 to 1979," *International Studies Quarterly* 28, no. 3 (September 1984): 329–48, https://doi.org/10.2307/2600634
3 Julian Wathen, "Reminiscences 1947–1987," 16, Barclays Group Archive (BGA) 1189/1.
4 Directors' Conference, 20. Ghana – Finance, 2 March 1966, Unilever Historical Archives (UHA) UNI/BD/DC.
5 Mr. Pedler, "Ghana – Unilever Policy for the Future," 3 May 1966, p. 136, UHA UNI/SC with TAC.
6 Annual Statement of Accounts, Chairman's Statement, p. 6, 1966, (hereafter Chairman's Statement 1966), Liverpool Records Office (LRO) 380 HOL II.
7 Chairman's Statement 1966, p. 6.
8 Douglas Rimmer, *Staying Poor: Ghana's Political Economy, 1950–1990*, ed. World Bank (Oxford: Pergamon, 1992), 147.
9 IDB Corner, Deputy General Mines Manager, "Notes on meeting," 9. December 1966, and DAR Hanvey, General Mines Manager, "Aide Memoire," 9 December 1966, London Metropolitan Archives (LMA) CLC/B/015/MS14171, vol. 166, Jul–Dec II, 1966.
10 Corner, "Notes," 9 December 1966, LMA CLC/B/015/MS14171, vol. 166.
11 Rimmer, *Staying Poor*, 110, 164.
12 Hanvey, "Notes on Discussions with Colonel Afrifa," 9 December 1966, 1–2, LMA CLC/B/015/MS14171, vol. 166.
13 Thomas J Biersteker, *Multinationals, the State, and the Control of the Nigerian Economy* (Princeton, NJ: Princeton University Press, 1987); Chibuike Ugochukwu Uche, "British Government, British Businesses, and the Indigenization Exercise in Post-Independence Nigeria," *Business History Review* 86, no. 4 (2013): 745–71, https://doi.org/10.1017/S000768051200181X; Ann Genova, "Nigeria's Nationalization of British Petroleum," *The International Journal of African Historical Studies* 43, no. 1 (2010): 115–36, http://www.jstor.org/stable/25741399; John D. Esseks, "Economic Policies," in *Politicians and Soldiers in Ghana 1966–1972*, ed. Dennis Austin and Robin Luckham (London: Frank Cass, 1975), 37–61; JD Esseks, "Government and Indigenous Private Enterprise in Ghana," *The Journal of Modern African Studies*, 1971, http://journals.cambridge.org/abstract_S0022278X00024666; Paul Collins, "The Political Economy of Indigenization: The Case of the Nigerian Enterprises Promotion Decree," *African Review* 4, no. 4 (1974): 491–508; LE Grayson, "The

Promotion of Indigenous Private Enterprise in Ghana," *Journal of Asian and African Studies* 9, no. 1/2 (1974): 17–28.

14 Rimmer, *Staying Poor*, 105, 114, 120, 123, 125–7.

15 Esseks, "Economic Policies," 46–7.

16 ERA Ocansey (Managing Director Service Advertising (Gh) Ltd.) to Ministerial Secretary, Office of Prime Minister, 22.7.71; KS Essah (General Manager & Director Graphics Corp.) and Moses Danquah (Ag. General Manager & Director New Times Ltd.) to RA Quarshie, Minister of Trade, Industry and Tourism, 25 June 1971. As Myles Hagan, the managing director of UAC (Ghana), was on the Advisory Committee, this is probably not surprising. JH Mensah to Editor, Daily Graphic, 19 August 1970; Public Records Administration and Archives Department (PRAAD) RG 6/1/190.

17 Quotation from NLC member in Esseks, "Economic Policies," 50. See also Rimmer, *Staying Poor*, 126; Fiona C Boyd, "Expropriation of Alien Property in International Law: A Study of Recent State Practice Concerning British Nationals" (University of Nottingham, 1988), 62–4.

18 Margaret Peil, "The Expulsion of West African Aliens," *The Journal of Modern African Studies* 9, no. 2 (1971): 205, https://doi.org/10.1017/S0022278X00024903

19 Esseks, "Economic Policies," 47–8. Ghana Enterprise Promotion Decree, p. 5; Ruoff, Mines Secretary, to General Mines Manager, "Monthly Report for November 1969," LMA CLC/B/015/MS14171, vol. 182, November–December 1969.

20 "Financing under the Ghanaian Business (Promotion) Act," n.d., PRAAD RG 6/1/190; Esseks, 50–1.

21 Rimmer, *Staying Poor*, xi, 101, 134; P Nugent, *Africa since Independence* (Basingstoke: Palgrave Macmillan, 2002), 213.

22 Rimmer, *Staying Poor*, 164–5.

23 Interview with Reg Dines, Hugh Norris and John Woodcock (Barclays Bank DCO), 17 August 2001.

24 For example, the Aid to Pioneer Industries Ordinance of 1951 and the 1958 Tax Relief Act. Biersteker, *Multinationals*, 53–4.

25 Biersteker, *Multinationals*, 73–4, 82.

26 David Kenneth Fieldhouse, *Merchant Capital and Economic Decolonisation: The United Africa Company 1929–1987* (Oxford: Clarendon, 1994), 474.

27 In May 1972 the government announced the acquisition of 60 per cent in the Port Harcourt refinery, followed by an agreement in July 1973 to take 35 per cent of the Shell-BP concession, with an option to increase this to 51 per cent, which was extended in 1974 (in line with developments in other OPEC countries) to a government share of 51 per cent in all major producers (BP-Shell, Agip, SAFRAP, Gulf, Mobil). BP's share was subsequently nationalized in 1979 in a political move over Rhodesia, and compensation was agreed in 1981. Boyd, "Expropriation of Alien Property," 81–4.

28 Biersteker, *Multinationals*, 97–8, 144–54.

29 Biersteker, 145. See also Collins, "The Political Economy of Indigenization," 505–6. Cases like the Ibru group of companies who acquired many indigenized firms and others can be found in Tom Forrest, *The Advance of African Capital. The Growth of Nigerian Private Enterprise* (Edinburgh, 1994).

30 Biersteker, *Multinationals*, 159–98.

31 Ankie Hoogvelt, "Indigenisation and Foreign Capital: Industrialisation in Nigeria," *Review of African Political Economy* 14 (1979): 57, 61.

32 Adeoye A. Akinsanya, *The Expropriation of Multinational Property in the Third World* (New York: Praeger, 1980); Kobrin, "Expropriation as an Attempt to Control"; Leslie L. Rood, "Nationalisation and Indigenisation in Africa," *Journal*

of Modern African Studies 14, no. 03 (1976): 427–47, https://doi.org/10.1017/S0022278X00053507; Chibuike Uche, "Oil, British Interests and the Nigerian Civil War," *Journal of African History* 49, no. 1 (2008): 111–35, https://doi.org/10.1017/S0021853708003393; Uche, "British Government, British Businesses, and the Indigenization Exercise in Post-Independence Nigeria"; Leslie L Rood, "The Impact of Nationalisation," *The Journal of Modern African Studies* 15, no. 3 (1977): 489–94, https://doi.org/10.1017/S0022278X00002081

33 Collins, "The Political Economy of Indigenization," 491, 501–2, 504–5; Biersteker, *Multinationals*, 284–99.

34 DCO Board Minutes, No. 14, 254. Nigeria, 27 March 1969, p. 94, and 589. Formation of Local Companies, 20 November 1969, p. 224, BGA 38/516.

35 Barclays was nationalized in Tanzania in 1969. Compensation was paid below a realistic market price but at a ratio that would later become the basis for negotiations in other nationalization cases. Margaret. Ackrill and Leslie. Hannah, *Barclays: The Business of Banking, 1690–1996* (Cambridge, UK: Cambridge University Press, 2001), 291.

36 J Crossley to F Seebohm, 17 December 1969, BGA 80/5839.

37 W Duncan, "Memorandum, 21 November 1968, Strictly Confidential: Future of Bank" and W Duncan to the General Managers, "Nigeria – A Plan for the Future," n.d., (hereafter Duncan, "Nigeria"), BGA 80/5318.

38 Duncan, "Nigeria," 1, BGA 80/5318.

39 Memo Nigeria, 24 March 1969, BGA 11/947.

40 "Minutes of the extraordinary general meeting of the company decision for conversion to a public company and to issue shares," 7 July 1969, p. 1–2, BGA 11/931.

41 Andrew Cohen, "Lonrho and the Limits of Corporate Power in Africa, c. 1961–1973," *South African Historical Journal* 68, no. 1, SI (2016): 31–49, https://doi.org/10.1080/02582473.2015.1118878; Chibuike Ugochukwu Uche, "Lonrho in Africa: The Unacceptable Face of Capitalism or the Ugly Face of Neo-Colonialism?," *Enterprise and Society* 16, no. 2 (2015): 354–80, https://doi.org/10.1017/eso.2014.31

42 Minutes of Special Committee, No. U.A. 47, 7. Participation, 2.2.1971, pp. 1–2, UHA UNI/SC with UAC (hereafter: Special Committee, "Participation").

43 Biersteker, *Multinationals*, 221–4, 238.

44 The last point refers to the pervasive control of remittances by governments that was introduced due to the balance of payments difficulties. Many states handled this power discriminately, preventing the remittance of dividends, i.e., the share of profits to be paid out to shareholders abroad. This in effect meant that local shareholders received their dividends whereas those abroad did not, hence the reference to a double standard. Special Committee, "Participation."

45 Lonrho Ltd. Report and Accounts, No. 64, 1972, 8 May 73, Lonrho Minutes 1972, Churchill College Cambridge (CCC) SPRS 1/209.

46 The government also had the option to acquire a further 20 per cent at the price of £1 per share. Opening statement by the Chairman of the Government Negotiating team, Negotiations between representatives of the government of Ghana and representatives of AGC in respect of a proposed joint venture, 21 August 1971, p. 1, Lonrho Minutes 1972, CCC SPRS 1/209 (hereafter AGC, "Opening Statement").

47 Minutes of Meeting between AGC management and Ghana Mines' Employees' Union, 20 March 1969, Ms 14,171, vol. 179, May–June 1969. On the Lonrho takeover and subsequent events see Cronje, Ling and Cronje, *Lonrho*, 54–66. Miners became increasingly disaffected in the late 1960s, see Jeff Crisp, "Union Atrophy and Worker Revolt: Labour Protest at Tarkwa Goldfields, Ghana, 1968–1969," *Canadian Journal of African Studies/Revue Canadienne Des Études*

Africaines 13, no. 1–2 (January 1979): 265, 267–93, https://doi.org/10.1080/00083968.1979.10803942
48 AGC, "Opening Statement."
49 AGC, "Opening Statement."
50 White paper on government participation in the mining industry, p. 6, n.d., Lonrho Minutes 1972 (hereafter Lonrho Minutes 1972), CCC SPRS 1/209.
51 Lonrho Minutes 1972, p. 6.
52 Lonrho Minutes 1972, pp. 2, 6.
53 Lonrho group budget operating results, three months ending 31 December 1972, Major General Spears at the board meeting on 22 February 1973, Lonrho Minutes 1972, CCC SPRS 1/209.
54 Minutes of Special Committee with United Africa Group, 7. Ghana, 20.2.73, UHA UNI/SC with UAC International.
55 Minutes of Directors' Conference, extract, 544. UACI – Timber interests, 2 November 1973, UHA UNI/SC with UAC International.
56 Extract from Minutes of Directors' Conference, 10 January 1976 and 5 December 1975, UHA UNI/SC with UAC International.
57 Rimmer, *Staying Poor*, 165–66; Naomi H Chazan, *An Anatomy of Ghanaian Politics: Managing Political Recession 1969–1982* (Boulder, CO: Westview Press, 1983), 169.
58 Thomas Callaghy, "Lost between State and Market," in *Economic Crisis and Policy Choice: The Politics of Adjustment in the Third World*, ed. Joan Nelson (Princeton: Princeton University Press, 1990), 257–319; Chazan, *An Anatomy of Ghanaian Politics*.
59 Fieldhouse, *Merchant Capital*, 466–7.
60 Report "Indigenization and Nationalization in Nigeria," n.d. [presumably 24 October 1972], The National Archives (TNA) FCO 65/1222.
61 PJ Roberts to AC Hall, British High Commissioner, Lagos, 19 December 1972, TNA FCO 65/1222 [hereafter Roberts to Hall, 19 December 1972].
62 Roberts to Hall, 19 December 1972.
63 Roberts to Hall, 19 December 1972.
64 Biersteker, *Multinationals*, 119.
65 Minutes of Special Committee, No. U.A. 70, 16. Nigerian Enterprise Promotion Decree, 4 April 1972; Minutes of Special Committee, No. U.A. 73, 27. Five Year Plan, 16 May 1972; UHA UNI/SC with Unilever International.
66 Minutes of Special Committee with UAC International, No. UA 92, 2. Nigerian Participation, 10 January 1974, UHA UNI/SC with UAC International.
67 AC Hall to J Wilson and JW McMeekin, 15 December 1972, TNA FCO 65/1222.
68 Extract from Directors' Conference, 1 March 1974; Extract from Directors' Conference, 15 March 1974; UHA UNI/SC with UAC International.
69 Minutes of Special Committee, No. UA 100, 26. Nigerian Enterprises Promotion Decree, 9 July 1974, UHA UNI/SC with UAC International (hereafter Special Committee, 9 July 1974); Fieldhouse, *Merchant Capital*, 656.
70 Special Committee, 9 July 1974.
71 Extract of Directors' Committee, 346 UACI – Nigerian Participation, 12 July 1974, UHA UNI/SC with UAC International.
72 Fieldhouse, *Merchant Capital*, 658.
73 Barclay Bank International board minutes, 13 May 1971, p. 9; 10 June 1971, pp. 24–5; 26 August 1971, p. 71; 13 April 1972, p. 217, Vol. 15, BGA 38/517.
74 Minutes of Special Committee, No. U. A. 124, 20. Ghana – Local Participation, 24 August 1976, p. 2, UHA UNI/SC with UAC International.
75 Geoffrey Jones, *Renewing Unilever. Transformation and Tradition* (Oxford: Oxford University Press, 2005), 79, 193–4; Fieldhouse, *Merchant Capital*, 620, 718, 721, 762, 774.

76 Biersteker, *Multinationals*, 198.
77 Special Committee, No. U.A. 123, 13 July 1976, UHA UNI/SC with UAC International. Biersteker, 290.
78 Special Committee, No. U.A. 125, 26. Nigeria, 7 September 1976, pp. 4–5, UHA UNI/SC with UAC International.
79 Biersteker, *Multinationals*, 192–3, 197, 220, 245–83; Fiona C Beveridge, "Taking Control of Foreign Investment: A Case Study of Indigenisation in Nigeria," *The International and Comparative Law Quarterly* April (1991): 320–1.
80 Biersteker, *Multinationals*, 290–1, 295–6.
81 Collins, "The Political Economy of Indigenization."
82 Frederick Cooper, "Africa and the World Economy," *African Studies Review* 24, no. 2/3 (1981): 1–86.
83 For a comparison to Latin America, see Bucheli and Decker, "Expropriations." For a discussion of economic nationalism in Canada, see Albert Breton, "The Economics of Nationalism," *The Journal of Political Economy* 72, no. 4 (1964): 376–86. For a comparison of economic nationalism in different contexts, see Harry Gordon Johnson, *Economic Nationalism in Old and New States, A Publication of the Committee for the Comparative Study of New Nations, University of Chicago* (London: Allen & Unwin, 1968).
84 Bucheli and Decker, "Expropriations."
85 Esseks, "Economic Policies," 48.
86 G Finlayson to KT Hall, 13 October 1972, TNA FCO 65/1222. Biersteker, *Multinationals*, 54–5; Boyd, "Expropriation of Alien Property," 178; Esseks, "Economic Policies," 50.
87 Minutes of the Special Committee and Directors' Conference of Unilever, 19 April 1974, UHA UNI/SC with UAC International.
88 PJ Roberts, file note on "Indigenous Businessmen's Seminar, Lagos, 28–29 September 1972," 5 October 1972, TNA FCO 65/1222.
89 Biersteker, *Multinationals*, 298–9; Boyd, "Expropriation of Alien Property," 186–90.
90 Uche, "Oil, British Interests and the Nigerian Civil War"; Uche, "British Government, British Businesses, and the Indigenization Exercise"; Uche, "Lonrho in Africa."
91 Stephanie Decker, "Less than an Empire and More than British: Foreign Investor Competition in Ghana and Nigeria in the 1960s," in *Imagining Britain's Economic Future, c.1800–1975: Trade, Consumerism and Global Markets*, ed. David Thackeray, Andrew Thompson, and Richard Toye (London: Palgrave, 2018), 183–203, https://www.palgrave.com/gb/book/9783319712963
92 UN Commission on Transnational Corporations, *Transnational Corporations in World Development – Third Survey* (UN Doc. ST/CTC/46, 1983), para 179.
93 Biersteker, *Multinationals*, 288. He refers specifically to an advisory committee set up on the initiative of KO Mbadiwe, federal minister of commerce and industry, in 1959, see pp. 53–5.
94 Peter J Burnell, *Economic Nationalism in the Third World* (Brighton: Wheatsheaf, 1986), 12–14; Independent Commission on International Development Issues, *North-South: A Programme for Survival: Report of the Commission* (London: Pan, 1980).
95 Obafemi Awolowo, *The Path to Economic Freedom in Developing Countries: A Lecture Delivered at the University of Lagos on 15 March 1968, Annual Lectures 1* (Ibadan, Nigeria: University of Lagos, 1968), 4–5.
96 Biersteker, *Multinationals*, 266, 280, 285; Harry Gordon Johnson, "A Theoretical Model of Economic Nationalism in New and Developing States," in *Economic*

Nationalism in Old and New States, ed. Harry Gordon Johnson (London: George Allen and Unwin, 1967), 1–16; Breton, "The Economics of Nationalism."

97 Fela Kuti, *ITT*, 1979. Translated lyrics from http://kalakutarepublic.free.fr/english/songs/itt.htm [accessed 7 March 2005].

98 Esseks, "Government and Indigenous Private Enterprise in Ghana," 26.

99 D Yergin and J Stanislaw, *The Commanding Heights: The Battle for the World Economy* (New York NY: Simon, 2002).

100 Bucheli and Decker, "Expropriations."

101 Jean-Francois Bayart, *The State in Africa: The Politics of the Belly* (London: Longman, 1993), 25; Frederick Cooper, *Africa since 1940: The Past of the Present* (Cambridge, UK, and New York, NY: Cambridge University Press, 2002).

102 Claude Ake, "Presidential Address to the 1981 Conference of the Nigerian Political Science Association," in West Africa, 25 May 1981, p. 1163.

103 Samir Amin, "Unequal Development: An Essay on the Social Formations of Peripheral Capitalism," *Science & Society* 42, no. 2 (1978): 219–22, https://doi.org/10.2307/532256; Walter Rodney, *How Europe Underdeveloped Africa* (London, UK, and Dar-Es-Salaam, Tanzania: Bogle-L'Overture And Tanzania Publishing House, 1972), https://doi.org/10.2307/484037

104 Biersteker, *Multinationals*; Collins, "The Political Economy of Indigenization"; Ronald Aminzade, "From Race to Citizenship: The Indigenization Debate in Post-Socialist Tanzania," *Studies in Comparative International Development* 38, no. 1 (2003): 43–63, https://doi.org/10.1007/BF02686322

105 AC Hall, British High Commission, Lagos, to JW McMeekin, Foreign and Commonwealth Office, West Africa Department, London, n.d. [27 July 1972]; PJ Roberts to AC Hall, 19 December 1972; TNA FCO 65/1222.

106 The equity in the Nigerian branches was not divested in 1986 as stated in the corporate history, but in the late 1980s as part of the group's strategy to reduce or divest minority holdings overseas. Information supplied by Nicholas Webb, Barclays Group Archive. Ackrill and Hannah, *Barclays*, 268–326.

107 Bucheli and Decker, "Expropriations"; Collins, "The Political Economy of Indigenization."

List of References

Ackrill, Margaret, and Leslie Hannah. *Barclays: The Business of Banking, 1690–1996.* Cambridge, UK: Cambridge University Press, 2001.

Akinsanya, Adeoye A. *The Expropriation of Multinational Property in the Third World.* New York: Praeger, 1980.

Amin, Samir. "Unequal Development: An Essay on the Social Formations of Peripheral Capitalism." *Science & Society* 42, no. 2 (1978): 219–22. 10.2307/532256

Aminzade, Ronald. "From Race to Citizenship: The Indigenization Debate in Post-Socialist Tanzania." *Studies in Comparative International Development* 38, no. 1 (2003): 43–63. 10.1007/BF02686322

Awolowo, Obafemi. *The Path to Economic Freedom in Developing Countries: A Lecture Delivered at the University of Lagos on 15 March 1968, Annual Lectures 1.* Ibadan, Nigeria: University of Lagos, 1968.

Bayart, Jean-Francois. *The State in Africa: The Politics of the Belly*. London: Longman, 1993.

Beveridge, Fiona C (neé Boyd). "Taking Control of Foreign Investment: A Case Study of Indigenisation in Nigeria." *The International and Comparative Law Quarterly* April (1991): 302–33.

Biersteker, Thomas J. *Multinationals, the State, and the Control of the Nigerian Economy*. Princeton, NJ: Princeton University Press, 1987.

Boyd, Fiona C. *Expropriation of Alien Property in International Law: A Study of Recent State Practice Concerning British Nationals*. University of Nottingham, 1988.

Breton, Albert. "The Economics of Nationalism." *The Journal of Political Economy* 72, no. 4 (1964): 376–86.

Bucheli, Marcelo, and Stephanie Decker. "Expropriations of Foreign Property and Political Alliances: A Business Historical Approach." *Enterprise & Society* 22, no. 1 (February 28, 2021): 247–84. 10.1017/eso.2019.66

Burnell, Peter J. *Economic Nationalism in the Third World*. Brighton: Wheatsheaf, 1986.

Callaghy, Thomas. "Lost between State and Market: The Politics of Economic Adjustment in Ghana, Zambia, and Nigeria." In *Economic Crisis and Policy Choice: The Politics of Adjustment in the Third World*, edited by Joan Nelson, 257–319. Princeton: Princeton University Press, 1990.

Chazan, Naomi H. *An Anatomy of Ghanaian Politics: Managing Political Recession 1969–1982*. Boulder, CO: Westview Press, 1983.

Cohen, Andrew. "Lonrho and the Limits of Corporate Power in Africa, c. 1961–1973." *South African Historical Journal* 68, no. 1, SI (2016): 31–49. 10.1080/02582473.2015.1118878

Collins, Paul. "The Political Economy of Indigenization: The Case of the Nigerian Enterprises Promotion Decree." *African Review* 4, no. 4 (1974): 491–508.

Cooper, Frederick. "Africa and the World Economy." *African Studies Review* 24, no. 2/3 (1981): 1–86.

Cooper, Frederick. *Africa since 1940: The Past of the Present*. Cambridge, UK, and New York, NY: Cambridge University Press, 2002.

Crisp, Jeff. "Union Atrophy and Worker Revolt: Labour Protest at Tarkwa Goldfields, Ghana, 1968–1969." *Canadian Journal of African Studies/Revue Canadienne Des Études Africaines* 13, no. 1–2 (January 1979): 265–93. 10.1080/00083968.1979.10803942

Decker, Stephanie. "Less than an Empire and More than British: Foreign Investor Competition in Ghana and Nigeria in the 1960s." In *Imagining Britain's Economic Future, c.1800–1975: Trade, Consumerism and Global Markets*, edited by David Thackeray, Andrew Thompson, and Richard Toye, 183–203. London: Palgrave, 2018. https://www.palgrave.com/gb/book/9783319712963

Esseks, J.D. "Government and Indigenous Private Enterprise in Ghana." *The Journal of Modern African Studies*, 1971. http://journals.cambridge.org/abstract_S0022278X00024666

Esseks, John D. "Economic Policies." In *Politicians and Soldiers in Ghana 1966–1972*, edited by Dennis Austin and Robin Luckham, 37–61. London: Frank Cass, 1975.

Fieldhouse, David Kenneth. *Merchant Capital and Economic Decolonisation: The United Africa Company 1929–1987*. Oxford: Clarendon, 1994.

Forrest, Tom. *The Advance of African Capital. The Growth of Nigerian Private Enterprise*. Edinburgh, 1994.

Genova, Ann. "Nigeria's Nationalization of British Petroleum." *The International Journal of African Historical Studies* 43, no. 1 (2010): 115–36. http://www.jstor.org/stable/25741399

Grayson, L.E. "The Promotion of Indigenous Private Enterprise in Ghana." *Journal of Asian and African Studies* 9, no. 1/2 (1974): 17–28.

Hoogvelt, Ankie. "Indigenisation and Foreign Capital: Industrialisation in Nigeria." *Review of African Political Economy* 14 (1979): 56–68.

Independent Commission on International Development Issues. *North-South: A Programme for Survival: Report of the Commission*. London: Pan, 1980.

Johnson, Harry Gordon. "A Theoretical Model of Economic Nationalism in New and Developing States." In *Economic Nationalism in Old and New States*, edited by Harry Gordon Johnson, 1–16. London: George Allen and Unwin, 1967.

Johnson, Harry Gordon. *Economic Nationalism in Old and New States. A Publication of the Committee for the Comparative Study of New Nations, University of Chicago*. London: Allen & Unwin, 1968.

Jones, Geoffrey. *Renewing Unilever. Transformation and Tradition*. Oxford: Oxford University Press, 2005.

Kobrin, Stephen J. "Expropriation as an Attempt to Control Foreign Firms in LDCs: Trends from 1960 to 1979." *International Studies Quarterly* 28, no. 3 (September 1984): 329–48. 10.2307/2600634

Kobrin, Stephen J. "Testing the Bargaining Hypothesis in the Manufacturing Sector in Developing Countries." *International Organization* 41, no. 4 (1987): 609–38. 10.1017/S0020818300027624

Lipson, Charles. *Standing Guard: Protecting Foreign Capitalism in the Nineteenth and Twentieth Century*. Berkeley and London: University of California Press, 1985.

Minor, Michael. "The Demise of Expropriation as an Instrument of LDC Policy 1980–1992." *Journal of International Business Studies* 25, no. 1 (1994): 177–88. 10.1057/palgrave.jibs.8490850

Nugent, P *Africa since Independence*. Basingstoke: Palgrave Macmillan, 2002.

Peil, Margaret. "The Expulsion of West African Aliens." *The Journal of Modern African Studies* 9, no. 2 (11 August 1971): 205. 10.1017/S0022278X00024903

Rimmer, Douglas. *Staying Poor: Ghana's Political Economy, 1950–1990*. Edited by World Bank. Oxford: Pergamon, 1992.

Rodney, Walter. *How Europe Underdeveloped Africa*. London, UK, and Dar-Es-Salaam, Tanzania: Bogle-L'Overture And Tanzania Publishing House, 1972. 10.2307/484037.

Rood, Leslie L. "Nationalisation and Indigenisation in Africa." *Journal of Modern African Studies* 14, no. 03 (1976): 427–47. 10.1017/S0022278X00053507

Rood, Leslie L. "The Impact of Nationalisation." *The Journal of Modern African Studies* 15, no. 3 (1977): 489–94. 10.1017/S0022278X00002081

Uche, Chibuike. "Oil, British Interests and the Nigerian Civil War." *Journal of African History* 49, no. 1 (2008): 111–35. 10.1017/S0021853708003393

Uche, Chibuike Ugochukwu. "British Government, British Businesses, and the Indigenization Exercise in Post-Independence Nigeria." *Business History Review* 86, no. 4 (2013): 745–71. 10.1017/S000768051200181X

Uche, Chibuike Ugochukwu. "Lonrho in Africa: The Unacceptable Face of Capitalism or the Ugly Face of Neo-Colonialism?" *Enterprise and Society* 16, no. 2 (2015): 354–80. 10.1017/eso.2014.31

Yergin, D, and J Stanislaw. *The Commanding Heights: The Battle for the World Economy*. New York NY: Simon, 2002.

Part II

Managing Postcolonial Transitions Internally

5 Africanization in Companies and the Civil Service

British business had successfully expanded under expatriate management during colonial times. Why did companies decide to follow the example of the British colonial administration and Africanize their senior staff in West Africa? Working with expatriates had several advantages for business: through the homeward passage, British managers were dependent on their employers; managers shared a common background and education and normally lived together in company housing.[1] Europeans were partly favoured because they had the requisite skills but also because of ingrained racism. Relying on expatriate staff, however, had its drawbacks, too: their salaries and accommodation costs were expensive, collusion between them against the interests of the company was hard to detect, their understanding of local conditions was limited, and they were less likely to identify and develop new business opportunities. Criticism of expatriates' affluence and of foreign control over the economy grew substantially after World War II when Africans gained a political voice that they had been denied previously. The response of British multinationals was determined by political events beyond West Africa and was part of an international strategy to create and maintain local goodwill in order to counter the rising economic nationalism in less developed host countries. Moreover, it was important to find ways of reducing the cost of foreign operations at a time when many companies were increasing their expenditure through expansion, investments and redeployment.

In the literature on West Africa, decolonization attracts a great deal of interest, whereas Africanization, both corporate and public, is often only treated in passing. Both Sarah Stockwell and Josephine Milburn treat corporate Africanization as a business strategy for decolonization, whereas Michael Burawoy connects it to Zambian independence.[2] Nevertheless, Stockwell remarks on CAST that Africanization there was 'largely a post-independence phenomenon'.[3] While the merchant companies were faster in giving responsibility to Africans, the process was not complete at independence. Even the civil services in West Africa were not fully Africanized at independence (apart from Nigeria's Western region). There is ample evidence that the Colonial Office regarded it as a way to showcase

DOI: 10.4324/9781003001058-7

its goodwill and regain the initiative.[4] In a similar way to the governments, British business sought to improve its local image by highlighting its commitment to the training and promotion of African staff, although few went as far as the UAC in regularly publishing its figures.[5]

This chapter compares the different rates of Africanization between the private and public sectors and among different companies. Although a convenient public relations tool, the advancement of local staff encountered internal resistance and created some unforeseen problems. Overall, administrative and corporate Africanization are generally portrayed as parallel or connected processes, but they have not been compared systematically. This chapter provides a brief overview of the central features of the changes in the public service in order to provide a benchmark for comparison with business. While both faced similar conditions, differences emerge between the public and private sectors and among companies. To explain those, the final part of the chapter addresses issues that affected the course of Africanization.

5.1 Why Africanize?

During the nineteenth century, Africans and Europeans had collaborated on an almost equal footing, and many administrative posts in West Africa were occupied by locals.[6] European attitudes underwent a noticeable change in the 1880s when colonial expansion intensified because of European rivalries and the rise of racism. While Africans were still employed by the administration and businesses, their promotion was increasingly obstructed, and they suffered from discrimination and abuse. Throughout the first half of the twentieth century, Africans were effectively barred from high-ranking positions, and despite renewed attempts from the late 1920s onwards to recruit more West Africans to the higher services, they still faced widespread racism.[7] IF Nicolson, a former British civil servant in Nigeria, somewhat naively remarked that it was 'something of a mystery' that only a few Nigerians reached senior ranks and cites the gradual estrangement between educated locals and foreign administration, rather than overt policy, as a cause. The Nigerian historian GO Olusanya, however, attributes it to pervasive racism. Nicolson's own description of the situation arguably vindicates Olusanya's view:

> There are many examples [...] of Africans tried out in senior posts, turning out unsatisfactory work, being warned and reprimanded, reacting in despair with lengthy protests and petitions alleging victimisation because of race, and [...] having thus added breaches of decorum to errors of judgement [...].[8]

This indicated that complaints by Africans were not favourably considered because they were 'bad style', possibly even a sign of irresponsibility and an attempt to shift the blame, rather than attempts at raising genuine concerns.

World War II changed attitudes significantly. In the public sector, finance was restricted, and the supply of qualified expatriates from the United Kingdom came to a halt. This alone does not explain why Africanization progressed decisively after the war when manpower became available again. The war had changed attitudes because racism became less acceptable, as West Africans had fought for Britain and because British imperialism had to prove its good intentions to the anti-imperialist superpowers (not to mention distancing itself from the Nazi racism driving the Holocaust). Advances in the civil service were at first slow but speeded up considerably once international pressure was combined with the nationalist challenge in the colonies. As constitutional devolution gathered speed, it became clear that the British colonial administration would leave soon, accelerating Africanization even more. The next section will outline the progress of Africanization in the civil service.

The following section focuses on the UAC as the British company that advanced fastest in terms of Africanization and published the most data on its progress. British business was not subject to the same pressures as the civil service and its political leaders. International opinion, for example, only turned against multinationals in developing countries in the 1970s. Most importantly, foreign companies intended to stay beyond independence. Although British managers had concerns about the trustworthiness of African employees, the rise of nationalism and popular criticism of the firms in West Africa led principals to slowly Africanize the lower managerial ranks as part of a wider strategy to ensure local goodwill. Corporate Africanization nevertheless remained slow. Files indicate a vicious circle based on the low expectations that British managers had of African staff performance, which was fuelled further by the insecure position of African managers. A similar argument has been made by the sociologist Burawoy for Zambianisation in the private copper mines, where expatriates had a low opinion of African staff, so they withdrew responsibilities and discretionary powers from new managers, thus undermining the successors' confidence.[9] Hence management assumptions about the unsuitability of recruits created conditions that made it harder for new managers to perform well.

5.1.1 The civil service

Africanization was not entirely new for the civil service. During the volatile 1920s, from both a financial and a personnel perspective, it became prudent to recruit a greater proportion of staff locally. Expatriates were costly, and government revenues were tight. Moreover, British recruits preferred the more prestigious Indian Civil Service over West Africa, which had a reputation for being unhealthy and badly paid.[10] Both Nigeria and the Gold Coast experienced their first Africanization drives, mainly enforced by their respective Governors, Sir Hugh Clifford (1918–1925) and Sir Gordon Guggisberg (1919–1929).

In the 1920s, Guggisberg's attempts showed results while he was still in office, but with his departure, further Africanization ceased.

While Guggisberg had drawn up a plan that projected further increases, Clifford's approach in Nigeria was more informal. He insisted that heads of departments repeatedly examine their staff with a view to substituting Africans for Europeans, and the rank that would only be filled with expatriates was set slightly higher in 1925. Nigeria's percentage of African civil servants was even worse than that of the Gold Coast: by 1945, only 75 Africans worked in the senior civil service with c. 1,300 expatriates (5.7 per cent), whereas in the Gold Coast, it was 89 to 960 respectively in 1946 (9.3 per cent).[11] Although this was only the beginning of the Africanization process, these figures illustrate just how small the number of Africans promoted actually was and how little this impacted the wider population.

It was also in the Gold Coast that the first Africans were appointed to the governor's executive council and to the administrative service as Assistant District Commissioners in 1942. This precedent forced the Nigerian governor to follow suit a year later with the appointment of three unofficial members to the executive council, two of whom were Nigerians. Moreover, the first two Nigerians entered the senior service in the Secretariat, but a Sierra Leonean had already been appointed earlier in Nigeria.[12] While this study uses Africanization as a general term to describe this process of replacing expatriates with African staff, the decolonizing countries preferred to think of Ghanaianization or Nigerianization because the policy of West African governments was not to employ any black Africans but their own nationals.

While Africanization in both countries was in some ways similar, the nature of politics and the availability of skilled manpower meant that some noticeable differences existed. Ghana was slightly more Africanized at the end of the war and tended to move somewhat faster than its larger neighbour (Figure 5.1).

In 1951 the CPP won the election in the Gold Coast, and Kwame Nkrumah became the 'junior partner' of the colonial government. In July 1953, Nkrumah announced the continued necessity of expatriates in the civil service in future years, followed a year later by an endorsement of their special privileges. This occurred despite general criticism of the slow rate of Africanization and demands for the immediate and complete removal of all European civil servants in the early 1950s.[14] At independence, further pressure from the CPP rank-and-file led Nkrumah to accelerate the rate of replacement of the 1,204 expatriates, the majority of whom were entitled to pensions. This was followed in 1963 by a parliamentary debate on Africanization, which revealed that in the previous year, only 39 Europeans remained.[15]

While Nigerianization was somewhat slower than Ghanaianization, this reflected the generally less developed economy of Nigeria with its lower per capita income and poorer education provision. Nigeria also lacked one national political party, which could be built up as a successor, and instead

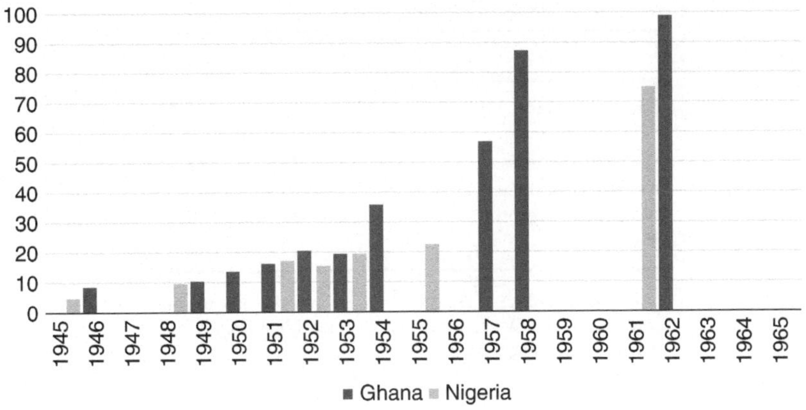

Figure 5.1 Percentage of Africans in the senior civil service, 1945–1962.

Note: For years that data could be found.[13]

saw regional and ethnic rivalries emerge in the form of party politics. Between these parties, there were differences over the terms and rate of Africanization, which the colonial government addressed by creating federal regions.

The federal structure of Nigeria makes it difficult to compare figures with Ghana, as most trained Nigerian civil servants were transferred to the regional services, so the number of Africans in the administration was lower in 1955 than in 1953, as figures after 1954 normally refer to the federal service. In colonial times, the Muslim North had rejected Western education through Christian mission schools and was governed, through indirect rule, by Emirs. This meant that the African civil servants working in the North were normally Christians, either Creole from Sierra Leone or the Gold Coast or Southern Nigerian. Northern Nigeria considered the faster development of the South as a threat and preferred an administration staffed by British expatriates. Instead of Nigerianizing, they aimed to Northernize the civil service. Hence at independence, the Northern region had made the least progress in replacing expatriate civil servants (Table 5.1). Although the Western and Eastern regions preferred recruits from their own regions, they focused more on Nigerianization as they competed to have the first fully local-staffed service; hence they employed positive discrimination for new appointments under the supervision of nationalist politicians. The Western region won this race by replacing all remaining British staff in 1960.[16] Despite the political rationale behind rapid Africanization, expatriates continued to play a role in West African administrations, particularly through the development effort, which even led to further overseas recruitment after independence by Ghana and Nigeria. It was not until the mid-1960s that most expatriate civil servants departed.

Table 5.1 Percentage of Nigerians in the senior civil service: 1954, 1960

	1954	*1960*
Unitary Service	17	
Federal Service		57
Western Region		82
Eastern Region		80
Northern Region		28
Total	17	62

Note: Presumably, these percentages include officers on contract, as the Western regional service Nigerianized the remaining top positions in 1960.[17]

5.1.2 UAC and the West African governments

Businesses were, such as the civil service, under significant nationalist pressure to Africanize their staff, but as the focus of West African decolonization had shifted decisively towards political control, foreign companies could afford to be slower – even had to be slower due to manpower constraints, as the staffing of government offices was considered more important. Commercial companies were also less likely than the civil service to lower standards to speed up Africanization due to concerns over profitability if insufficiently qualified personnel were appointed.[18] It is only the UAC that can reasonably be compared to the civil service because of its size, its publication of comprehensive data and its relatively fast Africanization. Nevertheless, the government employed many more senior civil servants than business employed managers (Figures 5.3 and 5.4). In 1949 in the Gold Coast, the government employed four times (c. 1,200) more senior personnel than the UAC (286), and in Nigeria in 1951, the company had a mixed managerial staff of 634, compared to the government's 3,679 (although at the time many vacancies in the civil service could not be filled) (Figure 5.2).

The Africanization rates of the UAC were initially better than those of the civil service. In 1949, the UAC was leading the government with 20 per cent vis-à-vis 10 per cent, but by 1952, UAC's ratio decreased to 17 per cent, while the government's doubled to 20 per cent. Two years later, the civil service had clearly improved, 35.8 per cent compared to the UAC's 19 per cent. Milburn omits this in her comparison of official and private figures, giving a more favourable impression of corporate progress, even though this information was available to her.[20] The ratio of Africans rose to 56.8 per cent in 1957, the year of independence, compared to 25 per cent at UAC. In 1962, the last year for which both figures are available, the senior civil service was Ghanaianized to 98.8 per cent and UAC's management to 39.9 per cent.

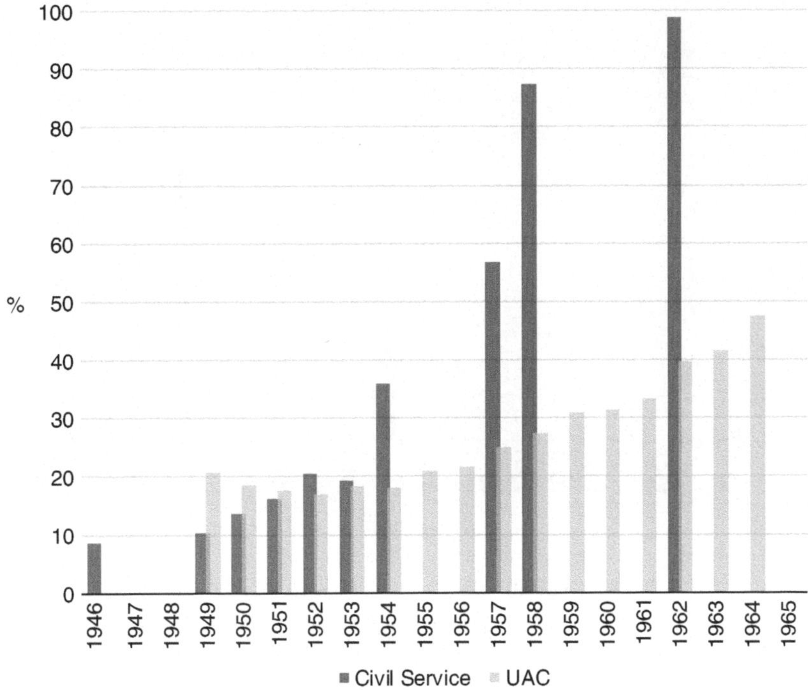

Figure 5.2 Percentage of Ghanaians in the senior civil service and UAC management.

Note: For years that data is available. Reproduced with kind permission of Unilever plc and group companies.[19]

In Nigeria, the civil service also pulled ahead from what appears to have been a relatively similar starting point: in 1948, it had 9.8 per cent of its senior staff Africanized (although this excludes unfilled positions and, if these are taken into account, the ratio falls to 6.5 per cent), against 8.6 per cent for the UAC in 1949. By 1951 government was leading with 17 per cent as opposed to 9.3 per cent at the UAC. In 1955, the federal service, after having ceded many senior servants to the regions, pushed the ratio up to 22.4 per cent in comparison to the company's 12.8 per cent. The last comparable figures are for 1961 (59 per cent government) and 26.3 per cent for the UAC.[22] Overall, in both the civil service and the UAC, the proportion of African managers was higher in Ghana than in Nigeria (Figures 5.3 and 5.4).

Ghana Africanized faster than Nigeria in both the civil service and business. While the UAC originally employed a similar percentage of Africans in senior positions, the civil service pulled ahead decisively in the mid-1950s. The next section compares the different companies and sectors and seeks explanations for the differences between them.

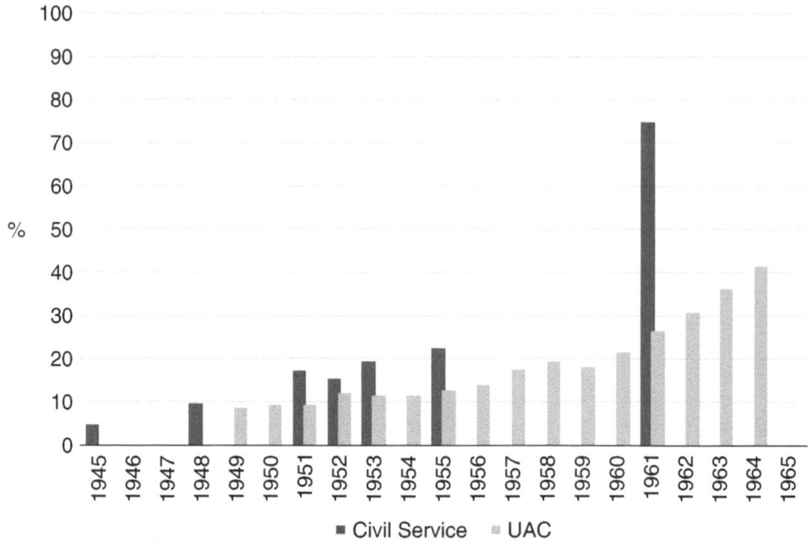

Figure 5.3 Percentage of Nigerians in the senior civil service and UAC management.

Note: For years that data is available. Reproduced with kind permission of Unilever plc and group companies.[21]

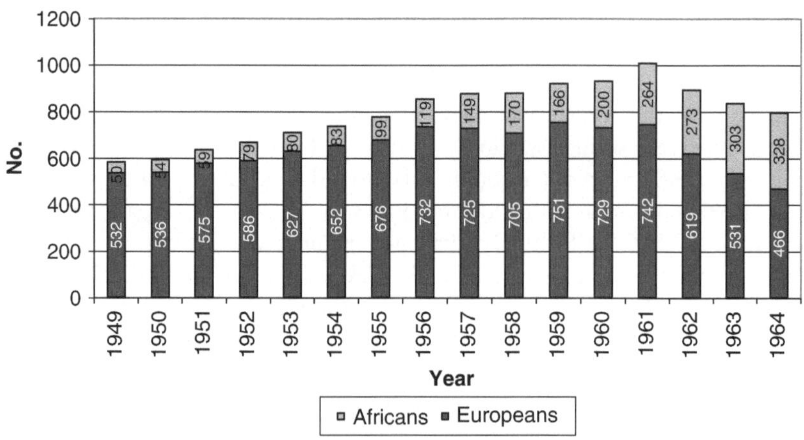

Figure 5.4 Africanization of UAC management in Nigeria, 1949–1964.

Note: Based on archival data from the Unilever Historical Archives. Reproduced with kind permission of Unilever plc and group companies.[31]

5.2 Corporate Africanization

Of the five companies in this study, the UAC Africanized most rapidly. As the largest West African trading firm, it was in a better position to attract recruits than others, but still, it did not keep up with the government. The origin of UAC's Africanization policy can be found in the Gold Coast riots when the firm was singled out for attack. To improve its public image, management focused on building up local goodwill through a variety of measures such as public relations policies and a pension scheme for African employees. Early Africanization formed part of these activities.[23] Other companies faced less pressure, but some sectors found it harder to recruit staff with the requisite skills (e.g., mining) or were dubious about the trustworthiness of Africans in positions that involved supervising finances or high-value production (e.g., banking and mining). This section will present the available data for the five companies and sketch the differences between sectors and individual firms.

Despite some differences, companies needed to resolve similar issues to Africanize successfully. The limited possibilities for education and training narrowed down the pool of sufficiently qualified applicants and led to increased pressure on governments and firms to fund scholarships to attend schools, universities or training, locally as well as overseas. In Nigeria, the politicization of regional and inter-ethnic rivalries affected companies almost as much as it did the civil service. Barclays Bank DCO, for example, had to protect its Igbo staff during the Kano riots of 1953 and increased its efforts to recruit Northerners in the 1950s, even approaching their main local contact, the Emir of Kano, to help them promote and put forward promising candidates.[24] The first part of this section looks at the commercial companies which generally Africanized faster than others, followed by the banks and, in the final part, the mining firm AGC.

5.2.1 Commercial companies: UAC and Holt

British companies were not under the same pressure to compile and release figures as the colonial governments were, and thus it was often unclear how well they performed in Africanizing their staff in comparison. While some authors claim that the preponderance of Europeans was stronger in business circles than in the civil service, others maintain that the UAC set a good example for other firms and even for some West African governments.[25] But beyond the UAC, it is much harder to determine the progress of Africanization in other firms, and there is hardly any evidence for Holt.

The UAC had, like the colonial governments and other West African merchants, a history of employing African managers. The company was formed through an amalgamation in 1929, and its predecessors had always employed African managers. By the late 1930s, they began to offer more training for locals, probably partly due to recruitment bottlenecks as the war approached.[26] The company appears to have been more successful in this than colonial governments (Figures 5.3 and 5.4), but that might also reflect governments' greater success in attracting expatriates. In 1948, UAC was one of the first firms to take Africanization seriously and sent the company secretary, ARI Mellor, to assess staff relations in response to the criticism it faced during and after the Gold Coast riots. He uncovered unfair and racist treatment of African employees and numerous other reasons for the firm's unpopularity. Based on this report, the UAC began to Africanize, restructured its commercial policies and introduced public relations measures.[27] Consequently, the company went on record during the hearings of the Watson Commission of Enquiry pronouncing its then progressive policy:

> The whole trend of our policy has been to maintain unchanged our position in the commercial life of the Colony but gradually to hand over to Africans the work for which they are suited as they become capable of it, while ourselves introducing and maintaining skills which are at present beyond them. The United Africa Company is probably well ahead of all other concerns in the promotions of Africans [...][28]

Firms had to be seen to be training and advancing in order to maintain local goodwill in West Africa and other decolonizing countries. At the UAC and Unilever, this was referred to as 'Ization', and the policy started in India in the late 1930s. By the late 1940s, it was becoming part of the company's global strategy.[29] In terms of corporate Africanization, the UAC is certainly the best-documented case, as the firm published statistics on staff and management for the 1950s and early 1960s. This openness about its progress was likely because it compared well to other companies in West Africa, which were less well documented.[30]

In both countries, management expanded overall until 1961, even though their total staff figures declined because the company centralized operations and sold off smaller trading posts. The UAC's expansion took the form of new ventures in manufacturing, increased focus on wholesaling, specialized trading and services, and department stores in major cities. The numbers of both European and African managers rose, but the latter increased more rapidly than the former (Figures 5.4 and 5.5). Africanization at first meant recruiting African managers in addition to the existing European managers. There are several explanations for this: overall expansion made it necessary to employ greater numbers, as did the extensive training programmes that accompanied the advancement of local staff. A similar process could be observed in the civil service. Burawoy suggested in his Zambian study that Africans were given the same title as the European they replaced but that the expatriate was simply promoted to supervise their successor and, in effect, still did part of their old job.[32] There is some indication that this dynamic was at play here, as a Barclays visiting manager claimed that the output of a Nigerian was only one-third to one-fourth of a British employee.[33]

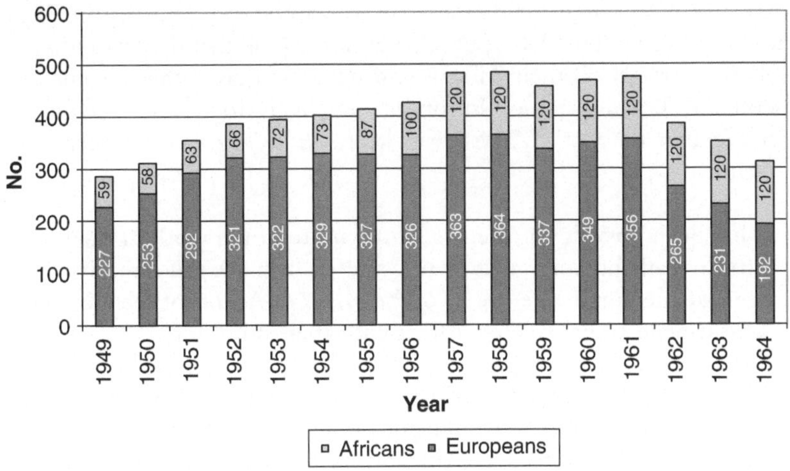

Figure 5.5 Africanization of UAC management in Ghana, 1949–1964.

Note: Based on archival data from the Unilever Historical Archives. Reproduced with kind permission of Unilever plc and group companies.[34]

From 1962 onwards, expatriate numbers at the UAC consistently decreased in both countries, which indicates that African managers now began to replace Europeans rather than being 'added on'. Another factor was that in Nigeria, independence was followed by a period of economic consolidation for many British companies.[35] Financial consolidation could easily be achieved by scaling down the use of expensive expatriate staff. Ghana introduced exchange controls in 1961 as its economy declined; hence fewer staff were needed, fewer expatriates were willing to work there, and companies cut down on the foreign exchange problems involved in paying expatriates salaries in freely convertible currencies.

Despite the absence of quantitative data for Holt, records show that Africanization was debated internally from at least 1938, when HL Rawlings, the General Manager in Liverpool, wrote to their agent in Accra

> I hope you will always make it clear to our African Staff that, in this Company, there is no bar to the promotion of any African to European posts merely because he is an African. [...] Only once in my experience has the African Staff ever thrown up a man who was potentially fitted to occupy a European post [...]. He was advanced by stages to considerable responsibility. Unfortunately, he failed to take advantage of the opportunity presented to him and disappointed us.[36]

In common with the civil service, European executives turned a blind eye to the pervasive racism in their organizations. Complaints by African staff were not investigated, and the difference between black and white was underscored by paying differential salaries – a common practice in West Africa.[37] However, by 1940, it became clear for Holt that they would have to rely increasingly on their African staff not only during the war but also subsequently because 'junior Europeans are likely to be unconscionably expensive after the war'.[38] Two years later, this policy had not been very successful:

> It has been possible to delegate a little more of the work to the senior African staff, but the greatest measure of help we have received has been by the employment [...] of the wives of Agents of the Company who happen to be in West Africa with their husbands.[39]

Holt's reasoning for this course of action focused on the untrustworthiness of Africans, who supposedly could not be left in charge of branch shops without supervision. Instead of Africanizing branches, the company preferred to withdraw from many trading stations and leave the retail trade to former African employees, who now became independent shopkeepers or middlemen supplied by Holt.[40] Despite these difficulties, some individuals were nevertheless promoted. One of the company's first Nigerian managers, SA Fajembola, had been a clerk in Ibadan, where he relieved the expatriate manager during illness in 1944. However, the exact date of his promotion is unknown, and he died in 1957.[41] By 1948 the company was offering management traineeships to Africans, but a regular training programme was only established in 1952. This was only moderately successful, and between 1953 and 1957, Holt employed only four African agents, one or two managerial assistants and four to five clerical assistants.[42]

5.2.2 Banking: Bank of British West Africa and Barclays

In banking, Africanization was generally slower than in the private sector. Unfortunately, hardly any material on staffing was found for the BBWA in their archives; hence this section is mainly based on Barclays' files. As both banks went through broadly similar developments in terms of branch expansion and staffing, it is likely the BBWA experienced similar pressures to Barclays.

Decolonization was a time of unprecedented expansion of banking. BBWA's overall staff on the coast (i.e., in Nigeria, the Gold Coast, Sierra Leone and the Gambia) increased from 461 at the end of the war to 1,107 in March 1953, of which 679, or 38.7 per cent, were Africans. At the same time, however, there was only one Africanized branch, Broad Street in Lagos, but by 1958, 13 African managers were in charge of branches, a figure that had doubled by May 1960.[43] In its company history, the bank actually admits to inflating management figures, suggesting that Africans were not given the same authority as their expatriate predecessors, who were probably kept in post at a higher rank, as suggested by Burawoy in his Zambian study.[44] Throughout the 1950s, expatriates became more expensive to employ; at the same time as both banks expanded their branch network and built new branches and expatriate housing.[45] As the banking boom ceased at the end of the decade, it is likely that overall staff figures dropped in the 1960s but that Africanization advanced further.

This rapid branch extension contrasted with the development of commercial companies, which followed a strategy of withdrawal from traditional retail and produce trade and could thus increasingly centralize and mechanize their operations. While there are no staff figures available for the BBWA, there is no indication in archival sources that it was noticeably more or less advanced than its competitor. Records for Barclays are patchy but indicate that the process of management Africanization was generally slower than at the UAC (Table 5.2).

The 16.9 per cent of Africans in Barclays' senior staff seems to compare well to UAC's figure for its Nigerian management in 1952 (11.9 per cent). However, in the case of the bank, this figure is entirely made up of the lowest rank within their senior appointments, B-signatories, who were not managers. In 1960 European managers still made up 15.7 per cent of the total staff (and not just management) for Nigeria. To some extent, this compared so poorly to the merchant companies because UAC's operations involved more unskilled labour, making up 45 per cent of its workforce in 1959.[47] It is difficult, however, to compare between sectors because the type of operations was different, as were their respective definitions of management and senior staff. In Ghana, the bank had 13 African managers in 59 branches (including 26 agencies), which suggests that 22 per cent of all branches were fully Africanized. However, six of the managers were ranked sub-managers, which means they were either second in command in a branch or controlling a sub-branch or agency under supervision from the main branch.[48]

5.2.3 Mining: AGC

Africanization was particularly slow in mining. The two main foreign mining companies in Ghana, the gold mine AGC and the Consolidated African Selection Trust (CAST), which mined diamonds, only began to put emphasis on Ghanaianization in the years immediately preceding independence.[49] AGC employed Africans mainly on a daily basis and offered contracts only to its expatriate staff. This changed in 1948 when the company responded to increasing industrial unrest by offering monthly pay in so-called African staff agreements in order to create 'a body of responsible workers loyal to the Corporation, so that in the event of any future strike we should not be left high and dry'.[50] While these agreements did not correspond to managerial appointments, they were limited to Africans in supervisory positions, and by 1950 about 140 were on a monthly salary.

Table 5.2 Africanization at Barclays Bank DCO in Nigeria and Ghana, 1952–1970

		Total staff					*Senior and managerial staff*				
			Local		*European*		*Managers*[1]		*Senior staff*		
Year	*Country*	*Total*	*Messen.*	*Clerical*	*Clerical*	*%*	*Europ.*	*African*	*Europ.*	*African*	*%*
1952	Nigeria	[231]					17	0	422	123	16.9
1960	Nigeria	937	790	147	15.7						
1966	Ghana	785	123	605	57	7.3		194			
1970	Nigeria	2,000			100	5					
	Ghana	800			45	5.6					

Note: Data drawn from Barclays Group Archives. Reproduced with the kind permission of Barclays Group Archives.[46]

[a]This category includes local directors, managers, branch managers, sub-managers (of branches and sub-branches) and accountants/clerks-in-charge. Senior staff comprises A- and B-signatories.

[b]Of which 13 are B-signatories, the lowest rank of senior staff.

[c]All B-signatories, see b.

[d]12 managers, one sub-manager and six sub-managers of sub-branches.

Designed as a response to industrial unrest, the Ghanaians on contract formed an African senior staff association, which, throughout its existence, took a very pro-management attitude.[51] The chairman, Edward Spears, however, objected to this on principle and released new contracts in 1961 to those members who filled 'European' posts on the understanding that they should not join any union because their expatriate colleagues were not unionized either.[52] Despite Spears' wishes, however, younger members of the African senior salaried staff founded a new association in 1966, which was placed under surveillance by the security officer. The need for an association was prompted by insecurities over whether the removal of Nkrumah would bring an end to the corporation's Africanization scheme and by the relative difference between the newer and the established senior staff.[53]

The corporate policy behind these changes was first formulated on the eve of independence, when Spears commented that 'the main danger lay in a sudden demand for Africanization, possibly as much as 5 per cent'.[54] In response, Spears insisted in May 1958 that Africanization would be a policy of replacement and that AGC sought to maintain an upper layer of expatriates for as long as feasible. While the intention to actually promote Africans into positions where they truly replaced Europeans, instead of being used as 'window-dressing', sounded promising, clearly, there was no intention to hand over responsible high-level jobs to Ghanaians any time soon. Spears expected Africanization to fall into two phases, first of the junior positions and, only after a significantly longer time, the senior posts. While CAST introduced its own consolidated training scheme in 1958, AGC continued to rely on the Chamber of Mines' school in Tarkwa. The gold mine became more proactive in 1962 when the company planned to publish a 'realistic' Africanization programme (Table 5.3). The guidelines were to replace approximately half of the European staff in the next five years but to avoid redundancy by relying on normal turnover. Over 30 European employees left the mine every year, and 15 were due to retire soon.[55]

Among the departments that submitted their plans, views differed over how achievable their suggestions were. The treatment plant, for example, aimed to Africanize all junior posts, but its head did not see any possibility that senior positions would follow suit soon.[57] The Mines Manager, PW Watson, estimated that of the projected African staff required, 29 would be available in time, but 54 needed to undergo further training. Of the clerical positions, the personnel and welfare office were fully Africanized, and the AGC's newspaper, the *Ashanti Times,* only had one European, the business manager, and one expatriate remained in the staff office, for whom a replacement was planned. The restaurant, catering mainly to European staff, was to remain under foreign management, and in the chief accountant's office, only three or four expatriates remained who were not due for replacement. Overall, PW Watson estimated that Africanization would proceed at pace: in a year's time, nine Africans were to be promoted, in three years 50, in five years 76, bringing the total number of senior salaried staff to

Table 5.3 AGC's Africanization forecasts from 1962 to 1967

Forecasts 1962–1967								
	Mining and technical				*Engineering**			
Year	*European* No.	*Ghanaian* No.	*Increase per year* %	*Africaniza-tion rate* %	*European* No.	*Ghanaian* No.	*Increase per year* %	*Africaniza-tion rate* %
1962	101	7		6.5	47	13		21.7
1963	94	13	85.7	12.1	44	16	23.1	26.7
1964	84	23	76.9	21.5	31	28	75.0	47.5
1965	70	37	60.9	34.6	26	33	17.9	55.9
1966	60	47	27.0	43.9	22	38	15.2	63.3
1967	52	55	17.0	51.4	16	41	7.9	71.9

Note: Data from the Ashanti Goldfield's archival deposit at London Metropolitan Archives.[56]
* Years run 1961–1962 etc.
+ For Engineering 1961–1962 represent actual figures.

Table 5.4 Africanization of personnel at AGC, 1961–1967

Date	*Expatriates*	*Africans*	*%*	*Total*
12.9.1961		11		
1.10.1962	181	19	9.5	200
1.01.1963	170	33	16.3	203
1.10.1964	150	58	27.9	208
1.10.1965	144	80	32.8	224
1.04.1966	145	84	36.7	229

Note: Data from the Ashanti Goldfield's archival deposit at London Metropolitan Archives.[58]

73 Europeans and 99 Africans. This was mainly based on figures supplied by the Mining and Technical and Engineers' department (Table 5.4).

While this programme sounded like an ambitious departure, the mine managed to get near its targets: in 1966, 84 African senior staff were employed, when the joint forecasts had been 85. By 1967 this figure had risen to 93, according to the *Annual Statement of Reports and Accounts,* rapidly increasing to 150 (79.9 per cent of total management) by 1970.[59] The takeover by Lonrho seemed to accelerate this process.

As the rising total figures indicate, there was probably still some 'adding-on' of African managers occurring, despite the reduction in expatriates and Spears' statement to the contrary. In his sociological study of the Zambian copper mines, Burawoy highlighted that bureaucratic planning approaches created a number of problems there that undermined the authority of newly-promoted Africans. Not all candidates were necessarily well-qualified or experienced enough for the posts, which led to what Burawoy called 'job fragmentation': responsibilities and discretionary powers were transferred from the African incumbent to an expatriate, who was installed in a newly devised managerial rung above the Africanized post. This undermined the legitimacy of the successor in the eyes of expatriate superiors and African colleagues and subordinates alike.[60] The relatively late and bureaucratic approach to Africanization at AGC, coupled with an overall increase in management numbers (which contrasted with Spears' official policy statement that Africanization would be a programme of replacement), indicates that this might have been a problem, although there was no direct evidence in the files. Job fragmentation explains why expatriate figures are maintained, as happened at the AGC. But at the UAC, for example, expatriate numbers were actually increasing in the 1950s. Another potential explanation was an increased need for expatriates to provide training for their African successors.

Despite the successful plan fulfilment, AGC was normally compared unfavourably to CAST, which had 40 Africans on its staff by 1954, and the gold mine was frequently criticized in the media.[61] The diamond mine's Africanization ratio remained around 32 per cent between 1961 and 1963 and then rose to 66.9 per cent by 1968, when 50 expatriates and 101

Ghanaians were employed as senior staff. Although AGC compared poorly to CAST in the early 1960s, the corporation's Africanization rate improved in the 1960s, from only 19 Africans in senior positions in 1962 to 84 four years later.

It is unclear whether the programme forecasts made in 1962 were published, but it is important to note that the year 1962 saw a spate of criticisms of AGC, particularly compared to CAST. Spears's defence was that for CAST's surface mining, it was easier to find or train qualified Africans than for AGC's underground operation.[62] Nevertheless, Africanization rates improved subsequently, suggesting that improved conditions were a response to public criticism, just as at the UAC and BBWA. The corporation's *Annual Statement* began to contain pictures of their Ghanaian senior staff, 15 in 1962, captioned with the claim that they made up 40 per cent (even though it was only 9.5 per cent according to the figures in Table 5.4). AGC had belatedly grasped that Africanization was an important tool for legitimization in a newly independent country.[63]

Africanization was clearly slower in mining than in commerce, but comparisons are difficult as definitions such as 'personnel', 'staff' or 'management' vary greatly. The percentages supplied by CAST compare well to UAC, which is interesting because the diamond mine trained relatively few Africans before 1956. A comparison between mining and commerce is generally difficult because they required different types of skills, as managerial positions in the former were predominantly technical and often based on engineering. West Africans with this background were rare, as colonial government education policy focused more on the clerical skills required for administration. While the academic focus of British colonial school curricula was often criticized at the time, it may have been more vocational than it was given credit for because English literacy and numeracy were the skills that were most demanded by employers.[64] However, in contrast to commercial firms, once technical staff were trained, they were less likely to leave mining, as there were only a limited number of employers, and self-employment was less of an option due to the heavy capital requirement.

5.3 Africanization and corporate legitimization

Why was Africanization such a relatively slow process, and what impeded the progress of local managers? Racism and the embedded ethnocentric preferences within multinationals were clearly issues, but these were accompanied by structural issues in the markets for skilled labour. Competition between employers for scarce manpower led to recruitment problems and high turnover. Glass ceilings limited African advancement in companies and made them a less desirable place to work when opportunities for promotion were better in the public sector. Africanization in the civil service also advanced more rapidly because expatriate civil servants had better exit options: they were offered better pension arrangements and loss-of-career compensation. While some firms sought to redeploy their expatriate staff, this was not always the case, and resistance to African advancement was clearly more pronounced if it was likely to end expatriate careers in the foreseeable future. Although discriminatory practices and salaries were increasingly abandoned, upon promotion, African managers still inherited expatriate privileges, creating an 'hourglass' structure of employment that created new inequalities.

5.3.1 Staff turnover

One of the major problems for commercial companies throughout this period was the loss of trained staff, who were tempted away by opportunities for further education, employment in government or other companies and self-employment. This was particularly striking in the private sector, which competed with the civil service for recruits. It was not only the better remuneration that attracted new entrants but also that opportunities for promotion were better, at least until independence, because Africanization proceeded more quickly. Expatriates in government were leaving West Africa more willingly than those in private employment, creating space for local recruits to advance to senior levels. There were a number of reasons for this: expatriate dislike of nationalist politics, a reluctance to serve under African ministers (an argument disputed by Nicolson), and generous incentives to depart. The colonial service offered generous pensions whenever a new stage of constitutional advancement was reached for 'loss of career', and the West African countries used pension entitlements to regulate expatriate resignations before and after independence.[65] These incentives were major factors in advancing Africanization rapidly, which the private sector could not match. While the UAC aimed to redeploy its expatriate staff from Africa to other regions, Barclays stated clearly in 1966 that they intended to use Africanization to replace those European recruits who did not make the grade:

> [...] the fact is that although 75 percent of the young men are quite first class, there is an element that ought not to be in the Bank. When these are identified, I feel that we ought to grasp the nettle and get rid of them. There is no place in the future of the bank for anyone who is not (a) loyal, or (b) potentially a large branch manager.[66]

Chairman Frederic Seebohm's comment on the Nigerian situation has to be seen in the light of much slower progress than at the UAC. It was only in the 1960s that the bank really had the option to replace Europeans with Africans to any extent. Both British banks had rapidly expanded throughout the 1950s and only began consolidating in the 1960s. The UAC had been more successful than other firms in terms of Africanization, and the deputy chairman FJ Pedler boasted about their reputation in Nigeria in 1965:

> [...] we are regarded as a company which [...] has done better than most in Africanization. A senior manager of another trading company expressed the greatest envy of the position we hold and it is clear that the pressure on them is more disagreeable than it is on us.[67]

Efforts to improve their local standing and to create goodwill were clearly paying off in the eyes of the company's principals. These activities were the result of the high level of public criticism the UAC faced early on, especially during and after the Gold Coast riots of 1948. However, although the company Africanized faster than its competitors, in the 1950s, it still suffered from a relative decrease and stagnation of African appointments (Figure 5.6), as trained staff resigned to form their own businesses or join the civil service.[68]

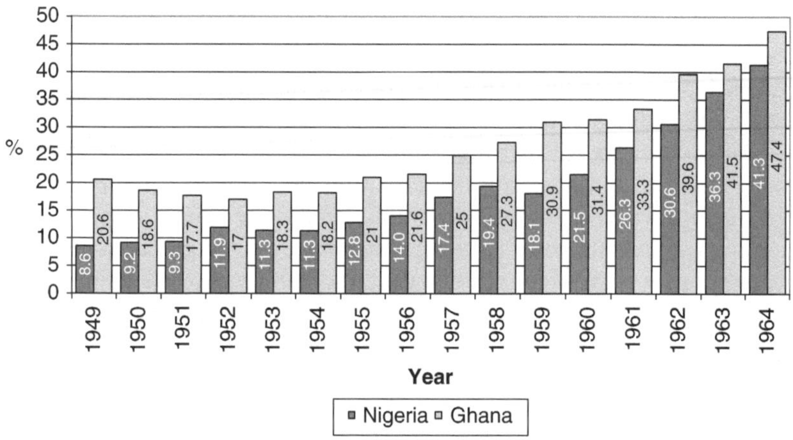

Figure 5.6 Comparison of progress of management Africanization at UAC in Ghana and Nigeria, 1949–1964 (in %).

Note: Based on archival data from the Unilever Historical Archives. Reproduced with kind permission of Unilever plc and group companies.[69]

The banks encountered similar difficulties, which JB Loynes of the Bank of England attributed to high turnover and institutional competition in 1958:

> The steady efflux of white officials from the regional administration had caused regional governments to offer attractive terms, including scholarships in the UK, to Africans. This had led to a serious drain on the promising African staff of Barclays DCO, doubtless BWA as well, at a time when the Bank needed to be at full strength to cope with its rapid expansion. The resignation of Africans had forced the

> Bank to import more European staff involving substantial outlays on housing etc.[70]

Indeed, there is evidence in Barclays' files that they were losing staff and recruits to other companies, most notably the UAC, which was the reference point for the expectations of Africans working in the private sector.[71] Barclays, for example, routinely overstaffed in order to overcome potential shortages and its Nigerian branches engaged 240 persons, an increase of 16.8 per cent in 1961. From March to May alone, when most school leavers looked for jobs, staff figures rose by 7.9 per cent, but during that half-year, 80 experienced clerks left the bank (5.6 per cent of the total). They either proceeded to better-paid jobs in Nigeria or had a chance to go to the United Kingdom for further training or education. In the same year, Barclays decided to increase the minimum salary for their higher-grade staff, as the bank realized that what they paid compared badly to other employers in the country.[72] BBWA's management was similarly aware of this problem. The bank's staff policy, however, received a boost after the takeover by Standard Bank, and from 1965/66 onwards, they began to proactively ask Ministers or Central Bank Governors to release promising employees under the condition to fast-track them in the bank.[73]

Firms competed with each other and with the civil service for school leavers and university graduates to fill positions in this time period. For West African recruits, there was a rank order of desirable employment, defined by income and reputation: government administration was followed by UAC and the trading companies in general, who offered better salaries and other benefits than the banks, with mining lagging behind.[74]

5.3.2 Ceilings

As Africans were promoted to responsible jobs in business, it became clear that invisible ceilings existed to their advancement. These were often obscured by debating the shortcomings of individuals, either in terms of their ability or 'character'. In 1945 Mr Pannel, one of Holt's managers, noted that the average Gold Coast recruit that '[…] he possesses the intelligence but too often lacks the integrity, understanding, initiative and sense of responsibility which make for the successful agent'.[75] Even W Arthur Lewis, the development economist, considered the supply of trained, efficient and enterprising managers as the weakest point of the Ghanaian economy.[76] But there is evidence that African advancement was limited by other factors. One of UAC's managers in the Gold Coast, George Cole, gave evidence at the Watson Commission of Enquiry into the 1948 riots and characterized the company's problems with Africanization as follows:

> For many years we have been doing our utmost to discover suitable African material for training to the higher posts of management. The

> results are disappointing to those who expect that fundamental changes in character can be brought about in a few years. Africans have risen to very responsible positions, but none of them has ever shown the capacity of challenge for the post of General Manager or anything approaching it.[77]

At Barclays Bank DCO, Julian Crossley debated the same issue with Frank Samuel from the UAC in 1951:

> [Frank Samuel] pointed out that their local African staff had not yet progressed far enough to take responsibility, even of a Store manager. He asked how far we had been able to give authority to local Africans, which is not yet very far, although they are quite good at routine duties. Although at a small branch the second man might be an African, we should not at present feel able to leave one in charge, even of a small branch.[78]

Despite differences in the progress of Africanization between those companies, there was a shared understanding in the early 1950s about the limits on African advancement. At Barclays in Nigeria, ceilings had shifted upwards over time but still existed in 1964:

> Though there are a number of good steady Africans in responsible positions, they nearly all seemed to me to lack the spark of real managerial ability; they might run small or medium sized branches adequately but would be unlikely ever to show the self-confidence and initiative needed to build up or expand a business.[79]

A new Ghanaian trainee in Accra, who joined Barclays in 1967, was convinced that glass ceilings existed, which obstructed the path into local head office. Some of his older colleagues successfully overcame this perceived barrier, however, and were the first Africans to be appointed to jobs that had formerly been a European reserve: AN Nortey became General Manager and SE Donkor General Manager Assistant.[80]

While the vicious circle of low expectations, insecurity, lack of initiative and strict supervision explains the existence of ceilings, it does not explain why they shifted over time. Political pressure and the spiralling costs of employing expatriates were certainly major factors that encouraged further progress. The existence of recognizable but moving ceilings also suggests that Africanization went through several distinct phases. After management and senior positions were effectively purged of Africans at the beginning of the century, the late 1930s and 1940s witnessed an opening of higher careers to a few chosen individuals. By the 1950s, most companies instituted general training provisions that allowed some level of general advancement, but it appears that measures such as the fast-tracking of trainees only really came into their own in the late 1950s and 1960s. For the banks, the mid to late 1960s was the time when staffing policy became focused on promoting African managers into responsible positions, a development that occurred earlier at the trading companies, particularly at the UAC. Myles Hagan was a UAC director from 1955 to 1961 and became chairman of Lever Brothers from 1961 to 1980 – the first African chairman of any Unilever or UAC company in Anglophone Africa.[81]

5.3.3 Salary structures

Africanization was also supposed to herald the end of the discriminatory promotion or salary structures based on race. In 1948 Holt assured its staff that African managers were to 'enjoy all the privileges extended to their European counterparts'.[82] However, this pledge was followed by a list of exceptions: higher incomes through overseas allowance, housing and free medical services were only provided for Europeans. The additional expatriate pay amounted to about one-third of the basic salary.[83] At the UAC, African managers received a salary of £350 per annum in 1948, whereas the Europeans were on £500 p.a. plus free housing and medical attention. In 1950, the BBWA was heavily criticized for paying its Port Harcourt branch manager a basic salary of £950 at a time when the average per capita income was as low as £20.[84] By the late 1950s, it was unusual for Europeans on the coast to earn less than £1,000 p.a., as well as being entitled to free housing and other allowances, when the equivalent job in the United Kingdom paid around £700.[85]

West Africa had never been a popular overseas area for expatriates, and finding suitable recruits in the United Kingdom appears to have been a problem. Europeans in West Africa were far from one united group: there was a rift between those actually serving on the coast and those who went to sea. The European sailors felt that expatriates in the colonies looked down on them. A former ship engineer from Liverpool commented that many expatriates would not have been able to get a job in Britain. Nevertheless, they considered themselves a 'cut above' everybody else, especially above the sailors, because they had African servants and lived a privileged lifestyle. In the interview, he remarked that he believed that it was not only as a result of recruitment problems that British companies paid high wages but also because executives were afraid that their employees would 'go Bush': if these mainly single men in the colonies could not maintain themselves socially, especially in the English clubs, they might start to go drinking with Africans and get otherwise involved with local people.[86]

Over time, salaries and employment conditions for African managers were equalized, and this was accompanied by British managers' ideas about socializing them into their firm's corporate culture. But even before pay parity, salaries for African managers were high in comparison to lower-grade staff, as they were required, like Europeans, to do a fair amount of networking and socializing at this level. Once companies began to offer free housing to African managers as part of a recruitment and retention package, one major expense also disappeared. Due to recruitment problems, it was not feasible to reduce senior salaries without losing personnel, and it became politically untenable to continue to pay salaries that were based on a racial bias. As British salaries could not be reduced, and African salaries could not continue to be discriminatory, basic salaries now consolidated a range of benefits at the higher end of the scale. However, this consolidation did not affect expatriate allowances. While Africans were now paid the same wages as Europeans in equal employment, wages in lower grade positions were not raised in line with the higher grades. The stark distinction between junior and senior service and the absence of an intermediate level effectively segregated the workforce into those who inherited expatriate positions and those for whom conditions stayed broadly the same. This quintessentially colonial employment structure was not reviewed after independence.

It marked the outcome of many years of African employees raising the fundamental injustice of discriminatory pay scales. Only in the late 1940s did businesses like Barclays begin to consider demands by local staff as potentially justified:

> It is my own humble opinion that an African whose work is considered good and who possesses the necessary qualifications should after 10 years be able to earn the initial salary of a European in the same employment.[87]

This letter by an African bank employee alludes to the mistrust that European managers showed towards their African employees, who had to prove themselves through years of loyal service before they could expect to be granted the same conditions as a European. By 1952, the nominal ethnicity pay gap in the basic salaries for senior appointments at Barclays was reducing: the average income at the lowest senior rank, a B-signatory, was £372 for Nigerians and £380 for British staff. In Nigeria, local staff constituted almost half of all B-signatories (12 local to 13 expatriates), but no one had been promoted higher than this, indicating that this constituted the 'ceiling' to African advancement at the time. However, allowances remained exclusive to expatriates and averaged £242, the minimum being £200 territorial allowance. For the lower ranks, this was significantly more than one-third of the basic salary and highlighted that the real ethnicity pay gap remained large.

It was also common for local staff to be older when reaching senior positions (45 years on average) compared to the average British age of 27.[88] Europeans continued to earn more, even when they were in a junior position and younger. In 1961 the British B-signatory DG Beecham (aged 26) earned more than his senior, the 34-year-old African accountant EU

Ukott, and this did not include expatriate allowances, which in 1965 ranged from £600 to £1850 (not including the housing provided by the bank).[89] Nevertheless, the average age of African A-signatories and sub-managers was now lower than the age of the B-signatories a decade before, with a substantial number of men being around 30. By 1970, African managers of a similar age eventually earned the same amount of money as their European counterparts in comparable positions.[90]

Access to other expatriate privileges, in particular housing, as well as car or entertainment allowances, were also not immediately granted. The first African manager of a Barclays' branch was Robert Mensah in Ghana in 1957, who took over Cape Coast and was subsequently appointed a local director in 1965, in a move that was reportedly well-received by African staff.[91] In Nigeria at independence, there were only sub-branches and agencies headed by Africans in acting positions. By 1962 the bank had appointed several Nigerian branch managers, among them a Northerner, Mallam Aba, who managed Funtua and was a distant relative of the Emir of Kano (one of Barclays' key political contacts). He even occupied a bank house, which had reportedly been a very controversial decision at the time. He was quite possibly the first Nigerian at Barclays to do so.[92] The reason why access to housing was such an emotive issue was because of the relative segregation of white expatriates in 'European' parts of African cities, a privilege that was coming to an end at the time.

Discriminatory treatment continued in British business, but African senior staff were increasingly entitled to many of the expatriate privileges and emoluments. As in the public service, those working in higher grades began to inherit expatriate standards in the 1960s. While it was apparently impossible to keep those expatriates needed in the administration and economy if their benefits were cut, it was equally impossible to restrict access to these benefits on a racial level indefinitely. Although racial discrimination in the payment structures did eventually come to an end, this continued the fundamentally colonial structure of employment: significantly higher incomes and other benefits became controversial once the West African economies slowed down or even contracted. The investigation of the Nigerian general strike of 1964 criticized these diverging salary scales as colonial structures that required reform.

5.4 Conclusion

Replacing European managers with Africans encountered numerous obstacles and perpetuated colonial employment structures in the economy. Although Africanization appears closely connected to decolonization, it commenced before constitutional devolution began and was only completed in the civil service in the mid-1960s and only significantly later in the companies discussed in this study. Africanization was a response to local pressure, a legitimization strategy to sway African politicians and public opinion.[93] Companies encountered several issues when implementing their Africanization policies, and these were often only addressed in the face of mounting public pressure for change.

By comparing corporate and official Africanization, differences in approach become clear. European civil servants were offered generous pensions and loss-of-career bonuses to induce them to leave, whereas some companies tried to redeploy men at an equivalent level in other areas or simply dismissed them. Business was also less likely to change discriminatory terms of employment and generally paid less well than the civil service. Combined with the higher prestige of working for the civil service, this ensured that the scarce supply of educated manpower drifted towards the public sector.

Different companies Africanized at different rates. The commercial firms, which had faced the worst public relations (especially the UAC), were the fastest to implement Africanization. Next came the banks, which became a focus of public criticism in the mid to late 1950s. Mining appears to have been the slowest, though the AGC performed particularly badly in comparison to the other major foreign mining company, CAST. This might have been due to the influence of the conservative chairman and managing director Spears. However, CAST was also part of a larger mining multinational operating in Africa and appeared to be more astute in assessing African opinion than the freestanding AGC. There is some indication that Africanization accelerated after the takeover by Lonrho, which was also a larger multinational conglomerate operating across many African countries.[94]

Notes

1 Geoffrey Jones, *British Multinational Banking, 1830–1990* (New York: OUP, 1993), 48–52.

2 Michael Burawoy, *The Colour of Class on the Copper Mines: From African Advancement to Zambianization*, Zambian pa (Manchester: Manchester University Press, 1972); Josephine F. Milburn, *British Business and Ghanaian Independence* (London: C. Hurst, 1977); Stephanie Decker, "Africanization in British Multinationals in Ghana and Nigeria, 1945–1970," *Business History Review* 92, no. 4 (December 1, 2018): 691–718, https://doi.org/10.1017/S0007680518001034; Stephanie Decker, "Postcolonial Transitions in Africa: Decolonization in West Africa and Present Day South Africa," *Journal of Management Studies* 47, no. 5 (July 2010): 791–813, https://doi.org/10.1111/j.1467-6486.2010.00924.x; Sarah E Stockwell, *The Business of Decolonization: British Business Strategies in the Gold Coast* (Oxford: Clarendon Press, 2000).

3 Stockwell, *The Business of Decolonization*, 173.

4 See CO554/400 no. 1, 13.3.53 (item 180), in Martin Lynn (ed.), *British Documents on the End of Empire (Nigeria)*, Series B (London: Institute of Commonwealth Studies, 2001), 510–15.

5 See UAC, Statistical and Economic Review, several volumes.

6 GO Olusanya, *The Evolution of the Nigerian Civil Service, 1861–1960: The Problem of Nigerianization* (Yaba and Lagos, Nigeria: University of Lagos, 1975), 3–5, 9. For biographies of several individuals in Sierra Leone, the Gold Coast and Nigeria, see K Arhin, DE Skinner, and GO Olusanya, *West African Colonial Civil Servants in the*

Nineteenth Century: African Participation in British Colonial Expansion in West Africa (Leiden, Netherlands: African Studies Centre, 1985).

7 See the account of Joseph Appiah on his time working for the UAC during the war: Joe Appiah, *Joe Appiah: The Autobiography of an African Patriot* (Accra, Ghana: Asempa, 1996), 111–44. For an earlier time period, DDA Coker, "Letter," in *Trading in West Africa*, ed. Peter N Davies (London, UK: Croom Helm, 1976), 157–72.

8 IF Nicolson, *The Administration of Nigeria 1900–60: Men, Methods, and Myths* (Oxford: Clarendon, 1969), 261–2; Olusanya, *The Evolution of the Nigerian Civil Service, 1861–1960: The Problem of Nigerianization*, 25.

9 Burawoy, *The Colour of Class on the Copper Mines*, 52, 99.

10 Nicolson, *The Administration of Nigeria*, 230.

11 Nicolson, *The Administration of Nigeria*, 234, 258.

12 Dennis Austin, *Politics in Ghana* (Oxford: Oxford University Press, 1964), 8 fn10; Jeremy White, *Central Administration of Nigeria* (Dublin, Ireland: Irish Academy Press, 1981), 278.

13 Austin, *Politics in Ghana*, 8, 158; FM Bourret, *Ghana: The Road to Independence 1919–1957* (Stanford CA: Stanford University Press, 1969), 43, 68; Milburn, *British Business and Ghanaian Independence*, 90–1; Trevor Jones, *Ghana's First Republic, 1960–1966: The Pursuit of the Political Kingdom* (London, UK: Methuen, 1976), 301 fn24; Nicolson, *The Administration of Nigeria 1900–60: Men, Methods, and Myths*, 258–60; IF Nicolson, "The Machinery of the Federal and Regional Governments," in *Nigerian Government and Politics*, ed. JP Mackintosh (London, UK: George Allen and Unwin, 1966), 187–9; JS Coleman, *Nigeria: Background to Nationalism* (Berkeley, CA: University of California Press, 1971), 313; S Phillipson and SO Adebo, "The Nigerianization of the Civil Service" (Nigeria, 1952), 37; K Ezera, *Constitutional Developments in Nigeria* (Cambridge, UK: Cambridge University Press, 1964), 86–7.

14 Austin, *Politics in Ghana*, 166; Bourret, *Ghana*, 178; Milburn, *British Business and Ghanaian Independence*.

15 Jones, *Ghana's First Republic*, 301 fn24.

16 Eme Onuoha Awa, *Federal Government in Nigeria* (Berkeley, CA: University of California Press, 1964), 161, 168–9.

17 Omorogbe Nwanwene, "The Nigerian Public Services Commissions," in *Studies in Nigerian Administration*, ed. DJ Murray (London, UK: Hutchinson, 1970), 201.

18 The lowering of standards was accepted in Nigeria by a Special Committee on Nigerianization in 1959, see Olusanya, *The Evolution of the Nigerian Civil Service*, 77, 86.

19 For data sources see Figure 5.1 and UAC, *Statistical and Economic Review*, 12 (Sept 1957), p. 40; 20 (Sept 1957), p. 41; 22 (January 1959), p. 51; 25 (March 1961), p. 62; 27 (June 1962), p. 57; 29 (April 1964), p. 68.

20 Milburn, *British Business*, 90–2.

21 Based on the same data sources as Figure 5.2.

22 See sources for Figure 5.1.

23 WTG Gates, District Agent, Kano, to Winter, District Agent, Lagos, 14.10.43, Rhodes House Oxford (RHO) Mss Afr. s 825, 232 (i).

24 Frederic Seebohm, 'Diary of Tours of several countries', 19.9.50–30.11.56, 23.2.54, p. 33, Barclays Group Archive (BGA) 277/1.

25 For the former view see Douglas Rimmer, *Staying Poor: Ghana's Political Economy, 1950–1990*, ed. World Bank (Oxford: Pergamon, 1992), 35. For the latter see Coleman, *Nigeria*, 44 fn47.

26 Milburn, *British Business*, 75.

27 David Kenneth Fieldhouse, *Merchant Capital and Economic Decolonisation: The United Africa Company 1929–1987* (Oxford: Clarendon, 1994), 338–41.

28 George Cole's testimony, cited after UAC's own files by Milburn, Ghanaian Independence, p. 76.
29 Andrew M Knox, *Coming Clear: A Postscript after Retirement from Unilever* (London, UK: Heinemann, 1976), 161–71.
30 Stockwell, *The Business of Decolonization*, 145.
31 UAC, *Statistical and Economic Review*, 12 (September 1957), p. 40; 20 (September 1957), p. 41; 22 (January 1959), p. 51; 25 (March 1961), p. 62; 27 (June 1962), p. 57; 29 (April 1964), p. 68.
32 Burawoy, *The Colour of Class*, 27–48.
33 RE Fleming and EV Whitcombe, "Nigeria and the Cameroons," 23 July 1960, p. 19, BGA 80/3466 (hereafter Fleming and Whitcombe, 'Nigeria and the Cameroons').
34 Same as Figure 5.4.
35 Barclays, which had expanded rapidly in the 1950s, assumed that independence and its aftermath was a period of consolidation. Subsequent policy confirmed this opinion: Fleming and Whitcombe, "Nigeria and the Cameroons," 6.
36 Holt's files at Rhodes House before cataloguing cited in Milburn, *British Business*, 71. The use of the term 'European post' only ceased after the Harragin Commission, and it seems that business adopted the new terminology of junior and senior appointments. Walter Harragin, *Report of the Commission on the Civil Services of British West Africa, 1945–1946* (London, UK: HMSO, 1947), 10.
37 Coker, "Letter," 168.
38 HL Rawlings to all District Agents in Nigeria, Accra, and Duala, 30 October 1940, Holt's Records file 8, Administrative Staff; and Pannel, "African Managers on the Coast Organisation," 10 April 1945, File 54, Holt's Records, both at Rhodes House before cataloguing, cited in Milburn, *British Business*, 72.
39 Chairman's speech, Ordinary General Meeting, for year ending 30 September 1943, 16 August 1944, pp. 4–5; Liverpool Records Office (LRO) 380 HOL II (hereafter Chairman's speech, 16.8.44).
40 Chairman's speech, 16.8.44, p. 2; LRO 380 HOL II.
41 Ibadan agent to John Holt, Liverpool, 'Quarterly Report', 18 September 1944, p. 3, RHO Mss Afr. s825, 232 (ii); Chairman's Statement at the Annual General Meeting, 8 March 1957, p. 16; 30 September 1950, p. 15, 30 August 1951, p. 18.
42 Milburn, *British Business*, 75.
43 It remains unclear whether these were acting or permanent appointments, working in full branches, or sub-branches and agencies, which were still under (normally expatriate) supervision. Richard Fry, *Bankers in West Africa: The History of the British Bank of West Africa* (London: Hutchinson Benham, 1976), 178, 190–1.
44 Fry, 193; Burawoy, *The Colour of Class*.
45 Fry, *Bankers in West Africa*, 191–2.
46 Dyson, "Mr Dyson's West African Tour – 1952," 15 February–25 March 1952, pp. 36, 39; and "List of Senior Staff – Nigeria," both BGA 80/4328; RE Fleming and EV Whitcombe, "Visit to Nigeria and the Cameroons," July 1960, BGA 80/3466; Letter, Barclays Bank DCO to J. Milburn, July 1966, from: Josephine Milburn, *Ghanaian Independence and British Business* (London, C. Hurst, 1977), p. 85.
47 UAC, Statistical and Economic Review, 22 (London: UAC, 1959), p. 4, Unilever Group Archives (UHA).
48 Stockwell, *The Business of Decolonization*, 143.
49 Milburn, *British Business and Ghanaian Independence*, 88.
50 Report of Staff Conference, 21 February 1948; Plans for these agreements had been made since 1946, see General Mines Manager OHG Gale to Manager and Secretary, 17 December 1946, London Metropolitan Archives (LMA) CLC/B/015/MS14171, v. 103, January–June 1948 and v. 100, July–December 1946.

51 General Mines Manager to EW Morgan, 27 February 1950; General Mines Manager to Spears, 15 and 28 November 1955; LMA CLC/B/015/MS14171 v. 107, January–June 1950; v. 122 July–December 1955.
52 EL Spears, 'Africanization', 23 May 1958; and Ag. General Mines Manager to Secretary, 23 November 1960; LMA CLC/B/015/MS24665.
53 Hamilton, "Intelligence Report," No. 412; General Mines Manager to EW Morgan, 24 May 1966, AD Appeah to General Mines Manager, 18 May 1966, General Mines Manager circular to senior staff, 21 May 1966, J. Beattie, "Intelligence Report on Proposed African Senior Staff Association," 23.5.66, J Beattie, "Intelligence Report," No. 4, 5 and 7, 18 July 1966, 23 August 1966 and 7 September 1966; LMA CLC/B/015/MS14171 v. 164 January–June 1966, v. 165 July–December 1966.
54 Staff conference, 2 March 1957, LMA CLC/B/015/MS14171 v. 127, January–June 1957.
55 PW Watson, Ag. General Mines Manager to Consulting Engineer, London, 18 August 1962, LMA CLC/B/015/MS24663, v. 3.
56 PW Watson, Mines Manager, 'Notes on Africanization of Mining Department & Technical Service', n.d.; A Hayes, Ag. Chief Engineer, to General Mines Manager, 'Memorandum Africanization, Engineering Dept.', 21 June 1962; LMA CLC/B/015/MS24663, v. 3 July–December 1962.
57 PW Watson, Mines Manager, "Notes on Africanization of Mining Department & Technical Service," n.d.; PW Watson, Ag. General Mines Manager to Consulting Engineer, London, 18 August 1962; Mr. Shearman, Ag. Production Superintendent, to Ag. General Mines Manager, 'Africanization at Pompora Treatment Plant', 22 June 1962; A Hayes, Ag. Chief Engineer, to General Mines Manager, 'Memorandum Africanization, Engineering Dept.', 21 June 1962; LMA CLC/B/015/MS24663, v. 3.
58 Minutes of Heads of Departments, 22 April 1966, LMA CLC/B/015/MS14171 v. 164, Jan–Jun 1966; Ag. General Mines Manager to Secretary, 12 September 1961, Ms 24,663, v. 1 July–December 1961; Minutes of Heads of Departments meeting, 15 February 1963, LMA CLC/B/015/MS24663, v. 4 January–June 1963.
59 AGC Photographs, LMA CLC/B/015/MS24661; Stockwell, *The Business of Decolonization*, 175.
60 Burawoy, *The Colour of Class*, 27–48.
61 PAL Greenhalgh, *West African Diamonds 1919–1983: An Economic History* (Manchester, UK: Manchester University Press, 1985), 132–7; Milburn, *British Business*, 85; Stockwell, *The Business of Decolonization*, 173.
62 EL Spears to George Cappendell, 21 November 1963, LMA CLC/B/015/MS24665. AGC's bad image: RD Power to EL Spears, 28 September 1963, LMA CLC/B/015/MS24665; General Mines Manager to Secretary, 5 May 1962, and Foli Armah to General Mines Manager, memorandum, 10 May 1962; Minutes of PR Committee, 9 November 1962, LMA CLC/B/015/MS24663, v. 2, January–June 1962; v. 3, July–December 1962.
63 Decker, "Africanization."
64 Rimmer, *Staying Poor*, 34–5. In Nigeria the improvement of spoken and written English was also prioritised in 1960, see Commission on post-school certificate and higher education in Nigeria, "Investment in Education: The Report of the Commission on Post-School Certificate and Higher Education in Nigeria" (Lagos, Ngieria, 1960), 86.
65 See CO554/400 nos. 1&2, March 1953 (item 126) in Rathbone, 19–25. CO554/1008, no. 84, 11 July 1956 (item 366) in Lynn, *British Documents on the End of Empire (Nigeria)*, 326–29.; Awa, *Federal Government in Nigeria*, 166.

66 F Seebohm, "Mr. Seebohm's Visit to Nigeria," 16–24 February 1966, 5, BGA 80/3375.
67 FJ Pedler, Report to Directors' Conference, UHA UNI/SC with Tropical Africa Committee, 10 December 1965.
68 Colin Legum, journalist for The Observer, at the Institute of Commonwealth Studies, University of London, 18 May 1958, cited in Milburn, Ghanaian Independence, p. 78. While the trading companies reduced their retail network and effectively supported former African agents to become independent retailers drawing on UAC as wholesaler, it was also not unusual that trained managerial personnel would begin their own business ventures.
69 Same as figure 5.4.
70 JB Loynes, "Nigeria," 26 February 1958, pp. 1–2, Bank of England Archives (hereafter BoE) OV 68/5.
71 GA Onagoruwa to General Manager (Staff), February/ March 1948, BGA 38/906.
72 DLG Davies to GNM Law, 16 June 1961; FA Boreham, 'Mr. Boreham's Visit to Nigeria', 3–19 July 1961, p. 2, BGA 80/4448.
73 Fry, *Bankers in West Africa*, 190, 256.
74 UAC, Economic and Statisticial Review, 25 (London: UAC, 1961), p. 62, caption under Africanization figures. The AGC admitted that the wage level was lower in mining than 'elsewhere': Col. Westmorland to EW Morgan, 8 March 1963 (dated 8 April 1963 in error), LMA CLC/B/015/MS24665; and strikers asserted that senior staff in Tarkwa were paid more than in Obuasi: Hamilton, 'Intelligence Report', No. 412, n.d., LMA CLC/B/015/MS14171, v. 122, July–December 1955. See also Awa, *Federal Government in Nigeria*, 173.
75 Pannel, "African managers on the Coast Organisation," 10.4.45, Holt's Rhodes House files before cataloguing, cited after Milburn, *British Business*, 72.
76 W Arthur Lewis, "Report on the Industrialisation and the Gold Coast" (Accra, Ghana, 1953), 24; Jones, *Ghana's First Republic*, 147.
77 UAC files before cataloguing, cited after Milburn, *British Business*, 77.
78 Julian Crossley's diaries, vol 9, 13 March 1951, 52, BGA 38/209.
79 RG Dyson, "Visit to Nigeria," January/February 1964, 3, BGA 80/4641.
80 Interview with senior executive manager of Barclays Bank of Ghana, 6 July 2004.
81 Fieldhouse, *Merchant Capital*, 379; Knox, *Coming Clear*, 171.
82 Milburn, *British Business*, 74.
83 Milburn, *British Business*, 74–75. Coker, in his letter from 1921, had claimed that Europeans earned on average six times more than Africans. Coker, "Letter," 168.
84 Milburn, *British Business*, 77; Fry, *Bankers in West Africa*, 175–6.
85 Interview with Roy Barlow (Liverpool-based ship engineer who sailed to West Africa from 1956 to 1960), 20 October 2005.
86 Interview with Barlow. Specific forms of 'involvement', however, were accepted: knowing local chiefs and politicians, later socialising with the African staff, and, less openly, prostitution. Interview with Reg Dines, Hugh Norris, John Woodcock (former Barclays Bank DCO expatriate managers who worked in West Africa), 17 August 2001.
87 GA Onagoruwa to Donald Carter, General Manager (Staff), February/March 1948, BGA 38/906.
88 Dyson, "Mr Dyson's West African Tour – 1952," 15 February–25 March 1952, pp. 36, 39; Dyson, "List of Senior Staff – Nigeria," BGA 80/4328. There were also differences in the number of dependants: Only two British signatories were married, without children, whereas all Africans are married, with an average of four children each.
89 FA Boreham, untitled salary list, BGA 80/4584.
90 AF Tuke, untitled list, BGA 80/4292.

91 "Ghana Board Members," BGA 80/3580.
92 Figures: RE Fleming and EV Whitcombe, "Nigeria and the Cameroons," 23 July 1960, p. 6, BGA 80/3466. Cade mentions in 1958 that Bashorun, who had been with Barclays at least since 1948, when he was one of the first three Africans to be suggested for a B-signature, had been manager of an Ibadan sub-branch. He later entered the newly established Central Bank as Assistant to the General Manager in 1960. See "Central Bank of Nigeria," 27 October 1960, BoE OV 68/13. Housing: C Fitzherbert to his family, Zaria 25 October 1962, BGA 38/993.
93 Decker, "Africanization."
94 Ayowa Afrifa Taylor, "An Economic History of the Ashanti Goldfields Corporation, 1895–2004: Land, Labour, Capital and Enterprise," *Department of Economic History, London School of Economics and Political Science* (University of London, 2006).

List of References

Afrifa Taylor, Ayowa. "An Economic History of the Ashanti Goldfields Corporation, 1895–2004: Land, Labour, Capital and Enterprise." *Department of Economic History, London School of Economics and Political Science*. University of London, 2006.

Appiah, Joe. *Joe Appiah: The Autobiography of an African Patriot*. Accra, Ghana: Asempa, 1996.

Arhin, K, DE Skinner, and GO Olusanya. *West African Colonial Civil Servants in the Nineteenth Century: African Participation in British Colonial Expansion in West Africa*. Leiden, Netherlands: African Studies Centre, 1985.

Austin, Dennis. *Politics in Ghana*. Oxford: Oxford University Press, 1964.

Awa, Eme Onuoha. *Federal Government in Nigeria*. Berkeley, CA: University of California Press, 1964.

Bourret, FM *Ghana: The Road to Independence 1919–1957*. Stanford CA: Stanford University Press, 1969.

Burawoy, Michael. *The Colour of Class on the Copper Mines: From African Advancement to Zambianization*. Zambian pa. Manchester: Manchester University Press, 1972.

Coker, DDA "Letter." In *Trading in West Africa*, edited by Peter N. Davies, 157–72. London, UK: Croom Helm, 1976.

Coleman, JS *Nigeria: Background to Nationalism*. Berkeley, CA: University of California Press, 1971.

Commission on post-school certificate and higher education in Nigeria. "Investment in Education: The Report of the Commission on Post-School Certificate and Higher Education in Nigeria." Lagos, Ngieria, 1960.

Decker, Stephanie. "Africanization in British Multinationals in Ghana and Nigeria, 1945–1970." *Business History Review* 92, no. 4 (December 1, 2018): 691–718. 10.1017/S0007680518001034.

Decker, Stephanie. "Postcolonial Transitions in Africa: Decolonization in West Africa and Present Day South Africa." *Journal of Management Studies* 47, no. 5 (July 2010): 791–813. 10.1111/j.1467-6486.2010.00924.x.

Ezera, K. *Constitutional Developments in Nigeria*. Cambridge, UK: Cambridge University Press, 1964.

Fieldhouse, David Kenneth. *Merchant Capital and Economic Decolonisation: The United Africa Company 1929–1987*. Oxford: Clarendon, 1994.

Fry, Richard. *Bankers in West Africa: The History of the British Bank of West Africa*. London: Hutchinson Benham, 1976.

Greenhalgh, P.A.L. *West African Diamonds 1919–1983: An Economic History*. Manchester, UK: Manchester University Press, 1985.

Harragin, Walter. *Report of the Commission on the Civil Services of British West Africa, 1945–1946*. London, UK: HMSO, 1947.

Jones, Geoffrey. *British Multinational Banking, 1830–1990*. New York: OUP, 1993.

Jones, Trevor. *Ghana's First Republic, 1960–1966: The Pursuit of the Political Kingdom*. London, UK: Methuen, 1976.

Knox, Andrew M. *Coming Clear: A Postscript after Retirement from Unilever*. London, UK: Heinemann, 1976.

Lewis, W Arthur. "Report on the Industrialisation and the Gold Coast." Accra, Ghana, 1953.

Lynn, Martin. *British Documents on the End of Empire (Nigeria)*. Series B. London: Institute of Commonwealth Studies, 2001.

Milburn, Josephine F. *British Business and Ghanaian Independence*. London: C. Hurst, 1977.

Nicolson, IF *The Administration of Nigeria 1900–60: Men, Methods, and Myths*. Oxford: Clarendon, 1969.

Nicolson, IF "The Machinery of the Federal and Regional Governments." In *Nigerian Government and Politics*, edited by JP Mackintosh, 138–99. London, UK: George Allen and Unwin, 1966.

Nwanwene, Omorogbe. "The Nigerian Public Services Commissions." In *Studies in Nigerian Administration*, edited by DJ Murray, 177–208. London, UK: Hutchinson, 1970.

Olusanya, G.O. *The Evolution of the Nigerian Civil Service, 1861–1960: The Problem of Nigerianization*. Yaba and Lagos, Nigeria: University of Lagos, 1975.

Phillipson, S, and SO Adebo. "The Nigerianization of the Civil Service." Nigeria, 1952.

Rathbone, Richard. *Ghana: British Documents on the End of Empire*. Series B. London: Institute of Commonwealth Studies, 1992.

Rimmer, Douglas. *Staying Poor: Ghana's Political Economy, 1950–1990*. Edited by World Bank. Oxford: Pergamon, 1992.

Stockwell, Sarah E. *The Business of Decolonization: British Business Strategies in the Gold Coast*. Oxford: Clarendon Press, 2000.

White, Jeremy. *Central Administration of Nigeria*. Dublin, Ireland: Irish Academy Press, 1981.

6 African Managers in British Businesses

Nationalists pressing British companies for further Africanization expected to increase local control over foreign businesses. Moreover, it created jobs for an emerging middle class in Ghana and Nigeria and ensured votes from skilled urban employees. During the first few years after independence, when relations between companies and politicians were generally good, there was relatively little dissent over Africanization and the speed at which it progressed. However, in the late 1960s and 1970s, when criticism of neo-colonialism and its 'stooges' was rife, the rate of Africanization became the focus of corporate anxieties and official pressure. Parliamentary debates, such as the following between Chief Festus Okotie-Eboh, Nigeria's Finance Minister and another member of parliament, Mr WO Briggs, challenged government policies regarding foreign investors:

Okotie-Eboh: The policy of the Federal Government can best be summed up as to '*Nigerianise* rather than to *Nationalise*'.

Briggs: The Minister of Finance advocates *Nigerianisation* and not *nationalisation* [...] Does he think that by merely Nigerianising the staff of some of these basic industries then automatically those industries will become Nigerian companies?[1]

While British companies hoped to develop a group of loyal African employees who could be entrusted with managerial responsibilities, most British executives were uncertain about the extent to which this could be achieved. The loyalty of African staff was an issue more complicated than a choice between employer and nation.

The role and experience of African managers are only slowly becoming the focus of historical research.[2] Prior research considered African managers who worked for foreign multinationals as part of an emerging middle class associated with foreign interests.[3] Conversely, studies of independent African businesspeople tended to highlight African agency.[4] Yet it was not unusual for African managers to leave their positions in multinationals to run their own companies.

DOI: 10.4324/9781003001058-8

Corporate Africanization created a group of employees distinct from the main body of employees. Their position within companies and among other groups of employees in British business changed significantly during and after decolonization. Singling out capable individuals for further advancement created a two-tier African workforce, and rapid promotion sometimes heightened tensions between different generations. Initially, Africanization indirectly created an equally two-tiered European workforce: those considered less promising, who were to be replaced in the short to medium term, and those who would go on to fill high-ranking positions either in international subsidiaries or in UK headquarters. While the first part of the chapter looks at the attitudes of European managers, who selected individuals for further promotion, the second section focuses on the problematic relationship between different groups of African workers in British business and the role of trade unions. The governments' position on Africanization changed in the 1970s, and companies came under increasing pressure to speed up Africanization. The combination of indigenization decrees (see chapter 4) and stricter expatriate quotas created many new opportunities for African managers in foreign companies, particularly in economically buoyant Nigeria.

6.1 Expatriates and Africans

Africanization not only fragmented the interests of expatriates and local staff but also changed how both foreign and local elites in business and politics interacted. By the 1970s, British executives were faced, for the first time, with the decision of whether to dispense with expatriates altogether in their management of subsidiaries. For many, the answer to this question depended on if they felt they could trust their African managers. This section first addresses how European executives suggested that they were separated from their African staff by a significant cultural and social distance. Such distance could be bridged, it was proposed, through in-house training as a critical socialization device to ensure the loyalty and trustworthiness of their African managers: 'expatriate managers tend to complain of the impossibility of training local staff but [...] in fact, with long term planning, indigenous staff are perfectly competent to run most businesses'.[5]

6.1.1 Cultural and social distance

The attitudes of European managers are important for corporate Africanization because expatriates essentially controlled and determined the recruitment, career paths and promotions of Africans within firms. UAC, for example, proudly published the achievements of its training and Africanization programme in its *Economic and Statistical Review* in 1959 and illustrated this with a picture of two Europeans interviewing a young African man for the post of apprentice (Figure 6.1). UAC review did not contain many pictures, and the

Figure 6.1 A job interview at UAC in West Africa, 1959.

Note: Reproduced with kind permission of Unilever plc and group companies.[6]

inclusion of this picture seems significant. It depicted two older European men, looking like senior managers, interviewing an African candidate. Their attentive postures emphasized their positive attitude to this process, contradicting claims that expatriates sought to obstruct the advancement of Africans in order to safeguard their own positions. The young man interviewed is in the forefront, aligned in the bottom right of the picture, the back of his head towards the viewer, all attention focused on him. His anonymity represented African applicants in general, and the fact that all parties in the image were men reflected the continued underrepresentation of women in business at this time. This image is interesting as an attempt to tell the UAC's side of the story of Africanization at the firm.

But images are always open to multiple interpretations.[7] Hence, the photograph can also be read as an illustration of who oversaw the process: white, normally British, men. The caption in the booklet informs the reader that the selection process is for an apprentice, underlining that Europeans were still in charge of recruiting even relatively junior positions. It also highlighted that Africans within the organization had not been advanced to a level where they took staffing decisions.

The fact that expatriates took these decisions highlights anxieties about who was to be allowed into the organization and whom to trust. Many British managers perceived an immense cultural distance between themselves and their African staff. Frederic Seebohm, who later became the chairman of Barclays Bank DCO, commented in 1954: 'It is very difficult for a European to assess the character and ability of an African.'[8] However, cultural differences seem to get cited more by expatriates than by local employees, who mainly maintained that expatriates understood their African subordinates perfectly well.[9] Concerns around cultural and social distance reflected the ideology of racial and cultural superiority that permeated colonialism. The modernization theory of the 1940s, 1950s and 1960s similarly only aimed to understand the local culture in as much as it was necessary to change it into something perceived as more progressive.

The changing attitudes were most obvious in the opinions of senior management. For example, Edward Spears admonished the European staff in Obuasi during a non-unionized strike in 1945: 'Each one of you must keep in touch and know what these people think.'[10] European managers' difficulties in dealing with labour troubles opened up opportunities for Africans later.[11] While Frederic Seebohm of DCO voiced his doubts about whether Europeans could actually understand local people in the 1950s, his attitude showed a stronger class bias by 1960: 'The top-class Nigerians are good company and much more interesting than most of the British that one meets abroad.'[12] Frederick Pedler of the UAC agreed:

> The ministers you meet and the senior civil servants are people of impressive quality. This, I think, has been a comment offered by other people who have come back from Nigeria.[13]

The social and cultural distance that was constantly being constructed within British companies was no longer upheld with regard to the emerging African elites, particularly in politics. The same occurred with attitudes towards senior African employees, although somewhat later. The British general manager of Dunlop in Nigeria, John Smith, was quoted saying in an interview in 1976: 'At the top, Nigerian managers are quite outstanding', but continued that 'the country lacked depth of management.'[14]

These attitudes were obviously affected by a broader social change that took place in West Africa. Colonial withdrawal gave Africans access to the top positions in the government and economy. Africanization increased the stratification of society by adding another rung or two to the social ladder. Europeans on the coast mostly fell into the higher strata, but during decolonization, Africans rose into the leading positions in society, not only drawing level but also outranking Europeans. In comparison to most Africans, however, Europeans continued to lead a privileged lifestyle. The greater social proximity of both groups of elites opened an avenue for cooperation, and this explains why expatriates changed their attitudes towards local elites but continued to distance themselves from African employees or, indeed, the locals in general.

6.1.2 Staff training and Africanization

In the immediate post-war period, British managers found it difficult to trust their African staff, and this effectively barred them from most responsible jobs. On the one hand, racist bias was more overt in organizations. On the other hand, British-based managers faced a principal-agent problem: they knew very little about the background of their Nigerians and Ghanaian staff compared to the expatriates. The latter were white middle-class men with similar educational credentials, being trained on the job by other trusted expatriates. Bonding was encouraged through joint accommodation in bachelors' messes or company housing. Companies had greater control of expatriates by deciding on when and how they travelled homeward, with the ultimate sanction being the non-renewal of contract, although this was normally only imposed for serious misconduct.[15] The same system of control and socialization could not be established for Africans, although housing was increasingly provided for managerial staff, and their membership in clubs was encouraged.[16] While some efforts at socialization were made, the treatment of European staff was changing at the same time, as careers were professionalized through structured training and more 'objective' assessment methods. Comprehensive training regimes for all staff were introduced in most companies, with a focus on preparing new African recruits for more responsible roles.

Particular attention was paid to training schemes for Africans in skilled or managerial positions. The old approach of unstructured on-the-job training was difficult to maintain in the context of commercial and industrial expansion during the economic boom in the 1950s, coupled with pressures to Africanize. Both British banks suffered from a lending crisis in the late 1950s, which was due to a large extent to the inexperience and lack of training of staff, both European and African, as well as a lack of control by head office.[17] UAC also recognized the need for organized and comprehensive training, which formalized the knowledge that African recruits had to acquire in order to advance. In an internal memorandum on 'ization', Andrew Knox, one of Unilever's directors, made it clear in 1956 that local staff's rise in the managerial hierarchies had to be accompanied by a thorough indoctrination into the corporate culture:

> […] the next stage which is to bring locally employed managers into the very highest positions in our business it becomes even more important that they should be 'Unilever' men in the true sense and not merely good local operators […] our task is not only, e.g. to Indianize our business in India but we must also Unileverize the Indians who have positions of authority in that business.[18]

Companies, not for the first time, believed they could instil corporate values into their employees, inspire a sense of pride in belonging to their organization and reap the benefits of their loyalty. In a practical sense, however, Knox's statement is more meaningful. Corporate culture is based on tacit knowledge of how things are done, how situations are appropriately handled and how risks should be dealt with. These tacit rules were not comprehensive or necessarily stable, but they had the advantage of limiting monitoring costs and allowing staff greater freedom in taking decisions. In this sense, the 'Unileverisation of Indians', and anyone else, was a precondition to promotion.

Training provision took different forms in different firms. UAC seems to have planned and publicized their efforts most comprehensively (Figure 6.2), opening its first training school in Nigeria in 1954 and a further five in West Africa. Barclays established a bank school that taught clerical skills in 1956 and gave limited support to potential managerial staff in preparing for their Institute of Bankers exams.[19] The mining companies in Ghana supported training schemes via the Chamber of Mines. CAST, the diamond mining company, had their own training programme. Training was an issue on which all sides could agree: African employees because it increased their educational credentials; European employers because they wanted to imbue the right character and ability in their foreign staff; and the trade unions, as it provided a service to their members. The close connection between training

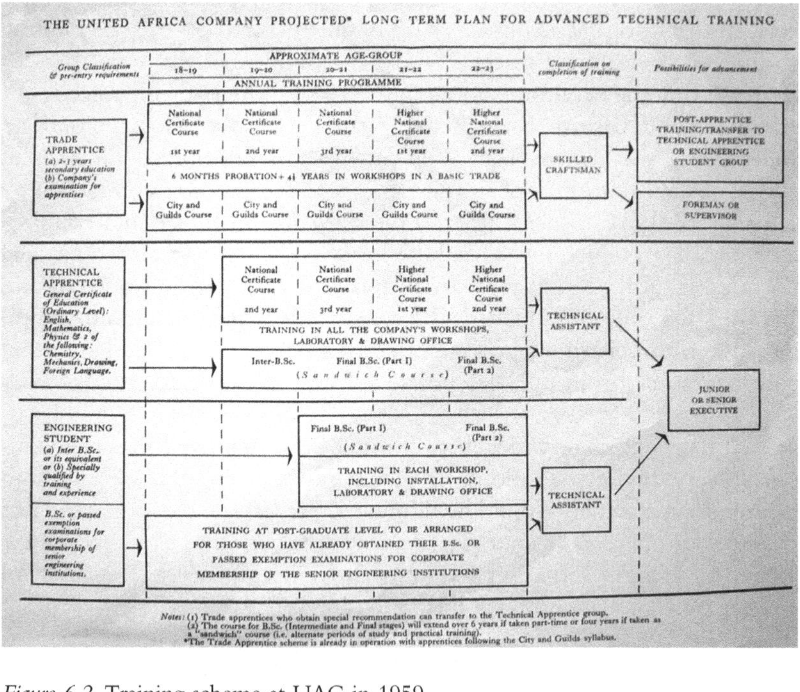

Figure 6.2 Training scheme at UAC in 1959.

Note: Reproduced with kind permission of Unilever plc and group companies.[21]

and Africanization is highlighted by the answer from a bank manager to the question of why she thought Africans began to replace Europeans: 'I think they [the expatriate managers] thought that the training was enough for the Africans to be able to manage […]'.[20] Using training as the main vehicle for the promotion of African employees had the advantage of being acceptable to both European managers and African staff.

African advancement, however, remained curtailed due to the existence of ceilings (see chapter 5.3.2), often based on sentiment and a vague notion of abilities. Clearly, this needs to be seen in the context of persistent racism. Curiously, there were some unlikely circumstances that significantly shifted European perceptions of African abilities. During the Nigerian civil war, only the UAC and the banks remained open in Biafra, apart from the oil companies.[22] At Barclays, all expatriates had been withdrawn, and the bank sent one of its local directors, John Okwesa, to Biafra in order to be the nominal head of the bank. The most senior Igbo manager in the East, Jibueze, took over as general manager. When an expatriate was sent over on a reconnaissance mission shortly after hostilities ceased, he remarked, 'amazingly, they did quite well'.[23] The Igbo staff kept books, continued nearly normal banking business, and accumulated deposits. Although the balances were wiped out by a currency change, the staff's committed work enabled the bank to continue business with only minor rebuilding delays. In conjunction with government pressure in both Nigeria and Ghana, the bank subsequently reassessed its policy of giving more responsibility to its African staff. The civil war provided the stimulus for several managerial careers in the bank.[24] In Ghana, Africanization also speeded up in the mid-1960, when Barclays began to recruit university graduates to fast-track them into management positions.[25]

In practice, certain positions in the central hierarchy of British firms in West Africa went to locals earlier than others. Highly visible posts such as public relations, or directorships on the local boards, became Africanized much more quickly than others.[26] This also included such unusual positions as the editor of the *Ashanti Times*, the AGC-owned newspaper, which always had a high proportion of Africans working for it. But the most common position for promotion lay in areas of personnel management dealing with African staff, positions that were often newly created for this purpose. Barclays' first attempt to promote an African into the Nigerian head office was E Inwang, who became Assistant (Staff) Manager in 1961 and shortly after the first-ever African Staff Manager. In 1957 at the AGC, there was also an African Personnel Officer, Alex Darko, who was by 1966 the Chief Personnel Officer, reporting directly to the General Mines Manager.[27] Positions of line authority over Europeans went only late, if at all, to Africans, and the same held true for higher-level technical and engineering jobs as well as those in central finance and accounting.[28] Which positions went to Africans earlier and which were only Africanized later, if at all, reflected the biases of European management.

6.1.3 Trust and loyalty

The lack of trust between Africans and Europeans was an intrinsic part of colonialism. For the senior management in the United Kingdom, loyalty and dependability were especially important issues. Any transgressions by African staff were noted and created noticeable anxiety with British managers. Over time, these issues became less pronounced, according to an African executive manager at Barclays: 'the expatriates we were working with were also flexible in their thinking. They knew that at the end of it all they will leave and [...] they were going to leave the bank in the hands of capable people.'[29] While this presents the relationship between expatriates and African managers in an unproblematic light, it took several years for most companies to establish a local cadre to which they were prepared to hand over. Frequently, outside political pressure was necessary to prompt the transfer of the most important position. These factors came together in the 1960s and 1970s.

Although the UAC had a good image in Nigeria because the firm had 'really responded to the call for industrialization' and 'had done better than most in Africanization', according to a report by Pedler in 1965, trusting their African employees remained a managerial concern.[30] And while their success in recruiting competent and promising African staff was celebrated, Pedler was concerned over an especially successful staff choice:

> We have one most extraordinary character there – a Nigerian called Ojora who is 33. He has been a director of UAC of Nigeria Limited for two years. He is the head of the Public Relations Department; he knows so much about some of our businesses and is so intelligent that he could give you very helpful advice as to marketing problems, financial problems, etc. He reckons to have a private talk with the Prime Minister every six weeks or so and, in fact, the Prime Minister welcomes it as a way of keeping himself informed. He walks in and out of any other government office as he pleases and it is to be recognised that this man has immense power to do us good but, at the same time, the potential to do us harm if he were so minded. By virtue of his personality and performance he really does constitute a major management problem and one wonders what he is going to do with the rest of his life.[31]

It is interesting that Pedler viewed one of the most outstanding and promising Nigerian managers, who also had extensive political contacts, as a threat to the organization 'by virtue of his personality and performance'. As opposed to a promising European, promoting an African to a high-level position at the head office in the United Kingdom, or circulating them internationally, was apparently not an option and potentially even a waste of Adekunle Ojora's political contacts.[32] Being an African manager in a

European multinational was clearly never going to be sufficient for an exceptionally talented Nigerian. Pedler's worries about Ojora's future were, however, unnecessary – he subsequently had an illustrious career as a director of several companies and was accorded several titles in Nigeria, Britain and Italy.[33]

British businesses found it hard to gauge the loyalty of their African staff towards the newly independent regimes, which took the credit for having promoted Africanization. Some of Barclays' political contacts in Ghana fell out of favour with Nkrumah, most notably CPP veterans such as Komla Gbedemah and Kojo Botsio, who had become too conservative for Nkrumah's increasingly left-leaning politics. The former was attacked in the press for having pressed an expatriate bank into giving him a five-figure loan for a business venture. The local director of Barclays in Ghana, Julian Wathen, commented:

> It is a little disturbing that the extent of his loan from us, which was £18,000 should be public property, but with the existing line that the Party is 'supreme' it is probable that other loyalties will go by the board and we shall not be able to trust any of our staff not to disclose facts to the Party which they feel are in the Party's interest.[34]

At a time when nationalist parties in West Africa were deliberately seeking to politicize educated urban employees, management was concerned about the implications for loyalty to one's employer or adherence to an industry's code of conduct. But while it only required one person to have leaked the information to the media or a CPP politician, the European leadership again made blanket assumptions. After the removal of Nkrumah, it became clear that African managers, even though they were dubious about the political achievements of the previous regime, still attributed the increased professional and social opportunities to political efforts. 'With the waygoing of Nkrumah the African feels and is expressing his apprehension that the European may not now feel so compelled to consider the African.'[35]

European managers took various initiatives designed to shorten the social distance that they perceived between themselves and African politicians and staff. As they controlled the recruitment, training and promotion of local staff, a pattern of employment emerged that first saw Africans appointed to the local boards, public relations or other highly visible positions in moves that appear to have largely been a form of window-dressing.

6.2 African staff

Africanization predictably created tension between European and African staff, as well as between different groups of African employees. Africanization created winners and losers, a fact which was not always considered by European managers, who would occasionally even use these internal rivalries as an excuse for their replacement programmes flagging. J Stanton of the UAC commented after a visit to West Africa in 1957:

> Africanization was proceeding smoothly in most centres, but there was a certain apprehension among junior European personnel in that they felt uncertain of their future [...] There were also some African employees who were apprehensive of the rapidity of the Africanization policy – they felt that their interests were safer in European hands.[36]

While corporate executives liked to give particular prominence to this because it provided them with a ready excuse for the faltering progress of Africanization, there is evidence that this was indeed an issue. Tensions emerged between different generations of African senior staff, the subject of the next section. Another faultline existed with African trade unions, which were caught between claiming to be a form of national, African representation and a social, class-based one.

6.2.1 The rise of African managers

Tension among African staff was indeed common in British business, and expatriates were quick to exploit this. In his testimony to the Watson Commission, George Cole of the UAC commented in 1948:

> Perhaps the greatest difficulty facing the most ardent advocate of Africanization is getting African staff to cooperate wholeheartedly with African Managers. They often distrust them, sometimes oppose them, and have been known to do everything possible to bring them down.[37]

Political pressure, however, ensured that Africanization proceeded nevertheless, despite issues in terms of customer acceptance in some businesses. While Holt claimed that 'the African understands the mentality of his compatriot far better than a European can hope to do and can converse with him freely in his own language', the BBWA maintained that their 'African customers were at first reluctant to bank with a branch that had no European manager'.[38] Barclays was advised by the Asantehene Prempeh II that African chiefs and farmers would fear that 'there is no secrecy where there are African employees' and that 'their heirs might learn too much about the financial position and decide to dispose of them'.[39] The banks introduced local managers only under the regular and visible supervision of a European manager from a nearby branch.

Newly recruited African trainees faced the potential disapproval of their colleagues, who sometimes felt bypassed in the fast-tracking process. The Ghanaian politician Joseph Appiah recounts in his biography an encounter in the army when the African instructor made it clear that he disapproved of plans to introduce black officers, arguing that if all black men were equal, none should have the privilege of crossing the colour bar. Eventually choosing a career in the UAC, Appiah found colleagues equally touchy about a new recruit earmarked for management fast-tracking, interpreting what he considered respectful behaviour as snobbishness.[40] Appiah's background and upbringing were different as his family were considered Ashanti nobility.[41] But Appiah's experience also reflected a degree of intergenerational conflict, as young and inexperienced new recruits were rapidly promoted above and beyond the positions to which the older generation could have aspired.

Generally, promotion can be based on either seniority or performance.[42] The colonial nature of the economy with its lack of educational opportunities meant, however, that these two factors rarely overlapped, as the following statement illustrates:

> [...] there were one or a couple of local managers, black, Ghanaian managers [...] they lacked qualification, they didn't have what it took to be managers. They just came through the system and some of them were just there. You know, they had reached their peachiest point, [...] age was a factor because I was fairly young and I was leapfrogging these fairly old people who had been in the system for so long. [...] Because, don't forget, those people were promoted more on the length of time they spent in the bank as opposed to their own performance. So when I was performing and they were promoting me, of course that created a bit of a problem for them.[...] that was the time [the late 1960s and 1970s] when [...] barriers were being removed and people were being rewarded and promoted based on their performance.[43]

On the one hand, seniority and age were important for status in Ghanaian and Nigerian society. On the other hand, the companies' promotion policy was predicated on the length of service and demonstrable loyalty. The changing economic and political conditions in the late 1960s, however, saw the introduction of more performance-based human resource management approach. There is some indication that rivalry indeed existed and presented a significant hurdle. The senior executive manager mentioned above, for example, remarked that he threatened to quit at one stage due to the resistance he encountered from other Ghanaians and only remained because he was encouraged by an expatriate.[44]

Some well-educated newcomers, such as Appiah, had the attitude to match: his wealthy and educated upbringing left him with a sense of superiority when faced with the illiterate army instructor, who only spoke pidgin, 'this new version of the King's English', or with the head of the UAC's Kroo labour in Accra.[45] In 1966, AGC's security officer reported on the discontent of the younger Ghanaian senior staff, who had formed their own association, with respect to 'the presence of a number of near illiterates in the senior staff. The more educated ones see this as a brake to management's wider consideration of their greater social aspirations'.[46]

Literacy, particularly in the Ghanaian mines, also had an ethnic dimension because it was normally miners from the Northern Territories, working underground, who could neither read nor write English. They were, moreover, those with the greatest practical experience of mining operations but were unlikely to undergo formal technical training because of their illiteracy. Surface workers, however, were mostly Asante or Southern Ghanaian, a larger percentage of whom had attended school.[47] Hence this classic tension between surface and underground labour was compounded by an ethnic dimension. While southern Ghanaians were also more likely to support nationalist parties, miners from the Northern Territories (or indeed from the neighbouring French colonies) were less politically active and primarily concerned with the immediate improvement of their working conditions – an attitude more palatable to the expatriate mine's management.

6.2.2 Trade unions and African managers

In mining, where labour was stronger than in other sectors, trade unions added another dimension. At the AGC, the Africanization of supervisory positions in the manual, non-clerical departments was often accompanied by so-called discipline problems. In 1960 C Moshie, the president of the Mines Employees Union (MEU), commented at a local branch meeting at Bibiani 'that everybody should pay more respect to their senior Africans than to the Europeans'.[48] However, relations between the union and the African senior staff were far from straightforward, as the MEU considered itself an African trade union. The position of Africans in what used to be 'European appointments' created several problems, for example, whether the trade union-supported African superiors enforced industrial discipline over its members?

In Ghana, this became a particularly thorny issue once the CPP had taken control of the trade union movement in 1958.[49] In 1961, there was an incident in which an African foreman was singled out by the union for disciplinary action after trade union members complained about the treatment of workers in the carpentry shop at Obuasi. The apparently strict regime in the shop was due to the European in charge, Mr Kellaway, but he and 'his African Foreman, Mr Marful, have joined hands to mistreat the workers' and union members claimed the foreman used the shop steward as a scapegoat.[50] Although the European was ultimately responsible for the situation in the workplace, the shop steward had the job of ensuring the welfare of workers; the union singled out the African foreman on the basis of race and superior position. In a meeting of the Obuasi branch of the Mines Workers' Union, two speakers made the position of the union clear: '[Mr] Acqua said there is no hatred between Europeans and Africans but the hatred comes, when Africans start to undermine each other and that, the union shall never sit aloof to allow this foreman to carry everything into his hands.'[51] The second speaker, Mr Mills, stated:

> That he blames Marful, as he is an African and should know the feelings of his fellow Africans [...] Mills warned all the official learners that they should not consider themselves as Europeans and forget all the facilities given them on arrival to take up appointments and get themselves closer to the union, which is the only mouthpiece of the workers in this country.[52]

The union threatened to expel Marful and wanted to see him dismissed from his employment and indeed have him barred from any further employment in any 'Labour Centre'.[53] This appears to have been an occasion where the weakest link was singled out. As an African, Marful could not count on the same support from the corporation that expatriates had. As he held a supervisory position, his interests were also at odds with the trade union, although he was still a member. It is interesting that in a dispute about work discipline and practices, the union sided with workers' complaints at a time when they publicly exhorted the need for discipline and increased productivity.[54]

The relationship between salaried African senior staff and daily rated, waged miners' union members had been difficult since the 1950s due to the staff agreements that precluded senior staff from joining the union. In 1953, Daniel K Foevie, General Secretary of the MEU, stated categorically 'that difficulties confronting the Union in Obuasi stem from the non-participation of the Salaried Staff in Union activities. This matter would be taken up with the Directors, who would be asked to cancel all Staff agreements'.[55] While this demand was predictably rejected, it remained part of Foevie's policy to gain the support of senior Africans. During the 1955 strike, the salaried staff and the striking miners clashed over the issue. The president, Buachie, complained at a rally that

> [...] a very annoying letter had been received by the Union Executives from the salaried staff, who said that they were not members of the Union and would have no benefits from the increases in pay that the Union were now demanding. This, he said, was stupid as the Union were fighting for all workers, including the salaried staff. [...] the salaried staff have always shared the increases in pay which have resulted from the efforts of the Union but they must be prepared to forfeit them in future.[56]

The union members present fully agreed with this, threatening 'that the salaried staff could man the mine if they wanted to, but there would be trouble if they also received increases as a result of the strike. [...] They [the miners] were determined to stop the salaried staff from working as they were all mines' employees and they must sink or swim together'.[57] The representatives of the African Salaried Staff Association told the General Mines Manager that they had been approached by the union to support the strike because 'this was an issue between African and Europeans, and that it was essential that if they were to achieve their object, the Africans should put up a united front'.[58] The president and secretary, however, assured the General Mines Manager that they had bluntly refused this.

Despite this failure to mobilize the senior staff, Foevie tried again in 1963:

> He [Foevie] had heard that there was a lack of interest amongst African Senior Staff at Obuasi in union affairs, and stated that without the Union there would be no African Senior Staff. Mr Foevie said 'What group do African Senior Staff belong to? You are not for the animals and you are not for the birds. In other words you are not for the Union and not for the real European Staff on the mine.[...]' [...] African Senior Staff were urged by Mr. Foevie to forget that they were not members of the union, and to submit their complaints to the union.[59]

At an earlier meeting, Mr A Quagraine, the branch secretary for Obuasi, had voiced similar views, criticizing the fact that senior staff did not make any voluntary contributions to the union's funds as happened at other mines and repeating the point that the advancement of the senior staff had been a result of the union's efforts. He also condemned AGC's redundancy policy, which had meant that after every pay increase Africans were discharged but never Europeans, again underlining the racial underpinning of labour politics.[60] There was indeed ample evidence that trade union activity improved the wages of African salaried staff, as the negotiation certificates specified an upper wage limit above which the union could not represent mines' staff anymore. By pushing this level higher, the companies were forced to improve their managerial wages in order to avoid having the union represent their own management staff. This limit increased from £600 per annum in 1959 to £625 three years later when the union applied to raise it again to £685.[61] That Foevie should have aimed to represent African managers is hardly surprising, as, by 1963, he was a manager himself. At the same time, he was also the 'Life General Secretary' and Treasurer of the Mines Workers' Union (MWU, previously the Mines Employees Union) and a director of the Ghana State Mining Corporation (GSMC) from 1960 onwards, as well as a CPP member.[62] Hence he was in the remarkable and exceptional position of representing the trinity of employers, employees and government all at the same time. The AGC, nevertheless, opposed his proposals.

> Again it cannot be accepted that senior African Staff should belong to the Union. When the Staff Agreement was prepared it was made clear that entering into a Contract was not compatible with Union membership. [...] Subscribing to Union funds must denote membership, in practice at least. I do not see how a man can in a crisis be loyal to his contract if he is a subscriber to the Union. The essence of staff engagements is that they

> should be outside the Union and no distinction should be made between Europeans and Africans.[63]

This strict differentiation between white and blue-collar staff was based on how British managers' viewed the organization of mines, and they successfully replicated this tradition at the AGC.[64]

The relationship between the trade unions and the AGC was not generally as difficult as these incidents might suggest. Both the MEU and the AGC considered labour relations in the years from 1956 to 1963 as very good, mainly at the expense of the gold mine: wage levels increased by 40 to 50 per cent.[65] Nevertheless, the legitimacy of the miners' union was gradually eroded through its close association with politics, particularly the CPP. It seems that this was less drastic at the AGC than at the state mines, where miners rioted in 1968 against management, both European and African, and trade union officials.[66] At most Ghanaian mines, however, the relationship between management and trade union representatives was already close in the early 1960s, as an episode at the AGC underlines. The British labour attaché actually advised the mine's management to be seen as reluctant to grant wage increases in order to give union officials the possibility to 'overcome' the firm's intransigence and strengthen their own position.[67]

Africanization did not necessarily serve everybody's interests, as it only created a limited number of opportunities. Those who were too old and without the necessary education were excluded. The promotion of promising young staff in fast-track programmes also clashed with the prior principle of seniority: firms used to train on the job and rewarded those who had shown a long-term commitment to the firms. Long-serving employees felt threatened by this change in promotion criteria from the length of service to performance. Africans mostly agreed with promotion by merit, but there was a noticeable expectation that seniority would be rewarded: miners, for example, often asked for promotion on the basis of their length of service.[68] The tendency to recruit African senior staff into positions of personnel supervision at an early stage brought them into conflict with lower-ranking employees and the trade unions. The harder Europeans found it to contain conflict, the more convenient it became to promote Africans on the assumption that they were more likely to handle this successfully.[69]

For European managers, however, this step was only possible once a basic code of behaviour was established. Absolute reliability in case of a strike was the backbone of AGC's Africanization strategy, and this illustrates the importance of two issues: first, trust and loyalty, and second, the company's attempts to distance its African senior staff from the common miner and the Obuasi township. Similar developments occurred in other British companies. Africanization was not only effective as a public relations measure, but it also served to break the ranks of African trade unions, as the neat alignment of European supervisors and African subordinates was unsettled, introducing a class dimension to African labour that previously had been irrelevant.

6.3 African management and economic nationalism

The promotion of indigenous enterprise that began in the late 1960s in Ghana and early 1970s in Nigeria had a direct impact on the position of African managers in foreign business. Because the 1970s was a decade when foreign firms faced expropriations across the globe, these internal changes have often been overlooked by researchers more interested in issues of ownership and control. However, the two issues, expropriations and Africanization, also interacted in ways that require further research. The economic nationalism of the 1970s benefited African managers to a considerable extent, which makes a simplistic assessment of whether host state or European business owners retained greater control more complex.

Training of locals was intensified in response to indigenization requirements. This was particularly noticeable in Nigeria, which experienced an economic boom due to oil wealth in the 1970s. It is, however, also applicable to Ghana, but the country suffered severe political and economic upheaval in the 1970s and 1980s. Most companies were increasingly willing to hand over to African managers in the smaller country because no profits could be remitted, and the country had gone into a deep recession. The impact of the Nigerian Enterprise Promotion Decrees (NEPDs) was studied in great depth by Thomas Biersteker, a sociologist, who identified that it was particularly Western European firms, the majority of which were British, that offered greater training opportunities to their staff. This expansion of training was to ensure the complete Africanization of many firms, and Biersteker notes that a number of Nigerians were promoted to senior management positions in response to NEPD II in particular.[70] In the 1980s, he went so far as to argue that Nigerian managers were the main beneficiary and pressure group for further economic nationalism:

> The combined effects of token personnel indigenization at the very top of indigenized firms and the anticipated return of large numbers of trained and highly qualified Nigerian managers will provide pressure for further personnel indigenization. There has already been a great deal of pressure within companies to speed up the process, especially from the junior ranks dissatisfied with the pace of promotion. This kind of tension will intensify unless relieved by other policies or programs.[71]

The indigenization programmes were also beneficial for local managers in other ways. In Nigeria, most British companies gave preferential share deals to their own employees when forced to indigenize.[72] As in the late 1940s, when the change in commercial policy had aided incumbent African businessmen to make the transfer from being agents of trading firms to independent retailers, or in the 1950s when the increased training and promotion opportunities led to more staff resignations in order to run independent businesses, the indigenization programmes also enabled managers to become businessmen in their own right. Biersteker notes this in particular in Nigeria, where a buoyant economy in the 1970s and later import restrictions in the 1980s aided local ventures.

> One multinational manager complained about the loss of several local managers who were trained by his office in Europe and upon their return to Nigeria went off and set up their own competing concerns, one in the production of toothpaste, another in the production of paints. Another foreign manager complained about a similar incident in which one of his former employees established a food-processing company that copied the packaging and labelling of one of his firm's most successful consumer products.[73]

While Biersteker's survey encountered a few examples, there is further indication that this was common, as Barclays Nigeria actually tailored an advertising campaign towards these 'new executives' (Figure 6.3). It is also noteworthy where the bank ran this advert: the Nigerian Institute of Management, which published the magazine *Management in Nigeria*, was a body that was funded by subscriptions from private businesses and offered management and technical training courses. This was a forum for Nigerian middle management, whether individuals saw their future in multinational employment or only considered it a springboard to self-employment. How far this also played a role in Ghana, which was in the depth of an economic crisis, is less clear. Political pressure to Ghanaianize senior management was certainly equally strong in the experience of a senior executive of Barclays Ghana, who worked for the bank at the time:

> I think they knew that at the end of [the] day it was inevitable that the Africanization programme was going to be [the] name of the game, because, remember, we are talking about the sixties and the changes in the economic environment and the government placing emphasis on the private sector, and also divesting state organisations. So the private sector was given the impetus and the Ghana government wanted its own people to be in charge of operations, so those of us who had the chance … That's why they offered us the chance, because they knew it was inevitable, that they need to train people to take over when they were not there. It was in their own interest, in the interest of the business.[74]

Economic nationalism was a key factor in improving Africanization levels in British business because it was important to preserve local goodwill and

Figure 6.3 Barclays Bank of Nigeria 'Our kind of people ... ' advert.

Note: Reproduced with kind permission of Barclays Group Archives.[77]

ensure the legitimacy of foreign business.[75] Despite the similarities between the two countries, companies and international observers tended to focus on the larger and wealthier Nigeria. For example, Anthony Tuke, the incoming chairman of Barclays, described Africanization and localization as problems that the bank faced in both Nigeria and Ghana, but that Nigeria was most important to the bank and hence the focus of their policies.[76]

In Ghana, an NLC report in 1967 on the promotion of Ghanaian business featured relevant excerpts from the writings of economic development experts, including W Arthur Lewis's argument from 1953 that foreign investment could aid African entrepreneurs through knowledge transfer but that they had to escape from this dependence as soon as possible.[78] In both Ghana and Nigeria, the early indigenization legislation was built on long-standing criticism of foreign firms and intended to improve the opportunities available to local managers and entrepreneurs. The boundaries between managers, businessmen and politicians were often blurred in Africa.

Economic nationalism increased the autonomy of local subsidiaries vis-à-vis their UK head offices. Remittance restrictions and expatriate quotas curtailed capital and personnel flow between West Africa and the United Kingdom, increasing companies' dependence on local staff. As multinationals were reluctant to commit fresh capital to these areas, from which profits could not be remitted anyway, head offices were often content to leave the subsidiary in the hands of African management. In 1970, Barclays' incoming chairman expected that more responsibility would move to Lagos as a result of local shareholding. The UAC fought hard to retain control over its Nigerian subsidiaries, as their own overall results and, to some extent, those of Unilever as a whole depended on it.[79] In Ghana, however, Lever Brothers and later UAC were confident to leave a Ghanaian, Myles Hagan, in charge, who was regarded highly within the company and Ghana. The UAC also withdrew expatriates from Ghana in the 1970s without a fight – unlike in the 1960s or at the same time in Nigeria.[80] The importance of politics for a successful and profitable business venture in West Africa became paramount, making it necessary to give negotiators locally as much freedom and responsibility as possible. While overall strategic planning remained with head offices abroad, more and more decisions were taken locally by local managers.

6.4 Conclusion

Africanization created a two-tiered labour force that was moreover segregated along a colour bar. In both cases, those at the bottom lost out in the process – Europeans in junior positions who did not show sufficient promise and Africans too old or too poorly educated to be promoted further. Africans who did climb the ranks found themselves often posted to specific jobs: barely ever to supervise Europeans, but often to manage African staff, industrial or public relations. Africanization became possible as European managers found ways to diminish the social and cultural distance they perceived between themselves and their African subordinates. To achieve this, many companies insisted initially on long service to ensure that staff were sufficiently socialized into their corporate culture. Later this was increasingly replaced by comprehensive training programmes. Better salaries and provision of housing were further tools to achieve this. The question of where the loyalty of African managers lays remained a thorny issue. Companies, nationalist politicians and trade unions all claimed credit for advancing locals. By the 1970s, African managers were in a strong position to capitalize on the many options they had due to economic nationalism. The boundaries to other elite groups such as successful entrepreneurs and politicians were fluid.

African management as a group has not attracted the same scholarly attention as businessmen have, with a few exceptions.[81] However, those most critical of the failure to take control of foreign investment often listed the lack of technology and relevant skills as causes. Why then did research focus so much on ownership when the debate revolved around the issue of control? Modernization and development studies considered an indigenous, entrepreneurial middle class as the engine of autonomous growth. Dependency and underdevelopment scholars, however, often accused the same groups of not being truly national but a neo-colonial bourgeoisie, which had sold out to foreign interests.[82] Those who already worked for foreign commercial interests were not considered separately but would obviously fall into the same category. Hence the shifts within businesses towards greater local autonomy of subsidiaries were not relevant if they were still owned by foreign interests.[83] During the 1950s, when West African economies expanded, businesses tightened central control and introduced more expatriate staff and new techniques. As long as a business was profitable, like the majority of those in Ghana in the 1950s or in Nigeria in the 1960s and 1970s, management fought to retain control through expatriate top management. However, once it faced increasing economic difficulties or greater political pressure, many firms became more willing to cede greater autonomy to their subsidiaries and their local managers.

Notes

1 Nigeria, Federal House of Representatives, *House of Representatives Debates* (Lagos, 1961), 29 November 1961, cols. 3542, 3573.
2 A A Taylor, *Sam Jonah and the Remaking of Ashanti* (Johannesburg: Pan Macmillan South Africa, 2006); Dmitri Van den Bersselaar, "'Doorway to Success?': Reconstructing African Careers in European Business from Company House Magazines and Oral History Interviews," *History in Africa* 38 (2011): 257–94, http://journals.cambridge.org/abstract_S0361541300005660
3 Andre Gunder Frank, *Lumpenbourgeoisie, Lumpendevelopment: Dependence, Class, and Politics in Latin America* (Newy York, NY: Monthly Review Press, 1972), 1, 3–5, 8–9, 75–137; Samir Amin, *Neo-Colonialism in West Africa* (New York, NY: Monthly Review Press, 1973), 249–50.
4 Tom Forrest, *The Advance of African Capital. The Growth of Nigerian Private Enterprise* (Edinburgh, 1994).
5 Attributed to an ICI manager, see PJ Roberts, Filenote "Commercial in confidence – ICI," 27 July 1972, The National Archives (TNA) FCO 65/1222.
6 UAC, *Economic and Statistical Review*, 22 (London: UAC, 1959), between pp. 30–1.
7 Roland Barthes, "The Rhetoric of the Image," in *Image, Music, Text* (Glasgow: Fontana Press, 1977), 33–47.

8 F. Seebohm, "Diary," Ghana 31 January–9 February 1954, no page numbers, Barclays Group Archive (BGA) 277/1; similar claims were made by expatriates in Zambia, see Michael Burawoy, *The Colour of Class on the Copper Mines: From African Advancement to Zambianization*, Zambian pa (Manchester: Manchester University Press, 1972), 37.
9 Interview with senior executive manager of Barclays Ghana, 6 July 2004; interview with woman manager of Barclays Ghana, 29 June 2004. There is a similar suggestion in Burawoy, 75.
10 Minutes of Conference at Chairman's Office in Obuasi, 30 November 1945, London Metropolitan Archives (LMA) CLC/B/015/MS14171, v. 98 July–December 1945.
11 Frederick Cooper, "From Free Labor to Family Allowances: Labor and African Society in Colonial Discourse," *American Ethnologist* 16, no. 4 (1989): 758–9, https://doi.org/10.1525/ae.1989.16.4.02a00080
12 Seebohm's Diaries, "Visit to Nigeria," 29 January–16 February 1960, entry for 29 and 30 January 1960, BGA 277/3.
13 FJ Pedler, Report to Directors' Conference, Unilever Historical Archives (UHA) UNI/SC with Tropical Africa Committee, 10 Devember 1965.
14 Gab Oviogbodu, "At the top, Nigerian managers are quite outstanding. Interview with John Addison Smith," in *Management in Nigeria*, November 1976, pp. 8–9.
15 Geoffrey Jones, *British Multinational Banking, 1830–1990* (New York: OUP, 1993), 49–51, 209, 282.
16 "Meeting regarding West Africa visit February/March 1948," 2 April 1948, p. 1; BGA 38/906; Minutes of PR Committee, 9 November 1962, LMA CLC/B/015/MS24663, v. 3 July–December 1962.
17 Stephanie Decker, "Decolonising Barclays Bank DCO? Corporate Africanisation in Nigeria, 1945–69," *Journal of Imperial and Commonwealth History* 33, no. 3 (2005): 424–27, https://doi.org/10.1080/03086530500185894; Richard Fry, *Bankers in West Africa: The History of the British Bank of West Africa* (London: Hutchinson Benham, 1976), 213–15; Chibuike Ugochukwu Uche, "Accounting and Control in Barclays Bank (DCO): The Lending to Africans Episode," *Accounting, Business & Financial History* 8, no. 3 (1998): 239–60, https://doi.org/10.1080/095852098330404
18 Andrew M Knox, *Coming Clear: A Postscript after Retirement from Unilever* (London, UK: Heinemann, 1976), 167.
19 Sarah E Stockwell, *The Business of Decolonization: British Business Strategies in the Gold Coast* (Oxford: Clarendon Press, 2000), 142–3.
20 Interview with woman manager of Barclays Ghana, 29 June 2004.
21 UAC: *Economic and Statistical Review*, 22 (London: UAC, 1959), between pp. 34–5.
22 David Kenneth Fieldhouse, *Merchant Capital and Economic Decolonisation: The United Africa Company 1929–1987* (Oxford: Clarendon, 1994), 474.
23 "Barclays Bank Dominion, Colonial and Overseas: An Account by Eric Comley, of his career with Barclays International, from which he retired some fifteen years ago, and highlighting some of the more interesting experiences that he had during the time" (Recorded 1995/6 at the request of Barclays Group Archives), pp. 4–5.
24 AF Tuke, "Visit to Nigeria, Ghana and Sierra Leone," 23 November–4 December 1970, BGA 80/4292 [hereafter Tuke, "Visit to Nigeria, Ghana and Sierra Leone"].
25 Interview with senior executive manager of Barclays Bank of Ghana, 6 July 2004.
26 Sarah E Stockwell, "Political Strategies of British Business During Decolonization – the Case of the Gold-Coast Ghana, 1945–57," *Journal of Imperial and Commonwealth History* 23, no. 2 (1995): 288–9.
27 "Personnel/Labour Report for January 1957," 1 February 1957, LMA CLC/B/015/MS14171, v. 127, January–June 1957; and Labour reports in the vols 164, January–June 1966; 168, April–June 1967; volumes 172–182, March 1968–December 1969.
28 At the UAC 25 percent of African managers were classified as trading, 13 per cent as specialist/technical, and 30 per cent as administrative in January 1959. The rest

presumably had no specialisation. UAC, *Statistical and Economic Review* 22 (London: UAC, 1959), 14.

29 Interview with senior executive manager of Barclays Bank of Ghana, 6 July 2004.

30 FJ Pedler, Report to Directors' Conference, UHA UNI/SC with Tropical Africa Committee (hereafter TAC), 10 December 1965.

31 FJ Pedler, Report to Directors' Conference, UHA UNI/SC with TAC, 10 December 1965.

32 On the beginnings of international staff circulation in the 1950s or 1960s see Knox, *Coming Clear: A Postscript after Retirement from Unilever*, 169–70. Barclays definitely circulated African staff worldwide by the early 1980s. Interview with senior executive manager of Barclays Bank of Ghana, 6 July 2004.

33 See http://www.abujacity.com/influ.html [accessed 9 November 2005], https://en.wikipedia.org/wiki/Adekunle_Ojora [accessed 20 February 2022].

34 [Julian Wathen] to BF Macdona, 15 April 1961, BGA 11/2390.

35 J Beattie, Intelligence Report No. 4 of 1966, 18 July 1966, LMA CLC/B/015/MS14171, v. 165 July–December 1966.

36 Quote after Fieldhouse, *Merchant Capital and Economic Decolonisation*, 380.

37 Quoted after Josephine F. Milburn, *British Business and Ghanaian Independence* (London: C. Hurst, 1977), 77.

38 Pannel, "African managers on the Coast Organisation," 10 April 1945, Holt's Rhodes House files before cataloguing, cited after Milburn, 72; Fry, *Bankers in West Africa*, 191.

39 WW Milne, "General report on a Visit to West Africa" (Kumasi, 16 May 1946), 9.6.46, p. 6, BGA 38/906.

40 Joe Appiah, *Joe Appiah: The Autobiography of an African Patriot* (Accra, Ghana: Asempa, 1996), 108–11.

41 See the obituaries for Joe Appiah (The New York Times USA, https://www.nytimes.com/1990/07/12/obituaries/joe-appiah-is-dead-ghanaian-politician-and-ex-envoy-71.html [accessed 20 February 2022] and his wife Peggy Appiah (The Guardian UK, https://www.theguardian.com/news/2006/mar/06/guardianobituaries.mainsection [accessed 20 February 2022]).

42 Burawoy, *The Colour of Class*, 41–2.

43 Interview with senior executive manager of Barclays Bank of Ghana, 6 July 2004.

44 Michael Burawoy describes in his study how African managers encounter disapproval from both expatriate supervisors and their Zambian colleagues and subordinates. Burawoy, *The Colour of Class*, 40–8.

45 Appiah, *Joe Appiah*, 118–19.

46 J. Beattie, Intelligence Report No. 4 of 1966, 18 September 1966, LMA CLC/B/015/MS14171, v.165 July–December 1966.

47 PJ Foster, *Education and Social Change in Ghana* (Chicago, IL: University of Chicago Press, 1965), 117, 134, 148.

48 AGC and Bibiani (1927) were at that time still one company, although the latter was nationalized in 1960 together with three other mines that threatened to close down and formed the State Ghana Mining Corporation (SGMC). The chief intelligence officers at both mines compiled reports on African labour and trade union activities, based on information delivered against payment by African miners. Some reports suggest that the reliability of new informants was cross-checked with other sources and that some individuals were considered better sources of intelligence than others. Intelligence Report Bibiani (1927) No. 4, 25 August 1960, LMA CLC/B/015/MS24665.

49 Jeff Crisp, *The Story of an African Working Class: Ghanaian Miners' Struggles 1870–1980* (London: Zed Press, 1984), 128–9; Frederick Cooper, *Decolonization and African Society: The Labour Question in French and British Africa, Africa: Journal of the International African Institute* (Cambridge, UK: Cambridge University Press, 1996), 434–5, https://doi.org/10.2307/1161082.

50 J Beattie, Intelligence Report No. 1 of 1962, 9 January 1962; and J Beattie, Intelligence Report No. 10 of 1961, 29 November 1961, LMA CLC/B/015/MS24665.
51 J Beattie, Intelligence Report No. 1 of 1962, 9 January 1962, LMA CLC/B/015/MS24665.
52 Official learners were workers studying for promotion to managerial or supervisory positions. J Beattie, Intelligence Report No. 1 of 1962, 9 January 1962, LMA CLC/B/015/MS24665.
53 J Beattie, Intelligence Report No. 2 of 1962, 19 March 1962, LMA CLC/B/015/MS24665.
54 Crisp, *The Story of an African Working Class*, 125; Cooper, *Decolonization and African Society*, 435, 438.
55 Mr Jackson, Intelligence Report No. 241, 16 June 1953, LMA CLC/B/015/MS14171, v. 112, January–June 1953.
56 Mr Hamilton, Intelligence Report No. 412, n.d., LMA CLC/B/015/MS14171, v. 122, July–December 1955 (Hamilton, Intelligence Report No. 412).
57 Hamilton, Intelligence Report No. 412.
58 General Mines Manager to Spears, 28 November 1955, LMA CLC/B/015/MS14171, v. 122.
59 J Beattie, Intelligence Report No. 6 of 1963, n.d. [8 November 1963], LMA CLC/B/015/MS24665.
60 J Beattie, Intelligence Report No. 5 of 1963, 1 November 1963, LMA CLC/B/015/MS24665.
61 R Wilson, General Mines Manager Bibiani (1927) to Secretary of Bibiani, London, 12 May 1959; PH Brown, General Mines Manager AGC, to Secretary, 15.1.62; Secretary to PH Brown, 23 January 1962; LMA CLC/B/015/MS24665.
62 Crisp, *The Story of an African Working Class*, 133; Cooper, *Decolonization and African Society*, 435.
63 Secretary, London, to R Wilson, General Mines Manager, 23 August 1963, LMA CLC/B/015/MS24665.
64 A similar split occurred in the Zambian copper mines in 1953, see Burawoy, *The Colour of Class*, 74.
65 Memorandum to the Minister of Industries by the Ghana Chamber of Mines – Negotiating certificates, n.d. [presumably between late May to early June 1963], LMA CLC/B/015/MS24665. It is difficult to determine how this compared with the rest of the country. The most reliable figures are indices of real minimum wages for Accra, which rose by 8.5 per cent between 1956 and 1959. It is likely, however, that other wages increased more rapidly. Elliott J Berg, "Real Income Trends in West Africa, 1939–1960," in *Economic Transition in Africa*, ed. Melville Herkovits and Mitchell Harwitz (London: Routledge, 1964), 220–4.
66 Report of the Committee of Enquiry into the recent Disturbances at Prestea, 1968, PRAAD ADM 5/3/179; Jeff Crisp, "Union Atrophy and Worker Revolt: Labour Protest at Tarkwa Goldfields, Ghana, 1968–1969," *Revue Canadienne Des Études Africaines* 13, no. 1–2 (January 1979): 265, 267–93, https://doi.org/10.1080/00083968.1979.10803942.
67 R D Power, General Mines Manager, to EL Spears, 28 September 1963, LMA CLC/B/015/MS24665.
68 Clerical Department Committee Meeting minutes, 27 September 1946, LMA CLC/B/015/MS14171, v. 100 July–December 1946. There is also evidence from the SGMC that the trade union resisted the recruitment of graduates for senior positions in preference to longer established staff, see Draft minutes of the fifth meeting of the sixth Board of Directors of the State Ghana Mining Company, 31 July 1970, p. 2, PRAAD RG 7/2/79.

69 A similar argument has been made by Frederick Cooper about nationalist politicians. Cooper, *Decolonization and African Society*, 435–36; Cooper, "From Free Labor to Family Allowances," 758–9.

70 Foreign multinationals accounted for more than three-fourths of examples of extended training programmes but only for 43 per cent of the total interview questionnaire sample. Thomas J Biersteker, *Multinationals, the State, and the Control of the Nigerian Economy* (Princeton, NJ: Princeton University Press, 1987), 231, 265–6 fn32.

71 Biersteker, *Multinationals,* 281, 244.

72 Fiona C Boyd, "Expropriation of Alien Property in International Law: A Study of Recent State Practice Concerning British Nationals" (University of Nottingham, 1988), 181.

73 Biersteker, *Multinationals*, 271. Both interviewees were Europeans.

74 Interview with senior executive manager of Barclays Bank of Ghana, 6 July 2004.

75 Stephanie Decker, "Africanization in British Multinationals in Ghana and Nigeria, 1945–1970," *Business History Review* 92, no. 4 (2018): 691–718, https://doi.org/10.1017/S0007680518001034.

76 Tuke, "Visit to Nigeria, Ghana and Sierra Leone," 2.

77 Nigerian Institute of Management, *Management in Nigeria*, 11, no. 3 (September 1975), p. 8.

78 W A Lewis, *Report on Industrialisation and the Gold Coast*, 1953, reprinted in "Report of Committee appointed by the National Liberation Council for the promotion of Ghanaian Business Enterprise," 7 April 1967, pp. 67–8, PRAAD ADM 5/3/166.

79 Fieldhouse, *Merchant Capital*, 774; Geoffrey Jones, *Renewing Unilever. Transformation and Tradition* (Oxford: Oxford University Press, 2005), 57, 79, 197.

80 Knox, *Coming Clear*, 171.

81 Taylor, *Sam Jonah and the Remaking of Ashanti*; Forrest, *The Advance of African Capital*.

82 Amin, *Neo-Colonialism*, 249–50; Frank, *Lumpenbourgeoisie, Lumpendevelopment*, 13–16. Frantz Fanon's critique of colonialism and neo-colonialism was highly influential because he argued that the subjugation had a psychological effect, making it more insidious and a transition to a neo-colonialist system more likely. See Franz Fanon, *Black Skin, White Masks* (Newy York, NY: Grove Press, 1967) originally published in 1952; and F Fanon, *The Wretched of the Earth* (New York, NY: Grove Press, 1961) originally published in 1961.

83 Fieldhouse, *Merchant Capital*, 765–72.

List of References

Amin, Samir. *Neo-Colonialism in West Africa*. New York, NY: Monthly Review Press, 1973.

Appiah, Joe. *Joe Appiah: The Autobiography of an African Patriot*. Accra, Ghana: Asempa, 1996.

Barthes, Roland. "The Rhetoric of the Image." In *Image, Music, Text*, edited by Stephen Heath, 33–47. Glasgow: Fontana Press, 1977.

Berg, Elliott J. "Real Income Trends in West Africa, 1939–1960." In *Economic Transition in Africa*, edited by Melville Herkovits and Mitchell Harwitz, 220–24. London: Routledge, 1964.

Bersselaar, Dmitri Van den. "'Doorway to Success?': Reconstructing African Careers in European Business from Company House Magazines and Oral History Interviews." *History in Africa* 38 (2011): 257–94. http://journals.cambridge.org/abstract_S0361541300005660

Biersteker, Thomas J. *Multinationals, the State, and the Control of the Nigerian Economy*. Princeton, NJ: Princeton University Press, 1987.

Boyd, Fiona C. *Expropriation of Alien Property in International Law: A Study of Recent State Practice Concerning British Nationals*. University of Nottingham, 1988.

Burawoy, Michael. *The Colour of Class on the Copper Mines: From African Advancement to Zambianization*. Zambian pa. Manchester: Manchester University Press, 1972.

Cooper, Frederick. *Decolonization and African Society: The Labour Question in French and British Africa. Africa: Journal of the International African Institute*. Cambridge, UK: Cambridge University Press, 1996. 10.2307/1161082

Cooper, Frederick. "From Free Labor to Family Allowances: Labor and African Society in Colonial Discourse." *American Ethnologist*, 16, no. 4 (1989): 745–65. 10.1525/ae.1989.16.4.02a00080

Crisp, Jeff. *The Story of an African Working Class: Ghanaian Miners' Struggles 1870–1980*. London: Zed Press, 1984.

Crisp, Jeff. "Union Atrophy and Worker Revolt: Labour Protest at Tarkwa Goldfields, Ghana, 1968–1969." *Canadian Journal of African Studies/Revue Canadienne Des Études Africaines* 13, no. 1–2 (January 1979): 265–93. 10.1080/00083968.1979.10803942

Decker, Stephanie. "Africanization in British Multinationals in Ghana and Nigeria, 1945–1970." *Business History Review* 92, no. 4 (December 1, 2018): 691–718. 10.1017/S0007680518001034

Decker, Stephanie. "Decolonising Barclays Bank DCO? Corporate Africanisation in Nigeria, 1945–69." *Journal of Imperial and Commonwealth History* 33, no. 3 (2005): 419–40. 10.1080/03086530500185894.

Fanon, F. *The Wretched of the Earth*. New York, NY: Grove Press, 1961.

Fanon, Franz. *Black Skin, White Masks*. Newy York, NY: Grove Press, 1967.

Fieldhouse, David Kenneth. *Merchant Capital and Economic Decolonisation: The United Africa Company 1929–1987*. Oxford: Clarendon, 1994.

Forrest, Tom. *The Advance of African Capital. The Growth of Nigerian Private Enterprise*. Edinburgh, 1994.

Foster, P.J. *Education and Social Change in Ghana*. Chicago, IL: University of Chicago Press, 1965.

Frank, Andre Gunder. *Lumpenbourgeoisie, Lumpendevelopment: Dependence, Class, and Politics in Latin America*. Newy York, NY: Monthly Review Press, 1972.

Fry, Richard. *Bankers in West Africa: The History of the British Bank of West Africa*. London: Hutchinson Benham, 1976.

Jones, Geoffrey. *British Multinational Banking, 1830–1990*. New York: OUP, 1993.

Jones, Geoffrey. *Renewing Unilever. Transformation and Tradition*. Oxford: Oxford University Press, 2005.

Knox, Andrew M. *Coming Clear: A Postscript after Retirement from Unilever*. London, UK: Heinemann, 1976.

Milburn, Josephine F. *British Business and Ghanaian Independence*. London: C. Hurst, 1977.

Stockwell, Sarah E. "Political Strategies of British Business During Decolonization – the Case of the Gold-Coast Ghana, 1945–57." *Journal of Imperial and Commonwealth History* 23, no. 2 (1995): 277–300.

Stockwell, Sarah E. *The Business of Decolonization: British Business Strategies in the Gold Coast*. Oxford: Clarendon Press, 2000.

Taylor, A.A. *Sam Jonah and the Remaking of Ashanti*. Johannesburg: Pan Macmillan South Africa, 2006.

Uche, Chibuike Ugochukwu. "Accounting and Control in Barclays Bank (DCO): The Lending to Africans Episode." *Accounting, Business & Financial History* 8, no. 3 (1998): 239–60. 10.1080/095852098330404

7 Conclusion

British companies sought the maintain their organizational legitimacy with the colonial and later with the independent governments of Ghana and Nigeria. Consequently, they adapted their commercial strategies to fit in with development ambitions: commercial companies redeployed into manufacturing, wholesaling and specialized retail; banks expanded their branch network, mobilized deposits and increased their local lending, especially to Africans; the AGC in Ghana improved its welfare provision for workers and raised its gold output to allow the country to pay for imports necessary for investment. Based on this discourse, corporate and political elites began to build networks that allowed frequent informal audiences between leading politicians and business people, providing a platform for each to canvass opinions and put their case across. These networks facilitated the transition to independence for British business, as the new independent leaders were the old colonial incumbents.

Relying on the development framework to be accepted by host governments was a successful political strategy for British business, which also aligned with commercial rationale. But the development vision of the 1950s and early 1960s came undone by the 1960s, as world demand for tropical commodities flagged and industrialization projects did not deliver on their objectives. New ideas about dependency and underdevelopment rejected extensive involvement with the international economy because global capitalism had promoted underdevelopment through colonialism and neocolonialism. The indigenization programmes were a direct consequence of the loss of legitimacy by foreign companies, and a sharp increase in expropriations worldwide highlighted that this was an international phenomenon. Domestic economic nationalism in Ghana and Nigeria influenced the nature of expropriation programmes: while there were some cases of outright nationalization, most foreign companies were subject to indigenization decrees. Indigenization required firms to sell specific percentages of shares or assets to domestic Ghanaian and Nigerian owners and investors.

As the legitimacy of international business was undermined, its local African staff became an essential safeguard to foreign interests. African managers could deflect criticism from British companies; conversely, low

DOI: 10.4324/9781003001058-9

Africanization rates meant that firms were singled out for attack. But in the 1970s, African managers became more important because the take-over of parts of the equity by West African governments emphasized the official resolve to see Africans in charge of the economy. As the presence of expatriates was increasingly politically damaging, British companies improved their internal training for domestic managers to ensure that they could place their staff into responsible positions first, rather than having to accept government appointments.

Much of the debate around the role of multinationals in developing countries, and the goals of the expropriation decrees of the 1960s and 1970s, was couched to take control of the economy. While this led to a focus on ownership, the dynamics of foreign investment were more complex. Minority shareholding, and in some cases even a majority shareholding or complete nationalization, did not automatically equate to full control over operations. Skills shortages and proprietary technologies made it necessary to arrange management contracts. Transfer pricing and other accounting techniques circumvented attempts to tax multinationals effectively. Once governments had partially nationalized some industries, they saw their share of capital gains reduced by such taxation. As both avenues would mean a greater return for host governments, such income did not necessarily come to the same departments within the government. Many scholars concluded that control over investment remained elusive for most developing countries.[1]

However, reducing indigenization programmes and targeted nationalizations to the issue of control over foreign investment was overly simplistic. Expropriation programmes reflected internal conflicts over resource redistribution in new states. They were not solely aimed at multinationals but also against other foreigners such as African and Lebanese immigrants (see chapter 4). All nationalisms require an external foe, but the category of 'foreigner' was not stable and defined in juxtaposition to the entitlements of citizenship.[2] Expropriations are also frequently considered separately from other local content measures such as corporate Africanization. Africanization beyond the civil service remained important to independent governments, and both Ghana and Nigeria pressed for better representation by forcing the issue through immigration controls and direct appointments.

Ghana and Nigeria were not unique as host countries, and globally diversified multinationals faced international pressure to localize in formerly colonized regions. The decline of tropical economies, first witnessed in Ghana in the 1960s and starting in Nigeria in the late 1970s and 1980s, made companies more likely to give greater authority to African managers. Inflation further complicated the remuneration of expatriates. Former free-standing companies merged with larger corporations to spread their risk as economic nationalism challenged their continued viability in developing countries. Complex political configurations in host states also made it necessary to give companies' local negotiators greater freedom to find the best possible deal.

These changed the nature of corporate control of West African subsidiaries and further contributed to more localized decision-making. Such legacies of decentralized decision-making shaped these MNCs for many years to come.[3] However, the relationship between multinationals and host countries did not necessarily become more beneficial for host countries because Ghanaians or Nigerians were in charge. Regulating foreign investment has remained contentious in an era of globalization.

Four out of the five companies researched for this study changed the focus of their operations fundamentally in this period: the merchant companies moved from an export orientation towards producing goods and providing services for the host economy; the banks increased their local customer base, although they eventually moved away from raising deposits from small savers and returned to focus on large cities and dealing with government accounts.[4] In gold mining, no opportunity for redeployment existed. Overall, however, the national subsidiaries of multinationals became more dependent on the performance of their host economies – in the case of the UAC, and its parent Unilever the 1970s and early 1980s were a time of increasing dependence on Nigeria, which ultimately led to the incorporation of UAC business into Unilever's overseas operations.[5]

The emergence of development economics framed the postcolonial transition as a means to effectively manage the political economies of formerly colonized areas of the globe. The development orthodoxy of the 1950s and 1960s envisaged a very active economic role for the state in conjunction with private foreign investment. The development and modernization of tropical countries thus gave British business a legitimate reason to outstay the British empire. British multinationals participated in the development discourse through legitimization strategies such as redeployment of expatriate staff, spreading the savings habit through the expansion of bank branches, and ex valuable natural resources. As firms reconfigured their identity from imperial business to becoming multinationals, their internal management control systems became more decentralized. A more balanced relationship between headquarter and subsidiary management developed over the time period of the study, as overseas branches became subsidiaries and increasingly autonomous. This decentralization of management control was not just a response to constraints but, more importantly, a legitimization strategy to ensure that MNCs could continue to operate in former colonies.

Notes

1 A Hoogvelt, "Indigenization and Technological Dependency," *Development and Change* 11, no. 2 (1980), 257–72 (270–2); S Amin, *Neo-Colonialism in West Africa* (Harmondsworth: Penguin, 1973), 249–50, 273–4.

2 Ronald Aminzade, "From Race to Citizenship: The Indigenization Debate in Post-Socialist Tanzania," *Studies in Comparative International Development* 38, no. 1 (2003): 43–63, https://doi.org/10.1007/BF02686322; Ronald Aminzade, *Race, Nation, and*

Citizenship in Postcolonial Africa: The Case of Tanzania (Cambridge, UK: Cambridge University Press, 2013).

3 Christopher A. Bartlett and Sumantra Ghoshal, *Managing across Borders: The Transnational Solution*, 2nd ed. (Boston MA: Harvard Business School Press, 1998).

4 Interview with senior executive manager of Barclays Ghana, 6 July 2004.

5 Fieldhouse, *Merchant Capital*, 620, 718, 721, 762, 774; Jones, *Renewing Unilever*, 57, 79, 197.

List of References

Aminzade, Ronald. "From Race to Citizenship: The Indigenization Debate in Post-Socialist Tanzania." *Studies in Comparative International Development* 38, no. 1 (2003): 43–63. 10.1007/BF02686322.

Aminzade, Ronald. *Race, Nation, and Citizenship in Postcolonial Africa: The Case of Tanzania*. Cambridge, UK: Cambridge University Press, 2013.

Bartlett, Christopher A., and Sumantra Ghoshal. *Managing across Borders: The Transnational Solution*. 2nd ed. Boston MA: Harvard Business School Press, 1998.

Appendices

Appendix 1 Ghanaian Indigenization Decrees

1968 NLC White Paper Government Policy on the Promotion of Business Enterprise
GHANAIAZATION DECREE (December)

- Enterprises entirely reserved for Ghanaians:
    - Retail trade of less than C500,000 in volume
    - Wholesale trade of less than C1 million in volume
    - Manufacturing and transportation businesses employing less than 30
      AND employing simple production techniques
      OR with capital investment below C100,000
- Compliance: divest within two to five years (deadline June 1973)
- Supervision: Ghanaian Enterprises Committee

1969 GHANAIAN BUSINESS PROMOTION ACT (June)

- Revises deadline and extends affected enterprises from the first Ghanaiazation Decree
- 13 reserved enterprises in two categories
    - category: six enterprises, deadline 1 August 1970
    - category: seven enterprises, deadline 1 July 1971
- Ghanaian Enterprise Advisory Committee
- Office of Business Promotion (implementation of decree, support of Ghanaian businessmen)

1970 GHANA BANKING ACT

- Local incorporation of banks

1972 MINING OPERATIONS (GOVERNMENT PARTICIPATION) DECREE (November/December)

- Government nationalizes 55 per cent of the equity of AGC (Gold) and CAST (Diamond)

1975 INVESTMENT POLICY DECREE (came into force 1 January 1977)

- Threshold for businesses: C500,000 of capital employed or C1million of annual turnover
- Schedule 1: 100 per cent Ghanaian ownership
- Retail and wholesale trade under the threshold
- Schedule 2: Ghanaian participation of varying degrees required (affects 45 enterprise categories)
    - Require 50 per cent of equity to be owned by Ghanaians:
        - Retail and wholesale trade over the threshold
        - Commercial and industrial enterprises below the threshold
        - Production of basic necessities below the threshold
    - Require participation of 40 per cent:
        - Commercial and industrial enterprises over the threshold
        - Banking, mineral and timber production below the threshold
    - Require a 55 per cent participation by the Ghanaian state:
        - Production of basic necessities over the threshold
        - Timber and mineral production over the threshold
    - Special requirements:
        - Extraction and processing of bauxite and aluminium requires 30 to 40 per cent state participation
        - Mineral oil production requires a minimum of 20 per cent state participation
- Acquisition costs for government of foreign-owned mining and timber enterprises to be paid out of future profits
- Penalties against 'fronting': two years imprisonment, illegal to employ, directly or indirectly, the previous owner
- Supervision and organization of sales vested in Investment Policy Implementation Committee

GHANAIAN ENTERPRISES DEVELOPMENT DECREE

- Complement the Investment Decree
- Sets up the Ghanaian Enterprises Development Commission:
    - Financial and technical assistance to businessmen
    - Advisory service to businessmen
    - Power to reserve a proportion of shares for employees of indigenized enterprises

Appendix 2 Nigerian Indigenization Decrees

1968 Companies Decree

1969 Banking legislation: banks to incorporate locally and publish audited statement of accounts

1970 Second National Development Plan 1970–1974: Government's intention to acquire commercial and industrial equity to ensure participation of nationals in the economy

1971 Government acquires 40 per cent of three largest commercial banks, all foreign (April) Nigeria joins OPEC (July)

1972 Nigerian Enterprise Promotion Decree (NEPD I or First Indigenization Decree) – compliance within two years

- Schedule 1: 100 per cent Nigerian-owned
    - Reserved activities: advertising, gambling, electronics manufacturing, bread and candle making, road transport, laundering, municipal bus and taxi services, media, retailing.
- Schedule 2: 40 per cent Nigerian participation (if over a certain size)
    - Restricted activities: domestic air traffic, shipping, construction, wholesale distribution, travel agencies, range of basic commodity-producing low-tech manufacturers such as furniture, cement, matches and household chemicals.
    - Restriction on size: Aliens barred completely if business smaller than: £200,000 share capital OR turnover lower than £500,000 p.a., whichever deemed appropriate. If bigger, then alien participation restricted to 60 per cent.

1976 Adeosun Panel on NEPD I: only 33 per cent of business complied up to that date (convened November 1975, report submitted March 1976)

- Government announced intention to take over some 600 foreign companies

1977 Nigerian Enterprise Promotion Decree II (NEPD II or Second Indigenization Decree) – compliance within two years

- Schedule 1: 100 per cent Nigerian-owned
    - Formerly schedule 2: bus services, travel agencies, wholesaling of home products.

  - Completely new categories (generally small, local activities): film distribution, newspapers, radio and television, hairdressing

- Schedule 2: 60 per cent Nigerian participation

  - In general activities with an emphasis on manufacturing for domestic market.
  - New categories: fish-trawling and processing, food manufacturing, plastic and chemical manufacturing, banking, insurance.

- Schedule 3: 40 per cent Nigerian participation

  - Applies to many industries previously unaffected, more technology-intensive activities.
  - Manufacturing of chemicals, drugs, pottery, china, glass, metal. Also, hotel industry, oil servicing companies.

1981 **Number of activities reclassified from Schedule 2 to Schedule 3 to attract FDI**

Reclassified: metal containers, fertilizers and cement, sugar plantation, processing operations, 'cash crop' agricultural plantations

Appendix 3 Archival Sources and Oral History Interviews

Liverpool Records Office (LRO)
Acc 4888 (380 HOL II)

Barclays Group Archive, Manchester Wythenshawe (BGA)

11/947; 11/2390; 29/667; 38/382 (4); 38/512; 38/513; 38/517; 38/906; 80/3468; 80/3580; 80/3649; 80/4292; 80/4330; 80/4351; 80/4641; 80/5356 (2); 80/5666; 277/1; 277/3; 1189/1

Rhodes House Oxford (RHO)
Mss Afr. s 825:
232 (i); 232 (ii); 232 (iv); 232 (v); 421(v); 421 A (iii); 421 B (ii); 549

The National Archives, Kew, London (TNA)
FCO 65/1222

Bank of England Archives, London (BoE)
OV 68/5

London Metropolitan Archives (LMA)
[Files originally accessed at the Guildhall Library, London]
AGC files
Ms 14,170, Outward Correspondence, London to Obuasi:
Vols 82–83 (January 1945–July 1946)

Ms 14,171, Inward Correspondence, Obuasi to London:

Vols 97–105 (January 1945–June 1949);
Vols 107–108 (January–December 1950);
Vols 111–112 (January–December 1952);
Vols 121–123 (July 1955–March 1956);
Vols 127–128 (January–June 1957);
Vols 163–166 (January–December 1966);
Vol 168 (April–June 1967);
Vols 171–178 (January 1968–May 1969);
Vol 182 (October–December 1969)

Ms 24,661, Reports of the Annual General Meetings:
Vol 7 (1963–1968)

Ms 24,663, Confidential Mines Correspondence Inwards, Obuasi to London:
Vols 1–9 (July 1961–December 1965)

Ms 24,665

BBWA files
Ms 23,538; Ms 23,558; Ms 28,517; Ms 28,636

Unilever Historical Archives, Unilever House, London (UHA)

UNI/BD/DC: Directors' Committee Minutes, 1942–1962
UNI/SC with TAC: Special Committee Minutes with Tropical Africa Committee, 1965–1968
UNI/SC with UAC International: Special Committee Minutes with UAC International, 1968–1976

Archives Centre, Churchill College, Cambridge (CCC)
Papers of Edward Louis Spears:
SPRS 1/112; SPRS 1/209; SPRS 1/350

Public Records Administration and Archives Department, Accra, Ghana (PRAAD)
ADM 5/3/166; ADM 5/3/179; CSO 21/8/48; RG 6/1/190; RG 7/2/79

Oral History Interviews

- Interview with Hugh Norris, Reg Dines, Hugh Norris, John Woodcock (former Barclays Bank DCO expatriate managers who worked in West Africa), 17.8.01
- Interview with woman manager of Barclays Bank Ghana, 29.6.04
- Interview with male senior executive manager of Barclays Bank Ghana, 6.7.04
- Interview with Alhassan Andani (executive manager of Barclays Bank Ghana), 5.7.04
- Interview with William Atta Krofah (formerly a director of Unilever Ghana), 13.7.04
- Interview with Roy Barlow (Liverpool-based ship engineer who sailed to West Africa from 1956 to 1960), 20.10.05

Index